PATRICIA MACKIN

# The Reunion

ISBN: 1-4792-2522-3
ISBN-13: 9781479225224
Library of Congress Control Number: 2012916298
CreateSpace, North Charleston, SC

# CHAPTER ONE: MEETING

"A cold beer sure goes down good on a hot day", said Will.

"You got that right", said Tom.

Paul said nothing but downed his glass of draft in three gulps.

The three friends had met for lunch but were having a few beers first.

Will said, "I suppose the only time I'll get to see you guys, is for funerals, and don't expect me to come to many of them, not even yours." They all laughed. The three old friends were around seventy and losing friends frequently. They had been at a funeral the day before and were having a final beer with Will, who was flying back to Louisiana late in the afternoon.

"Did you see Molly Burke at the funeral yesterday?" asked Will. "Boy did she get old."

"Take a good look in the mirror Will", said Tom.

"It's the grey hair," said Paul. "She's put on a lot of weight too."

"She wasn't bad in her day," said Tom. "Her husband died of a fatal heart attack in his own bed last year. I heard she was good in bed. Think he went out with a smile on his face?"

They chuckled. "Jane Goodman was there too. She didn't look too bad," said Paul.

"Are you kidding me; she had more wrinkles on her face than the wrinkles in a pair of fat guy's sweaty pants", said Tom.

"She was a cheerleader when we were in high school," said Will.

"Well I wouldn't want to see her strutting any stuff now in a little short skirt", said Tom. "You know Ed Thompson died two months ago, and Norm's wife got killed in a car crash."

"We're just dropping like flies", said Will.

"We'll be next. We're in God's waiting room," said Paul.

"Or the Devil's in Will's case," said Tom.

"If there's no beer or loose women up there, I'm not going", said Will.

"Who are you kidding, I know you and you'd trade all the beer and loose women for her", said Paul.

"Do you think she's dead" asked Will. "I hope she's not dead."

"If she is, she's in heaven", said Paul, "she was always a nice person."

"Don't say she's dead; I don't want her to be dead" said Will.

"I don't know if she's dead; maybe her husband is dead", said Paul.

"If they're both dead and I die will I see both of them", asked Will.

"No, because you will not be going to heaven", said Paul

"But if I do go to heaven, what if her husband's there too" said Will. "What do you Catholics do then?"

"We believe that in heaven you have perfect happiness and it's different for everyone. Whatever makes you perfectly happy is your heaven. Your happiness could be spending eternity with her but her husband wouldn't be there," said Paul.

"Well how could that happen? Sorry, I don't believe that crap", said Will.

"Well you don't have to worry about it, Will, because you're going to hell and you'll piss everyone off down there too", said Tom.

Will Benton was by far the best looking of the three. At seventy-one, he looked to be in his late fifties. He kept in shape. He was always neat and so clean he shined. Will also had a knack for picking the right clothes and colors that flattered him. The pale green polo shirt matched his eyes and the jeans fit well and even had a crease. He was almost totally bald but had a handsome face with a dimple in his left cheek when he smiled. His smile could forgive him anything. He knew he had good looks He paid attention to his appearance. He had to; he was always looking for a new wife. He had already been divorced three times.

"So how are they hanging", asked Tom?

"Pretty low", said Will, "I am seventy-one years old".

"Can you still get it up?" Paul laughed.

"There was a time when all I had to do was look at her and it saluted" said Will.

"She could do that, couldn't she", said Paul.

"She was something else. She had stars in her eyes and always made me laugh. She was so pretty. Her boobs got to me mostly though. No one had boobs like that at thirteen. I wish I had given them a squeeze", said Will.

"Shut up you two" said Tom, "when you're fifteen all boobs look good."

"Whatever happened to her Will?" asked Paul.

"I don't know. Heard her husband became a lawyer. They had a bunch of kids."

"You were just children when you knew her. Get over it. No one marries their first girl friend", said Tom.

"You did." said Will.

"Yeah but I was a late bloomer. I didn't have a girl friend until college."

"I dated a few girls before I married Marie and I never looked back" said Paul.

"What's wrong with you Will? Why didn't you ever move on," asked Paul.

"He moved on, alright, right on top of three wives" said Tom.

Will replied "Yeah, well I dated her longer than any of my marriages lasted. I remember all the dances and dates and the fun at the lake. She was the best looking girl I ever went out with and the nicest. We had such fun; so many memories. When she broke my heart I was never the same. She ruined it for me. I could never love again, really."

"You are so full of bull shit", said Tom. "Do you think if you married her, things would have been different? You're insincere, insecure and immature."

"I am all those things because she left me", said Will. "She should have married me instead. I should have fought for her."

Paul said, "Let it go Will, it was fifty years ago. You're twisted but you may have always been twisted. She would have been wife number one, it would have failed and you would have ruined her life as well. You are what you are; addicted to sex."

"If she had married me instead, we'd still be married and I'd be the happiest man on earth."

Tom said, "That's the beer talking, you're shut off."

"No, it's not" said Will "I should have fought for her; now I live with regrets."

"Bull shit" said Tom, "She was just a girl you remember."

Tom Neeley didn't give a damn about his looks. He was the tallest, and leanest. He wore chino pants, a short sleeve red plaid shirt and leather working boots. That was his style. He should have been born at an earlier era because he resembled a cowboy. His white hair was full and longish. He had a full white moustache. His teeth were stained with coffee and tobacco. He had a low bass voice and was happily married to the same woman for more than fifty years.

"No, Tom, you're wrong, there was something special about her," said Will resuming the conversation.

"Give it up Will. That was fifty something years ago," said Paul.

"She never appealed to me," said Tom.

"That's because you were older and you had Susan," said Will.

"Well she appealed to me, but she never gave me the time of day," said Paul. "She only had eyes for you Will."

"A lot of good that did me", he said. "She married someone else. In those days she was my hard-on all day and my wet dream all night."

"What kind of pants did you wear then" asked Tom? "They must have been uncomfortable." They all laughed out loud.

"Did you ever do it with her" asked Paul, "you went together long enough."

"No regretfully, we never did it," said Will. "I respected her. I cherished her. She was Catholic. I wish we had done it. Now I really wish we had."

Paul D'Angelo was the youngest of them, just seventy. He was medium height, medium weight, with a slight beer belly. He had on a blue tee shirt and cargo shorts. Paul was Italian and had that beautiful, ageless olive skin, a nice smile and a St. Anthony bald spot. Paul was a widower. He had been married to Marie for forty-six years. They had three children and seven grandchildren. He was very religious man and family orientated. He missed Marie.

The three men had grown up in a small New England town. Although not the same age, they were only a couple of years apart and they attended the same public schools, were in the same boy scout troop, swam, played sports and had a lot of the same acquaintances. Their families knew each other. In the spring they fished with their dads and in the fall they all went hunting. After high school Tom went to Northeastern University and became an engineer, Will went in the Army and later worked for the Post Office and Paul went to Tufts University to become a dentist. They were all in each other's weddings and remained friends throughout the years. Now they were all retired. Tom and Paul lived in that same town, and on that same lake, only yards away from each other; Will had lived in that town too, for many years. His land had been on the other side of Tom's but Will's house was on the main road away from the lake. Will's back yard went down to the lake. The men had bought their homes from their fathers. Seven years ago Will left; he sold his home and moved to Louisiana when he retired to live with his son, Jack, his only child.

The three friends thought they were the only ones in the restaurant, a quaint little place in a nearby town. The restaurant overlooked a pond and was beautifully landscaped. Many weddings were held in the function rooms there. Known for its good food the men were contemplating items on the lunch menu. It was a weekday and unusually slow. Only one other person was present. She had arrived just as they were ready to order their food. They had not noticed the older woman come in and sit at the table near the bar. Their backs were towards her. Her back was to them. They were busy making small talk and deciding on sandwiches and beer.

Isabelle was sitting at a table with her back to the men. She was waiting to meet her cousins for lunch. She never arrived early for anything but there had been less traffic than she anticipated and so she decided to have a glass of wine while she waited. It was nice to have a few moments by herself before lunch and the conversation nearby was funny. She was enjoying the banter of the three men at the bar. She had missed the first part of their conversation; it was like coming into a movie half way through. They were men around the same age as she. She couldn't see them, but she had been to enough wakes and funerals herself lately and understood how old they were and what they were talking about.

Her own Tim had been buried two years ago and at first she grieved the loss bitterly. It had been a happy marriage that lasted forty-nine years. Isabelle had just turned seventy but looked much younger. She was a beautiful woman. She was plump, but neat and had a great smile. She had had a charmed life with a doting husband and six children. They had been partners in business and at home. He was an attorney and she ran the business end of it. When their youngest had turned eleven Tim left the large Boston law firm to go into business for himself. She learned how to use a computer for the first time. It was the old fashioned IBM type with the DOS version. Isabelle had become familiar with billing software, bookkeeping, legal briefs and much more. When Microsoft Word was invented she rejoiced. The law office thrived for more that twenty five years. They were able to help kids with college tuition, help pay for their weddings and help them with down payments on their homes. After retirement they did a little traveling, Bermuda, Ireland, a few cruises and many long weekends. Her husband was so close to the family that he couldn't stay away from the grandkids too long. His death was sudden, always hard on the family but easy on the deceased. He was a good man, always faithful, and loved the children. He was strong in his faith and principles and never drank or smoked. Tim lavished Isabelle with jewelry and gave her all the money he earned. There had been lean years in the beginning when he attended law school nights and she attended to three babies in diapers. But they were always happy and in love. As the years went by, she realized that it would be better if he died first. Tim was needy. She had spoiled him. She knew she could go on. She'd have to. Isabelle kept busy. She had a great family and good friends. She had a lot of hobbies and had worn rose colored glasses since birth. She knew she'd be alright.

As a young girl she laughed a lot. She had a winning personality, a pretty face and a smile that could light up a room. Isabelle had been short and slim in her youth with a full bosom. She once had medium blonde hair, long and usually in a pony tail. She used to like sports, swimming, and water skiing, bike riding, playing baseball and just having fun. She grew up in the city but spent all her summers on a lake in a small town. The summers were the best part of the year. She had so many friends at the pond and one special one. She fell in love for the first time at the pond. She was thirteen. He was fourteen. He was tall, and drop dead gorgeous. They dated for a long time, all through high school and later. She broke his heart to marry Tim. He immediately joined the Army and she never saw him again. That was history but she never forgot him. Your first love always has a piece of your heart.

Since Tim died she thought of the good old days a lot. Memories become more precious as we age. Every time someone dear to her died she thought of her own mortality. Did she long for her youth again or did she just try to prevent feeling old? Isabelle had many friends during her life, men and women. She had gone to her high school reunions and many classmates had passed away. When she saw her grandchildren with their sweethearts she thought of her teen years. She thought of him again. She wondered if he was still alive.

Two years had passed since Tim's death and now she was learning to enjoy the freedom she hadn't had since she was nineteen years old. Isabelle was her own boss now. She was emancipated. She could get rid of some of the decorating accessories Tim had bought without hurting his feelings. They were down right ugly too, like the metal brown and red geese duo that hung on the dining room wall or the inflatable four foot Easter Bunny Tim always placed in the entrance hall. Small things like boiling an egg for supper, sleeping late, having the TV remote all to herself, were bonuses. Not having to wash anyone else's dirty clothes was a good thing. Not having to watch only historical movies was good too. Of course the other pillow on the opposite side of the bed was empty and the house was sometimes lonely. His snoring was not missed but his hugs and kisses were. He had given her a family. He had always loved her. She was a good wife to Tim. She loved him as much as he loved her and held dear all the precious moments they had shared together. Isabelle could endure being alone; she like to read and garden and bird watch. All of her children and grandchildren lived in the same town so she never had to be lonely.

She was looking forward to the cousins' visit. Two of them were from Vermont although they had been born in Massachusetts, they moved to Vermont about fifty odd years go. The other cousin lived another small town near where her summers were spent. All of them were widows. Isabelle was the oldest and so she tried to look her best when with them. Isabelle was the prettiest, but her vanity made her try harder when she was going to be with these younger girls. The two girls from Vermont didn't give a hill of beans about fashion. They would wear shapeless dresses in drab colors and ugly sandals and not care. They both had grey hair; one a long braid and the other a very short cut. They were smart and kind and good. The other cousin, Kathy, was a city raised girl like Isabelle. Kathy's hair was dyed that reddish maroon color so many women over fifty like. She had a good hair cut. Kathy wore very stylish clothes, usually beaded or sequined blouses with wide legged pants but they were always black. Kathy was the youngest. She was outgoing, funny and smoked like a chimney.

Isabelle was no longer slim. Six children and age had taken care of that. She struggled with weight but maintained an average to plump figure and had a great hair cut that was colored light ash blonde. Her light blue eyes still sparkled and her teeth were still her own slightly crooked white ones. The smile was still the same. She had no illusions that she would win any beauty contest. What seventy year old woman could? She knew that if she took her bra off her nipples would hit her knees. She earned all the wrinkles on her face; too much sun when young. Arthritis lived in her knees. When she laughed too hard she peed. Her moustache had been waxed, her nails painted, her hair sprayed, all was right with the world. Isabelle wore a coral tee shirt and white Capri pants. She hated shoes of any kind and would prefer to be barefoot always. Even though she was short and needed the height she tried never to wear heels. Today she had on slip on sandals to show off the recent pedicure. She sipped her wine slowly and listened to the three men.

"So, how is it working out in Louisiana? Getting any?" asked Tom.

"I don't have time", Will answered. "My son's been out of work so I live with him and help him out. He has a wife and three kids. I pay half the mortgage and the rest of my retirement check goes to the last two wives' as alimony every month. I live off whatever savings I have. At least I made some good investments and sold the house for a good price, otherwise I'd be screwed. Jack and I never seem to see eye to eye. He's too much like his mother. His wife doesn't like me at all, but she likes the money. I pay so I stay. Jack finally got a new job last week. So things will get better. I hope Jack doesn't invite his mother for a visit. Don't want to see her. I will say the best thing she ever did was marry Charlie; otherwise, I'd be paying her alimony too. It's the least Charlie could do for me since I did find him and Jill in bed together when I came home from work."

"His mother was alright; she was just too young for you," said Paul.

"Looking back I think I married Jill because she reminded me of that other young girl I knew," said Will. "Jill didn't look like her but she was young and full of fun."

"It's one thing to date a seventeen year old girl when your eighteen but you were twenty–six when you married Jill and she was only seventeen," said Paul. "She was too young."

Tom added, "You had no right marrying a seventeen year old when you were twenty-six. You were perverted, robbed the cradle and should have been arrested. You were trying to relive your youth. You thought marrying a young girl would make you young again too and Jill would be that other girl."

"What are you a psychologist now" said Will? "All my wives were a lot younger than me. That's what has kept me young looking, and you two are just jealous. I've had my share of women, especially when I was between wives and you two can't stand it.

"Oh right," said Paul, "You're the only stud in the corral."

"Yeah, any minute now, flocks of young girls from all across America will be sauntering in here just to see you", said Tom. "Every woman you ever went out with dumped you".

"Shut up" said Will gulping his beer.

"Do you ever hear from wife number two", asked Paul.

"Oh, dear old Alice, no, and you'd think she'd thank me for all those monthly checks. She and her first husband are living together again. They deliberately don't re-marry so she can still get my checks. I was a sap. But she was a looker and fourteen years younger than me. You know when you're forty one, bald and single it's hard to find the right one and her folks had that nice hunting lodge in Maine. Boy we had some fun there boys, didn't we", said Will.

Tom said, "All I remember about her were those two wining little twin girls she brought to the marriage. And all Alice ever did was polish her finger nails and toe nails. Whatever happened to the girls?" asked Tom. "How much did she spend on nail polish?"

"Don't know; don't care. Her ex used to visit his twin girls all the time. I think he was banging Alice when I worked nights. She worked days. We never saw each other. But I did like the hunting lodge, the peace and quiet, the still lake; the moose. Remember the deer we brought back? If I had it to do over I'd still have married her just to get to that lake."

Tom said, "You're just a sentimental fool."

"Shut up, Tom".

"So tell us about Louisiana" said Paul.

"It's hot in Louisiana. They have nudist colonies," said Will. "Have you ever been to one?"

"Now why in the wide world of sports would I want to look at a lot of flapping body parts all day long, especially if you live in an over fifty community. Those nasty, sagging balls and tits bouncing around would make me puke". Tom answered.

"There are young people there too and they're worth looking at. I enjoyed looking. Sometimes I worry about you Tom."

"Don't worry about me, I don't need to look at a bunch of naked men and women playing volley ball just to get it up."

Will said, "Susan's a lucky woman; it must be magic being married to you."

Paul was quiet and then said "I think it might be sinful. I'd actually be quite uncomfortable walking around naked with strangers. Did you really do that?"

"You bet your ass I did, and some of the bodies were well worth the look." said Will.

"You're seventy-one, you can't seriously think anyone was looking at your used up parts", said Tom.

"I think a few of them were", said Will, "but you know my package ain't what it used to be. I let it all hang out just the same."

Tom said, "There must have been many grateful spectators; nothing like looking at your package."

"Package?" said Paul, "What package? Were you carrying something around with you?"

"Paul you can't be serious," said Will; "My privates! A man's privates are called his package."

Paul said, "I never heard that expression. My mother told me once not to forget to keep June, July and August covered when I was going swimming. She was quite a jokester. She was referring to my penis and two testicles. But I have to admit that "package" is a much better term. See I'm not too old to learn."

Tom said, "You have to get out more, Paul."

"Tell me do you just walk around staring at people's nakedness at the colony or are there other things to do there" asked Tom.

"Yeah, what do people do there," asked Paul.

"Same as everywhere else", said Will. "They play shuffle board, swim; play cards, tennis anything you want. You just do it without clothes. These nudists know how to stay cool. You don't have to bother with clothes or towels".

"Where do you keep your wallet" asked Tom "tied around your dick?"

Will said, "No, I had a string tied around my waist and attached the wallet to it at my side. I wanted everyone to see my big dick."

Paul said, "You have a lot of sins to answer for".

Will said, "I'm not Catholic; I don't know what a sin is."

"You're not anything", said Tom, "and you don't even know right from wrong".

Will said, "I met my third wife, Yvonne, there; she was part Creole, Indian and part Cajun, a dark little minx."

"How old was she", Tom said, "twelve?"

"Well no," said Will, "she was actually forty-seven. I was sixty three when I met her. No one younger was really interested."

"Must have hurt your poor, old, naked feelings" said Tom.

Paul asked, "How long were you married to her?"

"Only a year and a half; she didn't get along with my daughter-in-law. We lived with them. It wasn't going to last. She had a Brazil wax thing. Not a good look at the nudist colony. It was like walking hand and hand with a shaved cat. People stared. It was pretty freaky doing it with her too. One real hot night we damn near stuck together. There's either too much friction or not enough. One minute I'd be sliding off her the next our sweat would cause a suction cup effect. I like the way God made women; there's a furry buffer zone. Women just can't leave well enough alone", said Will.

Paul said "Enough! Please keep these private things to yourself. I'm getting mind images of you stuck to a shaved cat. She was your wife after all, have some dignity.

"Damn straight", said Tom. "Sometimes you just don't know when to shut the hell up"

Will continued, unabashed, "Our cultures were too different. Yvonne was into some heavy shit. She was into voodoo and stuff like that. Once we went on a Cajun boat tour where you traveled in an air boat through the bayous and a narrator told us about the legends of the swamp. It was supposed to be a paranormal experience. All we saw was a big alligator and some other little critters but I don't even know what they were. She wanted me to visit cemeteries in New Orleans and listen to a lot of jazz and eat gumbo and craw fish".

Tom looked at Will. "You are the biggest loser. Who marries someone you'd meet at a nudist colony? Your cultures were too different, my ass. You are the least cultured man I know and I hope she has a voodoo doll that looks just like you, and she sticks pins in it every day."

The bar tender brought their sandwiches and refilled their glasses.

"You know you're not God's gift to the world. Not anymore that's for sure. You're old" said Tom.

"I'm young at heart", said Will.

"You have no heart, said Tom.

"I do, it's just broken and it can't be fixed" answered Will.

"If some woman came in here now and was even remotely interested in you, your heart would be on the mend as fast as you can say intercourse. You'd be all over her trying to chalk up another point and adding her name to the long list of conquests", said Tom.

They were silent for a moment while they bit into their sandwiches.

"By the way, what is a Brazilian wax" asked Paul?

Will told him.

Tom said, "That must hurt like a bastard."

"I guess", said Will.

"If all the girls you dated band together in heaven someday, you'd be better off going to hell." said Paul. "You and that pretty face of yours have made a lot of enemies, mostly female ones."

"Yes, but think of all the memories I have", said Will, "and besides most of the girls I dated won't be going to heaven either."

Maybe you should write a book, "How to Make Every Woman You Ever Dated Hate You"; or "Memoirs of a Perverted, Twisted but Hopeful Gigolo" said Tom.

"No, said Paul, "since all your women left you for someone else, you should call it "Keep it in Your Pants, It Just Ain't Worth It."

"Screw you two", said Will.

It was at that point that Isabelle laughed out loud. Her wine almost came out of her nose. The men turned around and Will got off the bar stool and said, "Have you been listening to our private conversation for long? That's called eavesdropping. I don't believe this. You are a very rude lady."

She answered, "Yes, and I think you guys should take this comedy show on the road. I've been very much entertained."

Will threw back his head and roared with laughter. His smile was brilliant, and his dimple creased. Isabelle sat very still. She didn't think more than one person could have the same laugh, smile and dimple. But this man did. He was old. He was bald. It couldn't be him. Her heart was racing. She said nothing. She felt confused and a little dizzy. It must be the wine. She put her glass down.

Will approached her and said, "Can I buy you another?"

Tom said to Paul, "Oh no, the game is on again."

Isabelle suddenly felt like a school girl. She smiled that "light up the room smile of hers" and said, "No thanks, one is my limit. I'm driving."

Suddenly Will was at a loss for words. He'd seen that smile before but not on an old lady. He'd know those light blue eyes anywhere but not on a face that had wrinkles. It was still a very pretty face but wrinkled nonetheless. It was one of those awkward moments when there is total silence. Two senior citizens' brains were trying to focus on what was going on. Will and Isabelle didn't even breathe for a minute.

Paul and Tom didn't know what was going on. And then the cousins arrived. The maroon haired smoker and the grey haired Vermont girls sat down at the table.

"Been waiting long" said Judy.

"Only a few minutes," said Isabelle.

Her cousin, Kathy said "And already you've picked up three guys from the bar. Not bad for someone your age".

"I haven't picked up anyone," said Isabelle.

The third cousin dropped the bomb; gave away the lady's name; she said, "Hi Isabelle."

Then Will finally knew. Will grabbed onto the bar stool and looked at his two friends.

Then Tom said "Will, are you alright?"

"Will" thought Isabelle, "His name is Will" and then she knew too.

She stood up and faced him.

He reached for her hand.

She took his hand and said, "Hey, Big Guy, it's been a long time."

"Hey, yourself" said Will. How's Tim?"

"I lost him two years ago." Then there was silence.

Paul and Tom said, "Isabelle"??? They couldn't believe their eyes. They had just been talking about her and here she was. She looked good; still smiling, still pretty, still Isabelle. Will was right; there was something special about her. How hard had the last fifty years been for their friend? She still called him Big Guy. She still had big boobs. Maybe he wasn't just a womanizer but someone who lost at love and never recovered. Where was all this going?

The cousins all spoke together, "Will Benton, wow".

Kathy remembered the handsome boy who had won Isabelle's heart. She remembered the dances, proms, the years of dating. They were the epitome of childhood sweethearts. He worshipped the ground she walked on. She loved him. Everyone in their family thought she'd marry him. But she married Tim.

Whatever happened to Will Benton thought Judy. He was still a looker. She wondered how many women he screwed. He was probably a bastard like all the rest of the male population.

Carol was more romantic she was thinking destiny was playing a part in this reunion. Why now? Why indeed.

They all said hello to each other. They had all been together at the lake fifty odd years ago. They all knew each other when they were young.

Tom and Paul went back on their bar stools and ate their lunches.

Isabelle released her hand and sat back down at the table.

Will joined the men and ate.

The waitress came over and produced menus to the ladies. The place was very quiet.

Then Tom said "Finish up, Will, you have to get to the airport". Will glared at him, pulled out his cell phone and dialed Delta Airlines. He cancelled his open ended ticket for today and booked a flight for next week; told Paul he'd be staying with him for a few days and drank his beer. Paul said he had to get back to baby sit his grand child. Tom wanted to tell Susan he didn't have to drive Will to the airport and perhaps they could go out tonight. When the other two men were done the three of them rose to leave.

Will went to the ladies' table and said, "Isabelle, please write your phone number on this napkin". Isabelle looked at him and laughed.

She said, "What are we in the seventh grade again"?

He looked at her solemnly, with such sadness in his eyes but said nothing. She wrote down the number and could not say anything else. She handed him the napkin. The men left.

The waitress came back to their table and brought over two apple martinis for the Vermont girls, a Sangria punch for Kathy and a diet Sprite for Isabelle.

"Will Benton", the girls said in unison.

"Have you ever heard from him in all this time? Did you even hear anything about him in fifty years?" asked Carol.

"No," said Isabelle. "I was too busy raising my family and working to be interested in that."

"Did you ever think about him?" asked Carol.

"Yes, I did. I hoped he was happy."

"Oh shut up you to two romantics. He was happy alright probably getting laid every night of his life and by a different woman no doubt." said Judy. "Just look at how he dresses and keeps himself in shape, still hoping to jump in the sack with someone and probably with someone young. Men go on until they're ninety five, Bastards, Pigs!"

The girls all laughed.

They finished looking at the menus and ordered soups and salads. After the waitress brought the food and poured water into their glasses, she left them alone.

Kathy said, "We had a lot of fun at your summer place, Isabelle. We met all those guys and other kids. We learned to swim and fish. I loved watching you and Will together. What happy days we had."

"I remember those two brothers, Greg and Joe, who lived across the lake. They were hot and had the fastest boat. Will's cousins, Milton and John, were pretty cool too", said Judy, "but they always wanted to make out; especially that Milton. It figures; they were related to Will. The best part of the summer was your father teaching us to playing cards. I still love playing Scotch Bridge."

Carol said, "Times were simpler then. Holding hands was a big deal, and counting fire flies at night. Remember going to the carnival when my mother threw the dart to win the prize and it hit the parrot, which was the prize. She should have worn her glasses. The carnival had a great Ferris wheel too; boy how many times did we ride on that. There was cotton candy and hot buttered corn on the cob too. We could walk around the whole fair grounds without parents and without worrying about perverts and molesters. You couldn't let a kid do that today.

Kathy piped in, "Well, that was fifty years ago, a half of a century. Boy, are we old. You never even heard the F word then and now it's lost its impact. Remember your brother and his tape recorder and all of us writing stories and each of us taking a part and making recordings and thinking we were great. I loved playing monopoly and reading comic books, all innocent stuff. We really were sheltered and better off."

Isabelle smiled and said those were the best years any teenagers could have had; and how all the rest of the years had raced by. It seemed just yesterday we were playing miniature golf and riding go carts, squishing too many kids in the station wagon and going to the drive-in movie with Uncle Dick and water skiing all day long. All those Sundays we had cook outs and remember the baked hams Kathy's mother used to make and all our parents playing cards or just talking and Granny cooking and Pa watching TV.

"It was nice to see those guys today", said Judy. "Usually when you see old men they wear their pants up near their chests to keep their balls from hitting their ankles. They didn't do that. So their balls must be fine. Also I find that old men have big bunches of gross hair sticking out of their ears. Didn't notice any of that either. I think they all had their own teeth too, which is more than I can say for myself. I'd expect it from Paul of course since he became a dentist. At least I think that's what he became. He was going to dental college when I saw him last. Those three looked pretty good today. These guys aren't normal". She was shaking her head.

Carol said "I don't remember Tom so much. He was older and had a girl friend. She was always nice to me and Kathy. Paul was always nice and good looking, but too quiet. The Stanley brothers were OK and the Pike brothers too. But Will was the babe out of the whole lot of them; and he only wanted you, Isabelle. You should have married him. Why didn't you?"

Isabelle was quiet for a long time and then she simply said, "I married Tim".

"Do you regret it" asked Judy?

"No" said Isabelle.

The waitress cleared the table and asked if they wanted to see dessert menus. They all said "YES" in unison and told her they'd like coffee as well. They choose one strawberry short cake, two hot fudge sundaes and one bread pudding with whipped cream. They settled into the best part of the meal, licking fingers, spoons and getting every bit of the sugar high they could. Since smoking was not allowed in the dining room, they went out to the patio for their coffee. Kathy was having a nicotine withdrawal. They settled down in the sunshine, not too hot but warm. There was a gentle breeze and the view was spectacular with a v geese formation flying in the sky, lily pads on the pond, bees buzzing around them, and peonies and irises in bloom.

"What a day", said Isabelle "a glorious sky, sweet air, and best friend cousins."

"Here, Here" said Carol.

"You two are too sugary for me", said Judy. "There's a dead fly on the end of that table, cat or rabbit poop on that stone wall over there and the purple loose strife stuff is growing out of control all over the water's edge. Kathy's cigarette smells. Plus we had to meet three guys from our youth who all look better than we do."

"Speak for yourself" said the other three in harmony.

"I wonder what happened to Will during the last fifty years", said Carol.

Kathy said, "I met Paul's mother once at the supermarket years ago and she told me Will had just gotten his second divorce. I asked her what happened to the first wife. She said Will came home from work and found his first wife in bed with another man. The second wife had an ex- husband who was always hanging around. Will had a baby with his first wife; a boy I think. That's all I know about Will.

"What about the others" asked Judy?

"I know Paul did become a dentist. His wife died about four years ago, they were married over forty years and have kids. He took it hard. She had cancer. I don't know anything about Tom. I mean I know he married Susan but I don't know if they have kids or if she's alive, but I think she is" said Kathy.

"Well we all get old. There's no way to stop it. We can only make the best of what time we have left." said Carol.

"So what are your plans while you two are here from Vermont" asked Isabelle?

Judy replied. "I want to visit my grandson on Friday and I'm Carol's guest tomorrow. We are going on the Odyssey Ship with some folks from the telephone company, who used to work with Carol. It's a lunch cruise in Boston Harbor. Also I'd like to visit Plimouth Plantation and the sites down that way. Carol wants to go to Christmas Tree Shops and if you girls want to come, you are welcome. We have a whole week.

Isabelle said, "My son, Gerry, is having a big Fourth of July party on Saturday. He said to tell you all to come. He lives in South Weymouth but that's not far from Kathy's. There will be fireworks and food and games and you can see my family. Come if you can."

"It sounds good". They all said they'd come.

"I have a doctor appointment on Thursday and dentist on Friday, so it's good you two are busy those days," said Kathy. "But Plymouth and Christmas Tree Shops look good for early next week. Are you in Isabelle?"

"I'm free Monday so let's plan on that. OK?" said Isabelle.

They chatted and finished catching up with each others news. Carol took out her note book ant jotted down "Saturday Gerry's Party" "Monday with Kathy and Isabelle". They all agreed on Monday and paid the bill and then parted with hugs in the parking lot.

On her way home Isabelle had to pay attention to her driving. Her mind kept wandering back to Will. He was still handsome, older and somehow sadder. There was an excitement in the pit of her stomach she couldn't explain. She was too old for this. She was behaving like an adolescent but oh charming, funny, handsome, wonderful, Will. She had sixteen grandkids for God's sake. She was a widow. She was being tempted by nonsense. She must be strong. She must fill all her days and nights with things to do. She would visit the kids. She would shop. She would garden, go to a movie and go out so no one would be there to answer the phone. He probably wouldn't call anyway. She got home. Shed her sandals and stayed outside in the front yard and watered the flowers. When she finished she sat on the bench and sunned herself. The mail man came and she read the local newspaper that he delivered. She took her time. She didn't want to go into the house. She didn't want to hear the phone ring. If it did, she'd have to answer it. She was half dozing when a car pulled up and there he was charming, funny, handsome, wonderful, Will.

# CHAPTER TWO: WILL AND ISABELLE

"How did you find me" asked Isabelle.

"I used Paul's computer and went on the internet to reverse look up. All I had to do was put in your phone number and up came the address."

"You don't waste any time do you?"

"I don't know how much time I have left to waste. I'm seventy-one. Is there somewhere we can just sit and talk? I think we have a lot of catching up to do."

"We haven't seen each other in fifty years, what do we need to catch up on?"

"Us", said Will.

"There is no "us". That was a long, long time ago. We were just kids. I was very happy to see you today and I'm grateful that we're both alive and well. I hope you have been happy. It was good to see Paul and Tom too but that's as far as this reunion goes."

Will said, "There are things I need to say to you. Things that should have been said years ago before you left me."

"Why would they matter now a half of a century later?" asked Isabelle.

"They matter to me and I think I deserve to be listened to."

Isabelle hesitated she heard something in his voice. Was it anger, misery, regret? She couldn't tell but it moved her. She said, "Come into the back yard; it's quiet and private. I hope this isn't going to be a shouting match because you think I picked the wrong guy fifty-one years ago."

Will responded, "I will never shout at you, I just want to know what went wrong and why you chose Tim."

They sat in two comfortable chairs in the back yard. The sun was going down, the birds were feeding at the feeders; the early summer air was filled with pollen and the smell of honeysuckle. A squirrel drank out of the bird bath, a few leaves moved in the breeze. It was a beautiful late afternoon when the blue sky turns golden and pink, forecasting heat for the next day.

Will started. "You and I have known each other since we were kids. We could always say anything to each other. We shared so many wonderful times. We laughed and cried, mostly laughed. We were best friends and more. I hope we can converse as easily now as we did then. I have had a lot of time to think about our relationship. Any fool could plainly see that I loved you all those years ago. I wanted to marry you but we were so young and you wanted college. Even though we shared a few kisses, you never encouraged it or talked about intimacy. I never did either. A few times I held you in my arms and it was magic. I thought you were uncomfortable with it. I tried to be a gentleman and believe me it was the hardest thing I ever had to do. I wanted to kiss you all the time, and make love to you just like any other normal man. I wanted you to want it. I never wanted to force myself on you. I was patient and it was unbearable sometimes. When you introduced me to Tim I thought he was just a friend. I never suspected you loved someone else. I was blindsided. By the time I met him, you and he were already in love. When did it happen? How did it happen? I was sure you'd never do that to me. Then all at once you told me that you and Tim were getting married. That's it. No explanation. You had only known him for about six months. You met him at college. I was working and saving to buy you a diamond ring. You were falling in love with someone else. You married him and had a great life. I'm glad because I could never wish you anything but the best. I ran off and joined the Army thinking that after four years I'd forget you. I had to get away. It didn't work. I have never been able to move on. I have had so many failed relationships. I wanted to blame all of them on you but can't because I failed them not you. I could never get you out of my mind or out of my heart. A day hasn't gone by that I haven't thought of you. Sometimes when I made love to other women, even my wives, I'd pretend they were you. I could never find the right one because the right one was married to Tim. Please tell me what went wrong?"

Something moved in the tree, a blue jay. A yellow finch grabbed thistle from the feeder. The wind chimes tinkled, a car drove by, clouds slowly passed overhead and a dog barked the next street over. All the usual sounds and sights were around but this was not a usual conversation. This was a sad conversation about love lost.

Isabelle sat for a minute. She felt stung and mean. She had never meant to hurt Will. She told him her side. "I went to college and you went to work. Those were the choices we made. Maybe that was the start of a big mistake; I don't know. I met kids at college who were different from you and me. They made my eyes open. I grew up that last year we were together. I wondered why you never kissed me that much or tried anything else. I loved you. I wanted you to be demonstrative with your affections but I was too embarrassed to mention it. My sex drive finally kicked in when I was at college. Yours had already done so and yet you were decent enough to keep it in check. We talked about a lot of things but never those things. We should have. I should have. Because I was in college and taking psychology courses I believed every thing I read and heard. Most of it was crap. We were taught that the more compatible a couple was the less chance they had of divorce. I started thinking about us and what we had in common. How compatible were we?  I was from the city; you came from a small town. I was going to college. You worked. I was a Catholic you were not. I was Irish you were Yankee. Did I have everything covered, the environment, the education, the religion, the ethnicity? Shouldn't marriage be by the book? See what a little education does. Meanwhile Tim kissed me. He never took advantage of me. He was a gentleman but he had passion. I wanted you to fight for me but you didn't. I wanted you to have passion. I should have told you. You shouldn't have needed to be told. I didn't know how to tell you. I was in college I was trying to think with my head instead of my heart. I was trying to be a grown up. If I thought with my heart I would have married you, but I didn't; I thought with my head and married Tim. That's not to say I didn't love him. I did. But you were my Will. You were always my Will. There were tears rolling down her face and she took his hand. I can't change what happened. I made the choice I thought was best at the time and I lived with it. Tim and I were happy. Tim loved me and I loved him.  I had a husband and babies and made a home and a good life for my family. Did I think of you? Yes, every day. Should I have married you? I don't know. Is there anything to remedy this? No. If I never went to college would I have married you? Yes. I think that God has a plan for all of us. He knows every baby that is going to be born hundreds of years before it's born. He knew your child was going to be born. He knew my six children were going to be born. He had no plans for Will and Isabelle's babies".

They sat for a long time in silence, holding hands.

Then he said, "Want to go get an ice cream".

She said she did and a bird dumped a big poop right on the front of her shirt.

"I'll have to change my shirt", she said, "but I'd like an ice cream and don't tell me this is good luck; there's nothing lucky about it."

They went in the back door and she showed him where the bathroom was. He looked at her with a questioned look and amusement.

She said, "I'm used to men and their weak bladders, old prostates or whatever. Go pee."

She went upstairs and changed her shirt. She fixed her hair and dabbed a little perfume on and hurried down. He was still peeing. What is wrong with men? Well he did drink all that beer today and at his age, he's probably taking hydrochlorothiazide or some such drug for fluid.

She showed him where the ice cream place was.

Will said, "Is it still butter pecan"?

She said, "Yes."

She said "Is it still chocolate chip"?

He said, "Yes."

They got cones and sat outside on a picnic bench. She bit the bottom off the cone and sucked the ice cream out.

Will said "I wondered if you still did that".

They laughed. Then she suggested going to the beach right down the street. They walked on the sand in bare feet until the sun went down, Isabelle felt like a kid again. Will was in love. He dropped her off at her house at 9:30 PM and said he was staying with Paul for a few days and could they go out for the day tomorrow. Isabelle figured what could a few days hurt. He was good company and she had nothing on the calendar. Who was she kidding? She was happier tonight than she had been in a long time. He suggested the Swan Boats, a Boston Harbor cruise and an Italian dinner at the North End. She said lovely and he said he'd pick her up at 10:00 A. M. He told her he was not the same shy eighteen year old boy she left behind and that his life had been filled with passion so she better watch her step. She said at seventy one, unfortunately, she was sure most of his passion had been spent on other women but she didn't mind the leftovers. He told her to warn her kids that tomorrow night's newspaper may headline, OLDER COUPLE GETS ARRESTED FOR LEWD BEHAVIOR ON SWAN BOATS.

She said "Dream on" as he drove away. He was laughing out loud. She always made him laugh.

Isabelle was so excited going to bed that night she didn't think she'd sleep. She had laughed at women who said they had vibrators but now she wished she had one. She had not felt this good in years. She did sleep and she dreamt of Will. It was not the kind of dream the nuns at her high school would like to have heard about. In the morning she smiled and laughed out loud. She thought about them holding hands last night. She found herself remembering how big his hands were. Well he was a big man. Then she remembered her big boobs. Oh thank you God for the big handed man. She forced herself to calm down. I can't act like a silly school girl, I'm seventy years old. I'm a grandmother. Please God, make me less horny.

Paul was waiting, like a worried father, for Will to get home. "What happened", asked Paul.

Will told him. "We talked, had an ice cream cone, walked on the beach, watched the sunset and made plans to spend tomorrow together. That's all".

Paul said, "You didn't do anything else did you?"

"No, but maybe tomorrow", said Will.

"Are you out of your mind." said Paul. "She's seventy years old. She doesn't do it any more. You could hurt her. She's all dried up or closed up or something."

"What the hell is the matter with you? Seventy year olds do it."

"Oh my God, Will. Don't be sick. She's a nice lady. She may have sons. They could beat you up."

"Should I buy condoms?" asked Will.

"Please have some respect", answered Paul.
"OK, I'll splurge for the K Y Jelly too."
Paul said "Where will you keep all these things?"
"In my pocket, I'm not at the nudist colony anymore."
Will slept. It was the same wet dream he had fifty years ago.

# CHAPTER THREE: BOSTON

Thursday dawned with a beautiful blue cloudless sky. It was warm but not humid and there was a slight breeze; a perfect day. Isabelle took this to be a good omen. She was ready when Will picked her up. They drove to Boston and Will was surprised at all the changes since he had moved to Louisiana. They talked about places they had visited and he said he'd like her to see New Orleans. They parked the car at the underground garage at Boston Common and walked across the street to the Public Gardens where the Swan Boats were. The yard workers had done a great job this year, hundreds of colorful flowers were planted in raised beds and the lawns were carefully manicured. They sank into the deep seats of the boat and glided toward the footbridge. In the distance they could see the sun reflecting off the gold dome of the State House. They sat close like teenagers and held hands when they walked back to the car. When they got to Long Wharf, a harbor cruise was set to leave in ten minutes. They got their tickets and boarded. They kept looking up at the sea gulls remembering last night's bird dropping. Would today be another a "lucky" day? Isabelle pretended to be ducking from the birds aim. But the birds behaved and the narrator started speaking. He welcomed them to Boston and then pointed out places of interest.

At Rowes Wharf, the Odyssey was getting ready to launch into the harbor for a luncheon cruise. Carol and Judy were on board with Carol's former co-workers. Out of the corner of Judy's eye she saw the Boston Harbor cruise boat pass by. "Wasn't that Isabelle and Will on the deck?" she thought. The sun was in her eyes and her glasses in her hand bag so she couldn't be sure but she was almost sure. She went to find Carol. A waiter with a tray full of drinks stopped and offered her a drink. Judy took one and said, "Thanks". She dragged Carol back on deck to see if Carol could make out the two figures on the other boat. Carol was blind as a bat on most days and had on her sun glasses, not prescription, and so she had to dig into her pocketbook to find her other glasses. Judy was holding her drink and digging into her bag for her glasses. The wake of a tanker passing tilted the Odyssey and waves hit the starboard side of the boat. Both Judy's drink and Carol's sunglasses went overboard. They both cursed, although Judy's language was much more imaginative than Carol's and they stared finally bespectacled at the other small ship. They both thought they saw the backs of two people walking toward the bow of the boat. Judy and Carol, who never had sea legs tried to run to the stern of the Odyssey. That was where they'd get the best view of the other boat's bow. Carol almost fell but Judy saved her by yanking her silver braid and pulling her entire body back onto its feet. It must have hurt. By this time Will and Isabelle left the deck and had decided to sit under the awning because Will forgot his baseball hat and didn't want his bald head sun burnt. A waiter came by with drinks again and Judy grabbed one and said, "Thanks, I need this one." Carol squinting either from the sun or bad eyesight told Judy no one was on the deck except for a small girl and her mother. Judy said she could no longer see them, but she was sure one of them had on a pink shirt.

"Well it must have been Isabelle because men don't wear pink" said Carol.

"I'll bet Will does" said Judy.

She wanted to keep guard but the gong sounded and they staggered up the deck along with the motion of the waves like two drunks heading to the dining room. Spying on your seventy year old cousin's love life was one thing but it couldn't stand in the way of a good meal.

The narrator on Will and Isabelle's cruise mentioned all the islands in the harbor, pointed out the cruise ships lined up at the Black Falcon Pier and talked about the clean up of the water itself. He spoke about Boston's history, showed them the waterfront restaurants, Logan Airport and all the other normal things narrators talk about. Will and Isabelle enjoyed the cruise. The narrator was good, the day spectacular but most of all they were happy in each other's company. They watched the planes take off and land on the run ways. Fellow boaters waved and they waved back. It was as if fifty years rolled away. They said funny things to each other. Their faces were full of smiles. Will's eyes were not sad today. It seemed like just yesterday and they were young again.

The two boats were parallel at this time but not close. A tug boat moved between them. Isabelle saw two figures at the bow of the Odyssey craning their necks and staring at something in her direction. She turned around to see if something of interest was behind her. There was nothing. When she turned back the tug boat barred her view. Then she saw two figures at the stern of the Odyssey. They were looking at her.

She said, "Will, do you see two people staring over here from that boat?"

He was wearing his glasses but squinted anyway. "Looks like a short Native American with a braid and a grey haired man holding a drink," said Will. He shrugged.

Then the tug boat moved again, blocking them from sight and Will and Isabelle went to the other side of the ship. Carol and Judy saw two figures on the other boat but the sun was blinding them and they couldn't make out who they were.

"Drat that tug boat" said Carol, "I didn't get a glimpse of anyone."

Judy said "You'd think if the sun was going to work some magic it would at least reflect from Will's bald head and give us a clue. I don't even know if there was a bald man; or even a man, just two figures."

The Odyssey turned toward Rowes Wharf and docked about fifteen minutes before the Boston Harbor cruise got to Long Wharf. Judy and Carol got off and walked to the aquarium parking lot, retrieved their car and headed toward the expressway. The passengers from the Harbor cruise were disembarking at Long Wharf and as Will and Isabelle walked passed the Marriott Hotel, Carol and Judy spotted them as they drove by on Atlantic Ave.

Judy said, "That dirty little sneak. She went out with him."

"We both have our glasses on now and you were right, Will does wear pink", said Carol.

"I'm going to try to turn this car around and see where they are going," said Judy.

Carol said, "She's not a dirty little sneak, just someone in love"

"Oh my God, She's seventy years old. She's not a dirty little sneak she's a dirty old lady", said Judy.

"Come on, Judy, if Will Benton asked you out you'd go" said Carol

"No I wouldn't"

"Yes you would" said Carol.

"Yes I would; that lucky bitch".

They both laughed.

Isabelle and Will walked through Christopher Columbus Park and headed toward the North End, Boston's version of Little Italy. They talked about Italian food. Will said he missed Boston and again that he thought Isabelle would like a trip to New Orleans. He told her about the black ironed balconies that flanked the busy streets, the smells of spicy foods, the size of the shrimp and the music and the vastness of the Mississippi River.

She said she had never been there but it did sound interesting, full of history and she would like to see the flowers and scenery. Just then they saw a small black sedan driving slowly along Hanover Street with two grey heads wearing tinted glasses peering down the side street at them. Then the car sped up.

Isabelle immediately recognized them and said to Will, "I forgot they were going on the Odyssey today."

"Who" said Will?

"Miss Marple and her short side kick; my cousins, Judy and Carol", said Isabelle.

"They must have spotted us when they were aboard. I'll bet one of them already has a cell phone speed dialing Kathy to dish the dirt. When I see them on Saturday they are going to want a detailed review of our big date"

"They're just having fun playing detectives. What's happening on Saturday" asked Will.

"My son is having a big Fourth of July party at his house", said Isabelle, "I was going to ask you to come. There will be lots of people, food, music; fire works and games. It's just a family day. Say you'll come? You'd like one game it's a lot like the horse shoes we played a long time ago. They call it washer toss. It has two rectangular shallow boxes about two feet by five feet with three holes in each of them. You stand on the end of one box and try to toss three washers into the holes in the other box. If you get it in the first hole you get a point, the middle hole is three points and the one furthest away is five. They have a tournament with partners and a trophy for the winners. I play, but I stink. You were always good at horse shoes. I think you'll be good at it, although my boys will give you a run for your money. It's fun. I hope you'll come."

Will thought for a minute and said, "I'd like to meet your family. How will they fell about you bringing an old friend?"

"I have to be honest with you. They adored their father and they'll consider you a prospective replacement. Through the years I have told them about you and all the fun we had at the lake. Tim told them he met you, that I really could water ski and that you were a nice guy. He referred to you as "your mother's first boyfriend". They never quite believed I could water ski or had another boyfriend so you can at least confirm that."

"So you and your cousins are the only ones I will know there?" asked Will.

"What a chicken you are. My brother and his wife will be there. Bring Paul with you, if you need a side kick, he and my brother always hit it off and the cousins know him."

"I'm not a chicken but I'll ask Paul"

They both laughed.

They walked hand in hand toward the North End. They chose La Summa for their restaurant. They had red wine for their hearts as this would be the only healthy choice they made. It was a shared Caesar salad for their appetizer and Will had lasagna and Isabelle had Chicken parmesan. They walked to Hanover Street and finished their meal with cappuccino and a dessert at Mikes Pastry. Isabelle thought it is so comfortable to be with him. Will thought this is the easiest date I've ever been on; I can just be myself. They walked back to the parking garage and felt full, tired and old. It had been a long date. The day had been wonderful. The sun knocked them out. The boat ride was calming. The meal was delicious.

When they arrived at Isabelle's house Will said no to a cup of coffee. He was tired. They made plans to do lunch tomorrow and a lecture on John Adams to be given at the Weymouth Library by the author of a recently published biography. He said he'd pick her up at 11:30 A. M. He kissed her goodnight. It was a gentle kiss. A kiss you save for someone special but he held her for a long time. It melted Isabelle's heart. Will didn't even know where that kiss came from. He was usually a frenzied lover; ardent and passionate. He was used to getting his own way with women right from the start. Thank God he wasn't like that tonight he didn't want to scare this precious old girl away.

Will returned to Paul's home around 9:00 P.M. Tom had come over to watch the Red Sox game on TV with him, since Susan had gone to see a movie with their youngest daughter.

"Well if it isn't Romeo himself" said Tom.

"Want a beer, Will" asked Paul.

"I'll get it", said Will. "Thanks. You guys need anything?"

"I'm good" said Tom.

"Me too." said Paul.

"Who's winning?" asked Will.

"The Yankees are ahead eight to six. We might ask you the same question" said Tom.

"What's that supposed to mean?" said Will.

"Paul tells me you were going to buy KY jelly and condoms for tonight. How'd that work out for you, since you're home by 9:00 P M?"

"I'm taking things slow" said Will, "and it's none of your business. Paul you have a big mouth."

Paul replied, "Isabelle is my friend too. I'm concerned for her well being."

"Her well being is just fine and all her other parts too" said Will.

Will told them about the day he had, the Swan Boats, the harbor cruise and the North End. He said they had a great time and that he was a gentleman. He told them he felt fifty years younger.

"Yeah well you don't look it," said Tom.

He admitted he was tired and so probably looked his age. He told them he and Isabelle were meeting tomorrow for lunch and a lecture

"What in God's name will you do at a lecture?" asked Tom.

"It's about John Adams. You know, the second president. He was born in Quincy. He's popular in Weymouth. His wife Abigail lived there. I know some history, you know." said Will.

"Yeah I went to those school field trips too," said Tom.

Paul said, "They actually have a nice tour you can take in Quincy, bringing you to the home President Adams lived in and the church he attended. It's narrated and on a bus. Marie and I went there before she got sick. It's right in Quincy Square."

"You better behave yourself, Will, she may have sons that will kick your ass" said Tom.

"What do you think I'm going to do to her?"

"Don't make me spell it out" Tom said as he put out his cigarette.

Tom got up to leave. "I was just telling Paul that I've arranged for us to join a group going on a deep see fishing trip on Monday. We're leaving at 4:30 A. M. Paul's going. Interested" he asked.

"I'd like that. I'll be ready. What do I owe you?" said Will.

"We'll settle up on Monday."

"OK"

When Tom had gone, Will told Paul about the party on Saturday. Paul said that his oldest son and family were visiting in-laws for the Fourth. His other son and daughter both lived out of state. So he was free for Saturday and would like to see Isabelle's brother again, the cousins too and of course Isabelle. I sometimes see her brother, Bob, at church. He used to talk to my mother and my Aunt Joan. They were in the choir with him.

"Great, you holy rollers should get along just fine. Wonder what Bob's wife is like. Isabelle told me he didn't get married until he was sixty, after their mother died," said Will.

"Never met his wife" said Paul.

Judy and Carol got back to Kathy's before rush hour traffic started. They wanted to tell her all about their lunch cruise and about Will and Isabelle.

They relayed all the information they had and Judy said, "What do you think"?

"It sounds like you two had a great day. I was on the Odyssey once and I loved it," said Kathy puffing on a cigarette.

"No, what do you think about Will and Isabelle?" asked Carol.

Judy said, "I tried to call her on my cell but she has her phone off the hook. She knows we want to grill her."

"By the way I won the lottery today, fifty bucks, using my grand kids' birthdates" said Kathy. "I say leave her alone. He's going back to wherever he's from next week and we'll learn all about it then."

"You are maddening" said Judy, "how can you wait that long? Do you think his intentions are honorable?"

"He's seventy-one years old, what else can they be?" said Kathy.

"Right." said Carol.

"Oh what you two don't know about men" said Judy.

"I think Isabelle's intentions are honorable", said Carol. "She's always been a lady. I don't know about him."

Judy said, "Isabelle was always such a goody two shoes but he's a man of experience; a man of the world. She could be fooled and get her heart broken. I think she still loves him. I think she needs us to protect her".

"Maybe he still loves her," said Kathy, "and maybe we'll be brides-maids again. I need another cigarette."

"Do you think they'll do the dirty deed before they get married", said Judy.

"Never" said Kathy, "Do you"?

"Maybe", said Judy.

"I can hardly remember doing the dirty deed", said Kathy, "it was such a long time ago."

"God created the sexes so it shouldn't be called that, it's beauti-ful", said Carol. "I remember."

"Listen you two. I remember doing the deed and sometimes it was pitiful. My first husband, who's probably in hell as we speak, had a dick the size of a three year olds and he hummed the whole time we made love, if that's what you want to call it. I'm amazed he ever gave me two kids with that little thing. What a dork he was" said Judy.

"Judy, please don't talk about your private business and espe-cially when we go to Isabelle's son's house on Saturday." said Carol.

"He hummed", said Kathy. "He hummed?

"He hummed", said Judy, "believe me, he hummed."

"What song did he hum?"

"Who the hell cares, I don't think it was the same song every time. I tried not to listen. He just hummed."

Kathy was still laughing. Nothing was private with Judy.

# CHAPTER FOUR: THE LIBRARY

Friday was cloudy and cool but not raining. Judy and Carol went to Weymouth where Judy's grandson, Dillon, lived and picked up the boy. She didn't get to see him much since she lived in Vermont and the boy's parents were divorced. But his other grandparents were always cordial to Judy and knew she loved him. Judy was always on her best behavior when with them. Judy and Carol told him they would go to the play ground at the library for a while, then to Burger King, and then they would take him to the new Disney movie in the afternoon. He was seven. He was happy. His other grandmother bid them farewell and tucked Dillon's library card into his pocket, in case they went inside.

Judy and Carol sat on a bench in the park drinking Dunkin Donuts coffee while Dillon played on the slide and monkey bars. There were a few other young boys there too so he was having a good time. The women kept their eyes on him and chatted.

"Are you wearing something patriotic to the party tomorrow?" asked Carol.

"What, are we in grade school? No, I'm wearing something comfortable. I wish I could go braless but they might bounce too much if I try that washer whatever game Isabelle told us about," said Judy. "I think I'll skip the game."

"Well it is the Fourth of July. I'm wearing a tan colored tee shirt with the Statue of Liberty on it with my tan cargo shorts and please Judy, wear a bra."

"Suit yourself but don't stand up teary eyed and pledge allegiance in front of everyone. You get so emotional. You probably need hormones. I'll have to watch how much you drink tomorrow".

"You make me sound like a lush. You drink more than me and you behave worse even without the booze. Take care of your own hormones."

"I can always count on you" said Judy.

Dillon continued to play with the other kids and the women resumed sipping their coffee. They were facing the play ground and sand box with the library rear entrance directly in the background. The library was located at a park that had a play ground and a baseball field. There were lots of trees and a walking path and plenty of parking spaces. There were a few picnic benches near the ball field bleachers. A black bird was making a cawing sound and a fat robin was flying to its nest. A group of kids were playing whiffle ball at the baseball diamond and girls had a soccer game going on in the grass. It was a nice spot.

"Do you think Isabelle will bring Will to the party tomorrow?" asked Carol.

"Maybe, but her kids will be there and they may not like Mama having a boyfriend," said Judy.

"Isabelle's family is very close. The kids miss their Dad. But they all have their own families now. They must know Isabelle gets lonely."

"Lonely! She's liberated! Who wants to be tied down to a husband; and an old one, at that? She has sixteen grandkids for God's sake. No, I think she and Will are having a couple of dates before he heads home and she will resume her role as doting Nana and he'll resume his as the Playboy of the Western World" said Judy.

"Will loved her so much when we were kids. Perhaps he's carried a torch for her all these years. He could be very persuasive," said Carol.

Judy said, "We all loved someone fifty years ago. Believe me there's no torch, the only thing Will Benton carried for the last fifty years was his dick in his hand and a large supply of condoms."

"Sometimes I wonder if you've ever really been in love. You're so cynical," said Carol.

"I kind of loved my second husband", said Judy. "He was good to my boys. He wasn't perfect, he drank and gambled and his mother was a witch but he had a good heart until he left me."

"Did he hum?" asked Carol.

"Shut up".

When Will arrived at Isabelle's he found her in the front yard talking to a little girl. The girl was excited and shouting, "Nana, Nana, come see the big fish daddy caught." Isabelle went to greet Will and asked him to come next door with her. She said "Will this is my grand-daughter, Fiona, and she says her daddy has a big fish".

"Hello, Fiona" said Will.

"Hi" said Fiona.

They went in the yard next door to find her son filleting a large striped bass. Isabelle introduced the two men and her son, Kevin, was so engrossed in his catch of the day that he hardly paid attention to the fact that his mother had a male friend.

Will was full of praise. "What a beauty, how much does he weigh?"

"Oh, about forty pounds, this is the third one I've caught this year."

"What else do you get?"

"Mackerel, but I use that for bait, my freezer's full of it and I have a few lobster pots."

"Really, do you get many?"

"Some days are luckier than others, but I've gotten seven so far this season. I made a nice stuffed lobster dinner last week. I used some of the striper with crackers for stuffing and tons of butter. It was great".

Will was a fisherman himself. He and the younger man got on pretty well. Will said his friend had arranged a deep sea fishing trip for Monday and asked Kevin what kind of bait and hooks he should use? Will told Kevin he'd often fished near Minot's light but they were leaving from the lower Cape on Monday. Her son told him he liked Hull Gut but Isabelle knew no real fishing secrets would be given away. They said goodbye and Isabelle's son said "I hope you reel some big ones in on Monday." He seemed like a nice guy said her son to himself. Who is he and why is he with my mother?

Will opened the car door for Isabelle. She started to give him directions to the library. He told her that her son looked a lot like her. He had her light blue eyes but he was big like Tim. He wanted to know which son he was, the oldest, or the youngest? He was one of the middle ones she told him. He's forty five. She had him when she was twenty five. He was child number four. He was a teacher and had his summer's off that's why he went fishing so much. He was married and had four children. "Take a right at the end of this street" said Isabelle.

"My son, Jack, is forty five", said Will.

Will told her how he had seen Tom and Paul the night before and about their plans for the fishing expedition. She said she was glad to hear it and hoped they had a good time. She also said she had plans for Monday at Plymouth and Christmas Tree Shops with the cousins. "Take a left at the next light" she said.

Then he asked about the lecture. Isabelle told him that Tim had been a member of the Historical Society for years and although it was not her cup of tea they had once listened to an audio version of a book entitled "My Dearest Friend" which was a biographical account of the love letters between John and Abigail Adams. There had been thirty-two doubled sided cassettes and it took Tim and Isabelle months to listen to the entire story. It was wonderful. John and Abigail were remarkable, so intelligent, so brave, so in love and way ahead of their time. Isabelle said it made her like history and so now I want to learn more about them. This lecturer is an author who just published another biography about John Adams. I think it might be interesting. The Revolutionary War was such an historical event and tomorrow is the Forth of July, how fitting. So I thought this would be something to do and it's free. Then she said "The parking lot is on the right about fifty yards up".

"I need to return these library books first OK?" said Isabelle

"Sure" said Will.

"Oh my God," said Judy. "Do you see who I see? Will and Isabelle are going into the library. That is not the type of date I would ever picture Will going on. I'd picture him taking her to a strip joint so she could learn a few moves"

"Isabelle has arthritis in her knees she can't do any moves. Maybe she's just returning books and he's just looking around," said Carol.

"Go get Dillon and tell him we're going into the library. There must be a children's room. We have to see what they are doing here. I'm telling you, she needs our protection."

Carol went and told Dillon that they were going to play a game called Spy. They were going to find their cousin. See if you can find a nice lady wearing a light blue shirt. She brought the boy over to the bench and then the three of them approached the entrance of the library. There was a sign saying "Lecture Here – John Adams Review" first floor meeting room. They both said "No way would Will Benton go to a lecture". Judy headed for the adult library door. Will was wandering around the library while Isabelle returned her books and spoke with the librarian and then talked to a friend she met. There was an art exhibition there as well and Will perused the displays. He walked up and down the aisles of the book cases and felt like he was being watched. He saw a book he had meant to read and reached for it. In the gap that was left on the book shelf he saw an eyeball staring directly at him. The eye ball move away quickly. Will put the book back and went to the next aisle but no one was there. Judy had run around another aisle so as not to be seen. He went back to where the book was and a grey haired head popped out from behind the other end of the book shelf. "What the hell" said Will? This time he moved as fast as he could but she was elusive. She had hidden behind a newspaper at the reading table at the end of the book case. She had her arms extended and the paper opened wide covering her face. She looked like some innocent person reading the paper. She was peeking from behind it. In the meantime Carol had taken Dillon to the children's reading room. He selected a "Captain Underpants" book and was allowed to take it out with his own card.

He asked, "Carol, when does the spy game begin?"

Carol said, "What, Oh, now, I guess."

Carol and Dillon went to find Judy at the adult section. Isabelle came to find Will. Judy tried to peer over the newspaper without being seen. Carol and Dillon approached Isabelle. An innocent bystander with a stack of books in her arms was looking at the books on the same shelf Will was at. Judy's hand bag fell off the table spilling the remains of her coffee. She got up so quickly to retrieve her purse that she knocked over the four foot spinning globe of the world and soaked the newspaper at the same time. Dillon rushed the stranger with the armful of books, grabbed her and said "I found her". The woman dropped all of her books on the floor, looked down at the boy and said, "What are you talking about". Will, who was on his way to Isabelle, tripped over the fallen books and went face first onto the globe of the world and started rolling back and forth on it as if he was on one of those large exercise balls. He got up with as much dignity as he could muster for a seventy-one year old man, replaced the globe to its original position and glared at Judy. Librarians came running from all directions and if you've never seen an angry librarian watch out. Carol and Isabelle exchanged pained looks.

"We were playing Spy" said the boy "and I found the lady with the light blue shirt." Many apologies were made and they all left.

"I won" said Dillon, "do I get a prize".

"I'll get you something later" said Judy. Carol and Judy headed for the parking lot and Burger King.

Will and Isabelle went into the lecture.

Will said, "Do you think Sherlock and Watson are still here".

"I hope not", said Isabelle.

# CHAPTER FIVE: THE PARTY

The Fourth of July was gorgeous, eighty degrees and breezy. At noon Isabelle drove to her son's house with ABBA singing "Take a Chance on Me" on a CD. Judy, Carol and Kathy were headed to the same destination and still talking about the disaster at the library. Will and Paul were on their way as well and they used Paul's car since he had a GPS system.

Gerry's yard was big, his house was big, and he was big. Gerry was Isabelle's oldest son and he was ready for the party. He had the white party tent erected, a water slide for the kids, his pool had been vacuumed and tables and chairs were set up all over the place. His wife was in the kitchen arranging platters and getting food and drinks ready. His kids were helping him put trash bags in barrels and ice in coolers. The washer toss boards were in place and ready. He loved this party. Every year since he and his wife had been married they had the Fourth of July party. They played cards and games and ate good food and ended it with a large fire works display. His father had enjoyed it and Gerry missed him. He wondered if his mother was sad when the rest of the family was together and Dad wasn't there. Did she think there was somehow a hole in the family that couldn't be filled? She never showed her loneliness, but he knew she was a sensitive, kind woman, almost a romantic. She was always watching some old romance or musical movie on television and usually British. She seemed happy enough when he saw her but maybe she hid her feelings.

Kathy was driving her car, with Judy and Carol in the back seat. She had a large aluminum pan of pasta salad on the front passenger seat.

She pulled in to a convenient store and said, "I have to buy a lottery ticket.

There's a bonus game today; because of the Fourth of July".

"Want me to get you guys any?"

Judy said "Yes" and gave her a dollar.

Carol said, "No thanks."

Kathy got back in the car, started up; and handed Judy one ticket. She placed two other tickets, she had bought, carefully into her purse. She did not want to damage her newly filled and polished talons trying to scratch tickets, the nails could break; the lottery tickets could wait. Kathy lit up a smoke. She had all the windows opened for this reason. She was listening to the cousins recall yesterday's events.

Kathy said, "You two don't have to spy today. Will and Isabelle will both be here and you can watch them to your hearts' content. I'm glad Isabelle called last night. I was afraid after what you two told me that she might be angry."

"Why should she be angry", said Judy. "We're only looking out for her well being and Will Benton would like to do well with her being. He's a snake in the grass if ever there was one. I know."

"You're too hard on Will; and Isabelle is old enough to know what she's doing" said Carol.

Judy said, "Hard on" and "Will" in the same sentence is correct; "Isabelle" and "old", correct. Kathy when are you going to kick that vile habit? Your lungs must be black by now."

Kathy blew out two perfect smoke rings in response.

"I'm glad Isabelle told you Will was bringing Paul", said Carol. "I always liked him. He was good looking when he was young and now he's a widower. Did you know he goes to the same church as you Kathy?"

"I don't get there every Sunday but I know his mother used to be in the choir" said Kathy. "She was nice and he had an aunt, his mom's sister, who was nice too. I remember them from the lake."

"Oh God, Paul is alright but he tends to be a bit religious and a little wimpy; too much Catholic training. Isabelle and her brother can get like that too sometimes," Judy said. She went on "Thank God we only had public school in Vermont and our CCD classes were few and far between. It really didn't matter, none of us got married in the church and Mom went to the Episcopal Church in the end. Dad must be rolling over in his sweet little Catholic grave. We all prayed to the same God. What's the big deal? I'll bet Paul always let his wife get on top in bed. Marie was nice, but a bit of a priss and I think she was bossy. She could cook though. When Paul and Marie were dating she made meatballs for some party we had at the lake and I still remember them. Always marry and Italian if you like good food. That was fifty years ago when Will and Isabelle were still together. Boy they were good meatballs!"

"I recall that party," said Kathy. "I was hoping to get a boy friend there, but no luck. I was so much younger and always tried to look older. I got a new outfit a black three quarter sleeve jersey with a rhinestone trim at the neckline and black Capri pants with slits on the sides and flats with bows on the toes. It's when I wore my hair short in a pixie cut. I thought I looked like Audrey Hepburn."

"Well you didn't, you looked like Elvira. Why do you always wear black?" said Judy.

"It's slimming. I'm still wearing black. Maybe I'll find a boyfriend today" said Kathy.

"Give me a break", said Judy. "We're too old for boyfriends. Maybe Dracula will be there all dressed in black. You'd like that. Anyway I hope we can get a card game going I'd rather deal cards then deal with men."

"I rather like men", said Carol, "but there will probably be slim pickings if only relatives are invited. Maybe Gerry's wife's family will have some eligible old bachelors. Maybe there will be some interesting male friends and neighbors. I better put on some lipstick just in case," said Carol reaching for her pocket book.

Judy thought with those cargo shorts, the grey braid and the Statue of Liberty tee shirt, Carol's chances of hooking up were zero. For once she was polite and said nothing.

Paul was driving at a moderate speed. Paul did everything moderately. He wore tan cargo shorts and a tan tee shirt with a Statue of Liberty emblazoned on it. He had on olive colored crocks. Did men really wear these kind of shoes thought Will? Will noticed the outfit but said nothing. Paul had a lot of quirks but he was a nice guy. Will had on white shorts and a navy polo shirt. He wore a Red Sox baseball hat so people, who didn't know him, wouldn't know he was bald, also he looked good in the cap. He was a vain man. His white sox were dazzling. He sure knew about separating clothes for washing and used a lot of bleach. Not bad for a guy. He wore sparkling clean, white sneakers as well. He wanted to impress Isabelle's family. He may have gone too heavy with the aftershave.

Paul said, "I'm interested in this washer game Isabelle told you about. If it's like horse shoes I'll probably be good at it. Sounds like fun anyway. I hope there's a lot of food there. I don't get too many home cooked meals these days and I like to eat. Maybe there will be some Italian food, although that may not be patriotic. Isabelle's brother and the cousins will be there. Maybe we'll get a card game going".

"Isabelle will be there too. How come you didn't mention her", said Will.

"Isabelle will only have eyes for you. You'll be busy being scrutinized by her kids and then she'll be busy with the grandkids. Have you met any of them," asked Paul.

"I met a little granddaughter named Fiona and Isabelle's son, Kevin. She's sweet and he's quite the fisherman. He was gutting a forty pound striper when we met. He seemed like a nice guy. With six kids and their spouses and sixteen grandkids I don't know how I'll keep track of who's who. I'll never get them right."

"You'd better," said Paul.

"We should have brought something", said Paul, "you know wine or cookies. At times like this I miss Marie. She remembered all that polite stuff. Want to stop at a store?"

"I bought a case of Bud Lite and a bottle of Chardonnay last night and put it them in the trunk this morning," said Will.

Isabelle arrived first. She was still singing "Dancing Queen" when so got out of her car. She was wearing white Capri pants and a bright red three quarter v neck jersey. It showed some cleavage but not too much. Seventy year old cleavage is not a pretty site. She had little flag earrings in her ears and a red white and blue beaded elastic bracelet around her wrist. Gerry kissed his mother, grabbed the heavy pan with a huge baked ham in it and showed her into the house. Isabelle kissed his wife, Andrea, and produced a tray filled with tons of white frosted brownies with red, white and blue sprinkles on them.

"Thank you" said, Andrea.

Isabelle also had a clear plastic jar filled with gummy bears with a sign that said "Guess How Many?"

"Where do you want this" asked Isabelle.

"I'll take it," said Andrea.

"Everything looks wonderful as usual," said Isabelle. "I invited the cousins, you knew that, and I also invited two old friends. I hope you don't mind."

"No, the more the merrier" they said.

"Who are the two ladies", asked Gerry, "anyone we know?"

"Actually they're men. Two guys I knew fifty years ago at the lake we spent summers at. Will and Paul are their names", said Isabelle. "Paul still lives on the lake, he's a widower and Will lives in Louisiana with his son's family. The cousins and Uncle Bob know them. It will keep all the old people entertained."

"Will? The one Dad called your first boy friend" said Gerry.

"Yes, that Will", said Isabelle.

"I met them by chance when I joined the cousins for lunch last week. The men were good at horse shoes when we were young, maybe they'll kick your butt at washer toss."

"Two old geezers are no competition for me, Ma," said Gerry.

"We'll see", said Isabelle, "we'll see".

Judy, Kathy and Carol got out of the car and looked around.

"Wow, they sure know how to throw a party said Kathy. I wish I wore something with more bling"

Isabelle greeted them and introduced them again to Gerry and his family.

"I know we've all met before", said Judy, "but your mother was like the Old Woman in the Shoe, so we can never get all the names and faces together. You look like both of your parents but you're huge. Carol and I brought a couple of bottles of Sangria and a couple of liters of Coke and a little rum to go with it. Here you go." She handed the beverages to Gerry.

"Thanks," he said, "you must be Judy because I always remember Carol's braid and I see Kathy more so I know her."

He bent over to hug the three women and his wife took the pasta salad from Kathy.

Kathy hugged Gerry's wife and told her how beautiful the yard and house looked. She said hello to their children, two girls and two boys, and then convened to the back yard where the party was starting. Carol asked to use the bathroom and Isabelle and Judy joined Kathy outside. Lots of friends and family members were arriving all at once. Isabelle's two daughters came at the same time with their husbands and kids. They kissed their mother and the cousins. Judy had been the oldest daughter's god mother so she was referred to as Jeanne's Mother of God. Carol and Kathy were god mothers to two of Isabelle's sons but lost track of which one went with which.

Paul and Will came into the yard a few minutes later.

"Gerry, this is Will Benton and Paul D'Angelo. Boys this is my oldest son, Gerry", said Isabelle.

They were introduced to Gerry and he put the wine and beer on ice. Isabelle noticed Gerry stood a little taller and was actually sizing Will up. Will held his own. Gerry hadn't thanked them for the liquor.

Billy came over with his live in girl of the month and kissed his mother. He was already drinking. Billy was the second son, tall dark and handsome and a handful. He was wearing a red flowered island type shirt. He thought he looked like Tom Selleck without the moustache. He did have those long slim legs and wavy dark hair. He was always able to find nice girls too. He never wanted to stay with any of them very long. She named the right one after Will.

"Ma this is Jane. Jane this is my mother", said Bill.

"Hi Jane", said Isabelle, "welcome to the party. Bill and Jane this is Will Benton."

"Will Benton", said Billy, "I've heard that name before. Are you famous?"

"No, I'm not famous just an old friend."

"Old how old are you? Ha! Ha! Ha! You walked right into that one," said Billy. Catch you later Will. Settle it Ma." Bill and Jane walked away.

"Don't ask," said Isabelle, "Yes he's the one I named after you and he's a character like you too. It's a curse"

Will was pleased she named a child after him.

Over to the left, Judy said, "Oh my God. Paul D'Angelo is wearing the same outfit as Carol. Now those are two people who aren't slaves to fashion. Talk about making a patriotic statement and clothing disaster all at the same time. Whoa!"

"Hey look in the mirror, Sis, you're wearing a green jersey jumper that looks like a potato sack. And your body fills it so you look like a huge dill pickle with legs. And hot pink flip flops! Nice accessory! You are and American who does not love her country. Where are your colors", said Carol?

"The difference is that you think you look good," said Judy. "I could give a fat frog's ass."

"Now that you mention it you look like that too," said Carol.

"I need a cigarette", said Kathy, "and maybe a drink too. All you girls do is make fun of each other and of my black clothes. At least I'm presentable and in case you didn't notice there's a flag brooch pinned to my blouse. Neither one of you better say another word."

"The bead and sequin queen has spoken," said Judy.

"Ladies, Ladies," said Isabelle, "you all look beautiful. Paul and Will are here."

"Isabelle, where ever did you get that bra", said Judy, "those sagging girls are pointing heavenward. It takes strong straps to keep those babies hoisted. What support! They look real and spectacular"

"They do" said Will.

"There are children here", said Isabelle. "Behave yourselves. I'm an old grandmother"

Will said "My grandmother never looked so good"

Paul said, "Inappropriate Judy and Inappropriate Will".

"Oh God", said Judy, "you're not going to recite a gospel or psalm or something are you Paul? Relax. Chill out, take some deep breaths. Have a beer."

Judy added, "Oh Paul, here comes Bob maybe you two could lead us in the Rosary later."

"No amount of Rosaries could save you, Judy," replied Paul.

Isabelle's brother, Bob, and his wife, Esther, arrived and they sat with Paul and the cousins and got acquainted and re-acquainted. Carol told Paul she liked his outfit. He said the same to her. They were serious. Judy said she'd like to get a card game going.

Bob, who was a little deaf, said, "What, You like to get hard rain and snowing"?

"Cards, later", Judy said louder.

"I'll play", he said.

Bob and his wife wanted to hear and tell all the latest gossip. Kathy just smoked and listened.

Will and Isabelle stood to the side and he said to her, "Who is the young blonde woman who's holding the little girl's hand?"

"That's my youngest girl, Tricia," said Isabelle.

"I thought so. She looks just like you."

"No, I was never that pretty."

"Yes you were."

Jeanne and Tricia came over to their mother. Jeanne asked Isabelle, "Ma did you bring your camera? I forgot mine. Those freakin' sons of mine farted around and took so long getting ready, I forgot my camera and Dan takes forever in the toilet. He always has to take a dump at the last minute. I swear I'll never be on time for anything. I had to fight with them all to wear sandals, all their sneakers smelled like ass. One kid had a big rip in his fly and crotch area. He wanted to know why I was making him change his shorts. I told him I didn't want Tommy and the Twins in the spotlight. Just because they have no sisters, they forget they have girl cousins. I think they'd go around bare assed if I'd let them. The two older ones had no gas money and we all can't fit in one car anymore, so I had to dig through my bag for cash. If some young thing in a mini skirt walked by, they'd find money to take her out. Sean took forever with his weightlifting and then the half hour shower that followed. Jeez. Heaven forbid he missed a day of working out. All I wanted to do was get here early so I could practice for washer toss. If my brother, Joe, thinks I'm losing to the likes of him this year again he can forget it. Now everyone is practicing. Son of a bitch! I hate to lose."

"My camera is in my purse under the table, right near Judy's feet. Jeanne, Tricia this is Will Benton," said Isabelle.

"Will Benton, The first boyfriend? I thought you'd be dead by now," said Jeanne. She added "Humph, how do you do." Then she gave her mother a puzzled look.

"I do fine", said Will, "and I can't believe you said all that to your mother in one breath. You look like your Dad."

"Tell me something I don't know". Jeanne walked away. She went to get the camera in her mother's pocket book.

Will looked at Tricia. She was fair and had the same smile that would light up a room but her eyes were a darker blue.

He said, "You look so much like your mother."

"I used to hate when people said that, not because I didn't want to look like her but because, well, I'm forty and I don't want to look seventy. Now I'm so used to it I don't mind. I'm glad to meet you Will."

She kissed her mother and walked away.

"Jeanne's husband is the tall guy with the moustache standing with Gerry and Tricia's is the one in plaid shorts practicing washer toss", said Isabelle.

"My girls are totally different aren't they?"

"Yes"

"You know I'll never remember all these names, but I'll try," said Will.

Joe walked over with a pad of paper and a pen in his hand. "Hi, Ma, he said. Either of you up for the washer toss tournament? I'm taking names to make the teams"

"Will this is my youngest son, Joe", said Isabelle. "He introduced our family to washer toss. In fact, he built the boards. He's very clever. Joe this is Will Benton."

"Hey, Will, How Ya doin'", said Joe. They shook hands.

"Good to meet you Joe and I think you can put both our names down, right Isabelle?"

"Yes"

"Ma, you stink at it, but you keep trying. Good for you." Joe walked away and winked at his mother.

"That's Joe's wife, Erin, over near the pool, with the purple shirt", said Isabelle. "They have a boy and a girl, James and Lily. See the kids getting into the water?" said Isabelle.

They joined the others at the old folks' table. Judy was still trying to get a Scotch Bridge game going. She said that she always carried a deck of cards in her hand bag, just in case. Bob and his wife and Judy said "No" to the washer toss tournament. Carol, Kathy and Paul were in. There was no lull in conversation. Everyone was catching up with the last fifty years. Bob found it amazing that he and Paul attended the same Church and never ran into one another. Bob had seen his mother in Shaws supermarket a few times too. Bob had been in the choir for years with both Paul's aunt and mother and had seen a lot of them before they passed away.

"My mother said she had seen you a couple of times", said Paul.

"Who," asked Bob?

"My mother", said Paul?

"Where" asked Bob.

"At Shaws, I think or in the choir", said Paul.

"Your mother is at Shaws", said Bob, "I thought she died."

"She did die" said Paul.

"She died at Shaws", asked Bob?

"Talk louder", said Esther to Paul.

"Oh, she did die". Paul yelled "but she told me she had seen you at Shaws a couple of times."

"I told you I saw her, a couple of times." said Bob.

"Right," said Paul

Bob's wife, Esther, took a shine to Paul at once. She thought he was a nice guy. She wanted to know if he and Carol were together. She wondered if they had other matching outfits. Esther asked Carol. Carol said, "No, it's just a case of great minds having the same idea." Esther made no comment about the great fashion idea. She was a polite woman.

Esther knew Kathy since they lived next door. Isabelle's mom and Kathy's mom had homes built side by side around 1969 and when the two ladies died one became Bob's home and the other Kathy's. The Vermont girls were Bob cousins too, so Esther knew them. The noise was happy chatter and as the crowd grew so did the volume. It was good to be at a family party, with cold drinks, water melon, and apple pie. Flags were flying and hung on display for decorations. Most folks had on red, white or blue of some kind. After all it was the Fourth of July.

"I remember we tried to teach you to water ski, Bob. You really never got the hang of it," said Paul in a loud voice.

"I can't ride a bike either, I'm not agile" replied Bob.

"That's unusual because your sister could do all that stuff."

"My sister can do what stuff" asked Bob.

"Ride a bike and water ski" said Paul louder.

"She's just a show off. I can row a boat" said Bob.

"And he can sing" said his wife in defense of her man.

"That's more than you can say for Paul," said Will.

"I can sing and at least I still have some hair" said Paul.

"Ha, Ha" said Will.

Will had been talking with Paul, Bob and the others and meeting Bob's wife. It was like a reunion of old friends. He noticed Isabelle had strolled away and he went looking for her. There she was sitting on a chair in front of the kid's water slide. She was bare foot with a toddler sitting on her lap and two big young men standing at her back. She was serene and lovely. He wanted to take her into his arms.

"Hi, Nana," said one big kid.

"Hello, Nana" said the other.

They each planted a kiss on the top of her head. When Will approached she said, "Will, these two guys are my two oldest grandsons, Danny and Patrick. They'll be finished with college next year."

Will shook their hands and said, "How are you, I'll bet you two play a lot of sports."

"Football, wrestling and track" said one.

"Not since high school", said the other.

"Are you in the washer tournament?" Patrick asked.

Will said he was looking forward to it.

"Can't wait to kick your butt", said Danny. The kids smiled and walked away.

"They're big guys" said Will; "whose kids are they".

"Jeanne and Dan's", said Isabelle. "They're the ones who need gas money and make her late for everything."

Will laughed. "And who is this", asked Will, nodding toward the little boy on Isabelle's lap.

"He's Liam my youngest grandchild", said Isabelle, "his father is the one who caught the striper."

"He's a handsome boy," said Will.

Several children came sliding down the water slide yelling, "Nana, watch me." She did. She answered "Great," or "Good Job".

A couple of older kids were in the swimming pool.

The girl said, "Hey Nana watch me cannon ball". The girl jumped, with knees up, arms around them and splashed about a half dozen dry parents who were keeping an eye on their own kids in the pool.

Isabelle looked and said "Wow, good jump" to the girl as if she was the only child there. The other kid said "Nana I can stay under water for a whole minute." He was chubby and cute and about eleven years old.

"That's great, she said, but don't try it for any longer you'll pass out and I don't feel like jumping in today to save you"

"OK" he said.

Her daughter-in-law, Ann, came over to take the baby from her.

She said, "Thanks for holding him while I helped Fiona change into her swim suit."

"No problem", said Isabelle, and kissed the squirming baby and handed him to his mother. "Ann this is Will Benton" said Isabelle.

Ann said, "Nice to meet you".

Gerry's wife stood on the deck ringing a large cow bell to summon everyone to line up for food. No one needed to be asked twice. There was a stampede led mostly by teenage boys. Mothers got plates for little ones and the seniors were at the end of the line. Stacks of Styrofoam plates, plastic utensils and napkins were grabbed. There were tables covered with red, white and blue cloths and loaded with pans, bowls and platters of food. There were lots of choices to be made, salads, ham, fried chicken, sausages and peppers, rice casserole, mac and cheese, lasagna, meatballs, everything was there. No one would go hungry today. They all loaded their plates and headed back to the table. Will and Paul grabbed some beers and soft drinks. All had heaping dishes of food.

Carol and Paul not only had the same type of food on their plates; it was arranged the same way, like a clock. Twelve was meat balls, space; three was lasagna, space; six was sausage, space; nine was salad, one more space. The only exception was that right in the center of Paul's dish was a roll. We all looked at their plates in astonishment but Paul and Carol were oblivious to what was going on.

She said, "Oh, drat, I forgot to get a roll."

"I'll go back for one ," said Paul, "you can't eat Italian food without bread."

We were all looking at them. They had no clue. All the rest of us had different foods on our plates. All of us had piled a little of everything to our tastes wherever we could fit it, with no rhyme or reason. We were all looking at their plates. Then we looked at our own plates. Then we looked at their plates again.

When Paul returned with the roll, Judy said, "Carol, Paul, Stop," look at your plates".

Carol looked at them like she saw neatly folded clothes.

Paul looked and shrugged.

"What" asked Carol?

"So?" said Paul.

"You both have identical plates, and identical food placed at identical spots. Don't you find that strange," said Judy.

Paul said, "I'm seventy years old, I don't find anything strange anymore. I don't like my food touching each other that's all."

"Me too Paul," said Carol. "If I wanted it all to taste like each other I'd mix it all up. I like the individual tastes and I like Italian."

"Just the food or the people?" said Judy.

"Both" said Carol, shoveling food in her mouth.

Judy thought, "I know she's my sister and she's not a stupid woman but she really doesn't know what's going on all the time".

"Did it occur to you two that you both like horrible, holiday clothes and you're neurotic about your eating habits," said Judy.

They both said, "No".

Kathy said, "In their defense, they can eat whatever they like and wear whatever they want. I mean I wouldn't be caught dead in those outfits or be anal enough to arrange my food on my plate like that but what the heck, live and let live."

It went right over Carol's head, she said, "These are good meatballs"

Paul said, "They remind me of the ones Marie used to make."

Carol said, "Judy was talking about that last night. She said she remembered Marie made meat balls for a party we had when we were at the lake years ago and they were so good she never forgot them".

"Judy actually said something nice", said Paul.

"She gets like that once in a while", said Carol.

"Really, I never would have guessed" said Paul

Judy couldn't let it go. She blurted out, "Well I'm surprised Paul didn't make us all say grace before he dug into his organized Italian plate"

"I said grace to myself", said Paul raising the volume of his voice.

"Me too", said Bob, and then with a sly smile, "I hope my sister, Isabelle, did too. Sometimes I think her faith's not as strong as it used to be."

Isabelle replied loud enough, "Alas, I shamefully tucked in to my meal without saying grace and I hope that God and all the angels in heaven will forgive me and Sweet Baby Jesus and all the saints and martyrs will welcome me into their arms at the moment of my death."

Everyone was silent. Then Will threw back his head and produced one of his famous, handsome laughs that Isabelle loved, with the dazzling smile and the creased dimple.

Bob said, "Isabelle, I think that was a sacrilege."

"I think so too. You may be going to hell with Will," said Paul

"I'll be in good company," said Isabelle. The others all looked at her. Will was smiling.

Joe came over to announce the teams for the washer toss tournament. Joe took this game seriously and as long as he didn't lose to his sister, Jeanne, he was happy.

He said, "Carol, you are partners with my sister, Jeanne. Jeanne's good so you lucked out."

Carol said, "Joe, I think I'm your god mother. Will I need my glasses?"

Kathy piped in "No, I think he's mine and for everyone's sake wear your glasses."

"He's not yours; Kevin's yours, I think I remember now," said Carol.

"Which one is Kevin" asked Kathy.

Will said "He's the one who caught a stripe bass. He's over there holding the little boy".

"How big" asked Bob?

"The striper weighed about forty pounds I don't know how much the baby weighs", said Will.

Joe said, "Carol is my god mother, I remember."

"What a memory and he was only two weeks old. That's my smart boy," said Carol.

"Well Joe didn't catch the striper" said Kathy, "Kevin did".

Joe felt like he was in an insane asylum. He announced that Will and Danny were partners. Isabelle and Dennis, Tricia's husband, were partners. Paul and Kathy were partners.

"The partners were drawn from names in a hat so no changing teams," Joe said. "We have three boards going simultaneously. You will be called for your turn. If you lose you're out. The final two have a championship match. If you lose, Carol, be careful, Jeanne can get nasty. Good Luck."

"Carol" shouted Jeanne, "Come on over here we have to kick some butt."

"Who are we playing against", she asked.

"Paul and Kathy," answered Jeanne.

The game was explained and since Jeanne was the only one who knew what she was doing, she went first. She stood in place, tossed the first washer and it landed in the far hole. "Five points", she shouted. Then she tossed the second washer. "One point, she yelled, take that Joey". Then she threw the last one and it went on the grass. "Shit", she said.

Ok we have six points"

Paul let Kathy go first. He was always a gentleman. She threw the first washer and it landed in the middle hole.

"You got a three points", said Paul.

She tossed the second and it went on the grass. She threw the third and it just sat on the board.

"Oh well, three points are better than none," Kathy said.

Carol was up next she took aim and no one knows how it happened. The washer soared through the air with such force and speed that it smashed into Paul's forehead. It was a freak accident but the washer hit just at the right angle and hard. Blood spurted out profusely. Paul was dazed but did not fall. One of the guests was a nurse and said he'd be fine but should have a butterfly stitch. She took him in the house and cleaned and repaired the injury. Carol was embarrassed and felt bad.

Judy shouted, "Didn't you wear your glasses".

Carol said "Yes, I did. It was just an accident."

Paul came back with his butterfly bandage. On his shirt the Statue of Liberty's torch was red with his own spatter of blood. Carol apologized. They resumed the game. Carol got no points for her team but Paul got three for his. The score was tied six to six. Jeanne's team and Paul's team had to go again to break the tie. In the end Paul's team won and everyone was safe from Carol's aim or throw or whatever. Jeanne was not a happy camper since now she was out of the game for good. Her brothers all smiled and laughed. She gave them the finger.

Carol and Paul were talking over by the pool. Everyone figured she was still apologizing and feeling bad about splitting his head open with the washer. It was quite an animated conversation. Judy thought, maybe with those shirts on they were getting ready to sing the National Anthem or something. It would be fitting. They were both religious and patriotic. Maybe they'd sing "God Bless America". Carol did dress up like Kate Smith once for Halloween. She used grapefruits in a pair of socks tied around her neck for the boobs. My mind is wandering thought Judy. Neither of them can sing that well and I've had too much to drink. They should have Bob do the anthem while he's still here, at least he can sing. Where are Isabelle and Will? Is that cad making a move on my cousin? He's going home Tuesday so he'll probably be aggressive today. I have to keep focused. Thank God I'm not driving.

Will and Danny went next. "Looks like I won't get a chance to kick your butt, since were partners", said Danny.

"Well maybe will take the tournament," said Will.

They were good. They won their match easily. In the second round Kathy and Paul were eliminated. Isabelle and Dennis were eliminated. Joe was right, she did stink but Dennis did not and felt gypped. Will and Danny went to the end but Sean and Victoria got the trophy.

When Will came back to the table there was a card game going on. They all asked Will how he did.

He shouted, "Took second place."

"Second place is good," said Bob.

He looked at Isabelle and said, "Second place, story of my life."

They played cards and had coffee and day turn into night. Bob and Esther went home early they didn't like traffic, noise, or bugs.

"There go the two party animals", said Judy as Bob and Esther walked to their car.

They all faced their chairs toward the fire works and as Kathy fished in her hand bag for another cigarette she pulled out the red, white and blue sequined visor she meant to put on earlier.

"Well better late than never," she said. She plopped it on top of her head and said, "Paul and Carol eat your hearts out".

"That's the spirit", said Paul.

"I'm proud of you Kathy", said Carol.

"I think I'm going to puke", said Judy.

The mosquitoes weren't too bad and the kids were getting excited for the fire works. They were already holding sparklers while Gerry and Joe set the bigger fire works up. The explosions went off safely and beautifully. Judy, Carol and Kathy thanked Gerry and Andrea for a nice day and said good bye. They were standing by Kathy's car telling Isabelle to be on time Monday.

Paul and Will were ready to go.

As Paul got to his car Carol said, "Paul do you want to do lunch tomorrow"?

He was taken back but quickly said, "Yes".

She handed him a piece of paper. "I'm staying at Kathy's; call me in the morning after Mass."

He said, "OK"

She said "Good night".

Paul smiled.

Kathy drove along Route 58 heading home.

She said, "Carol, you shady lady. I didn't think you had it in you."

Carol said "Well he's so shy sometimes and I did hit him in the head with the washer. I want to make it up to him. Besides, we had on matching outfits and eat the same way. It must be destiny. Don't you think so? I knew he wouldn't make a move but he did talk to me a lot today and he's nice."

"I'm proud of you", said Kathy. "You go girl"

"We'll have to fix her up", said Judy.

"Get rid of the braid and put better clothes on her. You have to wear your glasses or you'll fall down. Too bad you can't get contacts. What do you think Kathy?"

"I'll be the one to fix her up, not you. I may wear bling, but it's better than the crunchy, granola, granny outfits your wear," said Kathy.

"Thanks a lot", said Judy.

"He wore the same outfit as me so he must like it," said Carol. "I'll go with my own feelings, thank you just the same. At my age all I have to be is clean and covered."

"Paul D'Angleo, Oh my God," said Judy. "He's an average man, average height; average weight; average everything; probably average in bed. He's a dentist for God's sake. You better floss and use mouth wash. He'll be looking at your teeth. At least you still have yours. Maybe that's why he likes you. He wants to get his tools on you. He's a dentist. How average is that? He's not even a doctor. He's just average".

"Well it takes more than that to resume a game and win after you've been injured", said Carol.

"Average wound" said Judy.

Back at Gerry's, Isabelle was saying good bye to Will. He held her and kissed her right in front of anyone who was there. He had balls, old balls, but balls none the less. Some of her kids were there. Her big son, Gerry, was there. Paul saw it all from the driver's seat. Where were her other boys? Would these guys thrash Will to protect their mother? Can Will fight any more? Could he ever? Will was a lover not a fighter. He was in the Army, he must know something. What am I thinking? Will was in the Army fifty years ago. I did box in college maybe I should jump out to be on the ready. What am I thinking? I was in college fifty years ago. Will you're on your own thought Paul. Will and Isabelle made plans for brunch tomorrow and Will got into the car. He said he'd call her later. Paul sighed in relief and drove away.

On the way home Paul told Will about his date with Carol tomorrow.

"Get the hell out of here", said Will. "You and Carol are going on a date?"

"It's just lunch. She's going back to Vermont next week. I'll probably never see her again. Besides, I think she feels bad about hitting me in the head," said Paul.

"She asked you?" said Will. "Well you do have stuff in common, the clothes and the way you put food on a plate. At least you have that going for you. How hard were you hit on the head?"

"I'm a lonely, desperate man. Why should you be the only one having fun?" said Paul.

"This is true" said Will.

They spent the rest of the ride home keeping each other awake. They were older than they thought.

The crowd had dwindled and the yard was quiet except for the crickets and a random fire cracker.

Isabelle was getting ready to go. She put her sandals back on and got her pocket book from under the table and started up the path to say good night to her family. They were all there, waiting. Some of the boys had their arms folded across their chests. She felt like she was facing a firing squad. Was she a defendant standing before the judge waiting for the verdict? Was this what it was like to reach the pearly gates and find St. Peter glaring at you and reminding you of all your sins? Oh boy here goes nothing she thought.

She thought they'd shoot comments at her like bullets. Comments like "Will Benton???" "Is this serious?" "When did you start seeing him?" "You're too old for this sort of thing" "I don't want a new daddy". "I hope you know what you're doing" "How long has this been going on." "Do you want that old man for a new husband"? "What do you really know about Will." "He might have been a nice boy fifty years ago but a lot can happen." "When's he going back to Louisiana" "Soon I hope" "You really don't know what men are like" "Be careful"

They said nothing.

Gerry said, "Did you have a nice time".

Isabelle said "Yes".

She kissed them all and went home.

The kids had been thinking all the comments Isabelle envisioned but they just looked at one another and said things like "It must suck to be old and lonely". "He didn't seem too bad". "He was pretty good at washer toss." "He likes to fish." "He brought a case of Bud Lite". "He said I was pretty". "He wore a Red Sox hat." "He told me I looked like Dad." "I mean at his age he must be pretty harmless" and "He's going back to Louisiana on Tuesday."

# CHAPTER SIX: SUNDAY BRUNCH AND LUNCH

The next morning Isabelle took care in her dressing for Church. She chose light weight black crepe slacks, a lavender blouse and black sling back sandals. The blouse hung over the waistband of the pants hiding a multitude of sins. She wore big gold hoop earrings and a plain gold chain with a cross on it around her neck. For once her unruly cow licks stayed in place and she used a little make up. She had had a nice time yesterday but today she wanted Will all to herself. She was glad they would be alone.

She attended the 8:00 AM Mass and hardly heard any of the readings. She didn't pay attention to the sermon. She went to communion only because the person next to her nudged her to move so she could receive communion herself. She was in a daze. Please God, give me a sign that I am doing the right thing. I love Will. I want Will. He lives in Louisiana and I live here. I have six kids who don't want their Dad replaced. I'm old and shouldn't be starting anything like this. Why did you bring him back into my life? Everyone else was standing for the final blessing. She stood quickly knowing she needed all the help she could get. Bob and Paul would say she didn't really attend Mass. She looked at the priest and blessed herself, In the name of the Father, Son and Holy Spirit, Amen.

She got home around 9:15 AM, gathered up her laundry and put some clothes in the washer. She used the bathroom. She checked her e-mails. One was an advertisement. She hit the delete key. Kathy had sent her a message. "Carol has a lunch date with Paul this afternoon. Did you know?" She typed "No, tell her good luck and tell Judy to keep her mouth shut." Then she hit the send key. Isabelle then played three games of Free Cell and looked at the clock. It was only 10:00 AM. She heard voices outside and so went out front to see who was there. Her grandkids from next door were playing in the side yard.

"Nana is that man your boyfriend", one of them asked?

"He's just a friend," she said.

Her daughter-in-law came out and said "You kids get over here we're all going down to the marina."

Then she said, "Hi, Isabelle, nice party yesterday"

"Yes," said Isabelle. They each went back into their own houses.

The phone was ringing. It was Tricia.

She said, "Ma, I don't want to interfere in anything you do. I want you to be happy. I'm on my way to Mass and I will pray that you make the right decision. Just don't rush into anything because you think you don't have much time. I love you." Isabelle assured her that she would not rush. She hung up.

The phone rang again. The door bell rang. She opened the door and beckoned Will to come in. She picked up the phone and heard Jeanne, in fact Will could hear Jeanne too.

"I don't know what fucking life crises you are in. You're certainly past mid life and menopause so I hope you know what the hell you are doing. I'm looking Will Benton up on Google as we speak and let me tell you if I can find one blemish, one flaw he's going to hear from me. Stay cool and for God sake, use a condom if old people still do that stuff. I might have to poke my eyes out at that mental thought." She continued, "You don't know where he's been. There are diseases around now that weren't even known about when you were young. Just go out and eat or watch a movie. No touchy feely. Good bye."

Will and Isabelle laughed. He took her in his arms and gave her the best kiss she had in a long time, maybe the best kiss he had ever given. He had been with a lot of women. He knew what women liked. She was not jealous. She was glad. Experience counted and she was reaping the benefits of his experience. After this long embrace they left for brunch.

Will looked handsome. He was wearing khaki pants with the crispest crease she had ever seen. The black silk dress shirt he had on was opened at the collar. He wore no hat and she hoped he would not get sun burned. He said that he had put sun screen on before he left. He told her Paul was in panic mode, worrying about what to wear when he met Carol for lunch.

"Why", said Isabelle, "they'll probably wear the same thing anyway".

They both laughed. He said Paul had called Carol this morning and they were going to some British Beer place in Hanover.

"Ever hear of it?" asked Will.

"Yes, said Isabelle "it's quaint and pub like. They'll be alright there."

"I think Paul likes her," said Will.

"And why not", she said. "Who would have guessed those two would get together?" said Isabelle.

They went to a restaurant across from Nantasket Beach; it was part of the Clarion Hotel. He reminded her of when they had come here on a date, when there was no hotel and it was Paragon Park all those years ago. He had taken her to Paragon Park when she was fifteen. She reminded him of how scared she was on the roller coaster. She had screamed out prayers on the ride and was crying hysterically. He told her he remembered it well.

The place was crowded but they got a table. The meal was served buffet style and they took their time. By the time they finished it was 1:00 P M. They decided to cross the street and walk along the sandy beach. The tide was low so they had plenty of time before their pant legs would get wet. They left their shoes in the car and walked the whole length of the beach heading back toward Gun Rock Beach. They stopped to sit on the beach wall for a while.

"Are you looking forward to the fishing trip tomorrow" asked Isabelle.

"Yes it should be fun. I hope I catch a forty pound bass like Kevin's. How about you? Are you looking forward to Plymouth; and the Christmas Tree Shop, whatever that is?"

"Yes, I love being with my cousins and Christmas Tree Shop is just a store where you buy things you don't need but they're pretty and the price is right. It's not a Christmas decoration place; you can get a variety of things there. It's a woman's store with gifts and odds and ends. I'll miss you tomorrow. You're leaving on Tuesday right."

"Yes, I am but not until late after noon. I hope to come see you in the morning and leave from your house. I need plenty of time to return the car rental. Maybe you can make me lunch. I want to see if you can cook? Did your kids say anything last night?"

"No, but I think they wanted to. The boys won't, I don't think. The girls called me this morning. You heard Jeanne and Tricia went to church to pray for me."

"I don't want to go back to Louisiana but I have to. My retirement check will be in the mail and my son and his wife will need the money for their mortgage payment. He's back to work now but I think he still needs help and I should pay my way if I live there. Then there are the two alimony checks that have to be mailed."

"I thought you were married three times said Isabelle. How come you only send two checks?"

"My first wife remarried, God bless her, and so she's taken care of. You know Isabelle, I want to marry you. I'm not going to waste any time; how much longer do we have? Will you marry me, Isabelle?" I don't want any answer now. I hope to come back in another month. We can e-mail or write or talk on the phone but we will straighten this out. I don't want to live the rest of my life without you. I don't expect anything from you. Any wealth you and Tim accumulated should be put in a trust for your children. I know Tim was an attorney and he did well financially. I don't want your kids thinking I'm after you for your money.  I have a nice retirement from the Post Office, I made some investments that did well and I sold my home for a nice profit. I can take care of the two of us, no problem."

Isabelle said, "First of all, most of my assets are already in Trust for the kids. I wasn't married to a lawyer for nothing. But don't you think you're rushing this?"

"No I don't. I've waited fifty years for you."

"From what I hear you weren't exactly waiting, you were busy.

There was silence.

"I have a big family that lives in Massachusetts and I won't leave them to live somewhere else," said Isabelle.

"If we get married, I'll move back to Massachusetts and maybe we could visit Jack and his family during the winter months when we want to go somewhere warm" said Will.

"Sounds like you've given this some thought," said Isabelle.

"I have and I want you to", said Will "We're not always going to be healthy or mobile. We're getting older. Let's have fun while we can, together."

Isabelle said nothing for a while. They held hands and watched the surfers in the water. The sea gulls were swooping down to pick up clams; they'd drop the clams onto the big rocks and then swoop again to pick out their food. The life guard sat in his high seat taking command of the beach and the tide kept coming in. Will put his arm around her shoulders and kissed her neck.

He whispered, "I love you" in her ear. She leaned against him and looked into his beautiful green eyes.

"I love you too", she said.

"Oh Will, my charming, funny, handsome, wonderful Will," but she said that to herself.

They sat for a long time letting the sun warm their old bones, feeling the ocean breeze and smelling the salt air. They were silent. There was no need for words.

Finally Isabelle broke the spell and said "I think we should get back. I need a bathroom."

"Me too", said Will.

They used the public facilities at the beach and walked back to the car. The ride home was quiet. They had had a beautiful day. They knew they loved each other. Isabelle just couldn't figure out what to do. Will was all for just getting married and the hell with it but she was more cautious. Isabelle wanted to be sure and she wanted what was right for both of them. He walked her to her door and kissed her again. This time it was more ardent and dare she think passionate. He held her close. He had strong arms and large hands. What a wonderful feeling to be in the arms of a man who loved you. Could he be thinking it was wonderful to hold a woman you loved? He could have been, but actually he was thinking he wished he didn't have to leave. He still had the condoms and the KY Jelly in his pocket. What would she do if she knew? She'd probably laugh and say it's good to be prepared. Isabelle was always a practical girl.

She wished him luck on his fishing expedition and told him to be careful.

She said, "Tom and Paul together don't have a brain. Don't do anything dangerous like hooking a shark, or getting hooks in you or drowning and don't drink too much beer out there. You're not as young as you used to be.

He laughed and said, "Thanks a lot. Have fun with the girls."

Will headed back to Paul's house.

Paul was waiting for him when he got back. "How was your day" he asked.

"Great, really great, I was with the girl of my dreams" said Will.

"Oh, good", said Paul absentmindedly.

"How about you, did you and Carol hit it off? Did you wear matching outfits?"

"What, No, but we had a good time. I never knew how smart she was. Did you know she was an executive for the telephone company?"

"Which one" asked Will?

"Oh, I don't know," said Paul, "the one that's in New York. Anyway, she married another big wig when she was fifty and he died three years later. Isn't that sad?"

"I didn't know she ever married," said Will.

"She's very interesting. She's an engineer. I bet Tom and her could talk shop. She knows all about politics, and has a green house and makes Irish bread, and she's been to Romania."

"I'm glad you had a nice time", said Will.

"I'm taking her to dinner and a movie on Tuesday night", said Paul.

"You sly dog" said Will, "want a beer?"

They drank their beers and at 8:00 PM Will said, "I'm calling it a night. We have to be ready at 4:30 AM"

"Goodnight Will," said Paul.

# CHAPTER SEVEN: FISHING

Promptly at 4:30 AM Tom was beeping outside. His head was out the window with a cigarette hanging from his lips. He greeted them with "Come on you land lovers let's go fishing." He drove an SUV. Paul and Will put Paul's stuff in the rear and got in. Will had a hat on, a sweat-shirt over his arm and sun block, his wallet and cell phone in his pocket. Paul had his pills, extra Dramamine, a hat, sun block, two sweat shirts, an extra pair of sneakers, hand sanitizer, tissue, a bag of snacks, three bottles of water, his bag of favorite fishing gear which included: rubber worms, lures, hooks, and an extra reel, a deck of cards, a pen and pad of paper, a first aid kit, a pair of pliers, a flash light, his cell phone, a large knife and a portable radio along with extra batteries and other good stuff. All of this was neatly packed in a duffle bag. Tom wore his sweat shirt with a hood and carried his wallet and cigarettes in his pocket.

"Paul", said Tom, "we're going deep sea fishing not camping. The captain who is taking us out, is a professional. He has everything we need on board. They even provide lunch. Why did you bring all this stuff?"

"You never know", said Paul, "and besides I like my stuff."

The drive to Onset was unremarkable. They talked about the Fourth of July. Tom told them he and Susan spent the weekend with their daughter and her husband in New Hampshire and the grandkids loved the parade and the fireworks. "My son-in-law grilled salmon on his gas grill," said Tom, "I don't know what he put on it. He said it was a dry rub or something but it was the best salmon I ever ate." He told them that his grand son, Nick, played on a baseball team and they got to go to one of his games. Nick was getting big and he was dark like his father. The girl, Nora, just lost her two front teeth. Susan loved being there, she held the baby almost the whole time. "It was a nice quite Fourth, just the way I like it," said Tom. "How about you guys?"

"We went to a party at Isabelle's son's house, big house, big kid, said Paul. "Isabelle's kids were all there, giving Will the evil eye. Her cousins were there too and her brother, Bob, and his wife. You remember

Bob, he sings in the choir. We met his wife, she's nice. They didn't marry until they were sixty. We played a new game. It's like horse shoes only it's played with washers. You try to pitch them into holes on a free standing board. Carol hit me in the head with one of the washers. I bled like a pig right on to my Statue of Liberty shirt. I almost needed stitches. Carol and I wore the same outfits and we put our food very orderly on our plates and we only ate the Italian food and she forgot her roll. We didn't know we did that. Judy told us. Kathy always wears black. Did you know that? Kathy and I lost washer toss tournament but Will came in second place."

"Doesn't he always" said Tom.

"Fuck off," said Will.

"What", said Paul, "Oh, anyway, Judy was there too, always making wise cracks, Will and Isabelle went to brunch at Nantasket Beach on Sunday, Isabelle didn't say grace before she ate and Judy got a card game going and we watched fire works and I took Carol to lunch on Sunday. Isabelle has a bunch grandkids and I don't think Will can ever get their names straight and I'm taking Carol to dinner and a movie Tuesday night and Will is going home tomorrow and he's in love with Isabelle big time and Kathy still smokes as much as you and the meat balls tasted just like the ones my Marie used to make."

"Take a few breaths, Paul", said Tom. "You're talking too fast and I don't know what in the world you're talking about. You're not making sense. Did you take medication this morning"?

"Well, just my regular high blood pressure and fluid pills and a Dramamine. Tell him, Will, tell him what a good time we had."

"We had a good time," said Will.

Tom pulled into the parking lot. He turned around and looked at Paul.

"Are you alright?"

"Yes".

"No he's not," said Will.

"Shut up," said Paul.

The three men unloaded Paul's gear and went to the dock to board the fishing boat. The captain greeted them and they all settled in. There was coffee and donuts for breakfast. They headed out to sea.

One of the hands was mixing a bucket of chum which Paul had to get away from since he was eating a donut and was getting sick.

The captain drove on watching his fish finder while steering. The mate started baiting the hooks, and passing out the rods. The boat finally stopped and they dropped anchor and lines and began fishing with gusto. The day was overcast and not hot. The sea air was refreshing. The three friends were sitting waiting for a bite. They were sitting comfortably holding their rods. Tom lit another cigarette and said, "OK, Paul, start from the top. What was the Fourth of July party like, slowly and from the start?

"We went to Isabelle's son's house. Her cousins were there and her brother, Bob, and his wife. I didn't know that her brother sang in the choir with my mother and Auntie Joan. Judy, Carol and Kathy came together and Carol wore the same out fit as me".

Tom looked stunned and said, "What did you wear?"

"Oh, a tan tee shirt with the Statue of Liberty on it, for the Fourth of July, and tan cargo shorts with my crocks."

"Nice", said Tom. The sarcasm was missed by Paul.

"You wear crocks?" asked Tom.

"Did Carol have on crocks too?"

"They're very comfortable and no Carol had sandals."

"What did Judy and Kathy wear" asked Tom?

"What does that matter", said Paul, "I don't think I can remember; but nothing patriotic. Wait, yes, Judy had some puke green dress on and Kathy always wears black, so something black with beads or something shining in the front. But to give her credit, Kathy had a sparkly red, white and blue visor thing she put on for the fire works."

"Well good for her" said Tom.

Then he asked Will, "Were you dressed up like Uncle Sam?"

"No, I looked like fucking Daddy Warbucks with my bald head, a navy shirt and white shorts. Since when did you become the fashion police?"

Paul said, "Actually, Will, you wore your Red Sox cap so you didn't look like Daddy Warbucks."

Tom said, "Ah Ha, you didn't want Isabelle's family to know you're bald. Poor little bear he has no hair. You sure fooled them."

"Screw you."

Tom went on, "Last time I spoke to you two, Will was getting the condoms and jelly ready for the little lady. Any luck there Romeo."

"Mind your own damn business."

"Testy, mustn't be getting any" said Tom.

"They haven't done it yet," said Paul. "When Will came home last night and emptied his pockets on the counter. The box of condoms and the jelly were unopened."

"Thanks Paul," said Will.

Tom laughed out loud and Will stood to take a whiz of the starboard side of the boat.

"You know, Will, there's a head on this boat", said Tom. "Why are you always whipping that thing out? Paul and I aren't impressed."

Paul said, "I hope you don't whip that out in front of Isabelle like that. I don't know what she sees in you. You are no gentleman and you're such and exhibitionist. Were you always this bad or have you gotten worse with age?"

"All that time at the nudist colony", said Tom.

"Screw the two of you. If you have to go you have to go. I'm an old man; I have to pee all the time. You're lucky I'm standing where I am or piss would be blowing back in your faces. See, I am a gentleman" said Will.

"Paul" said Tom, changing the subject, "what's this I hear about you getting hit in the head?

"Carol was on the opposing team in that washer game with a very aggressive woman, who is Isabelle's oldest daughter, must take after the father. Anyway, I was pretty good at the game, right Will."

"Right".

"Carol went to toss the washer, and what a powerful little arm she must have, because it split my head open. The washer was only about three inches in diameter and it didn't weigh that much. It hit just right, like a ninja star or something. A nurse, one of the guests, fixed me up and I went right back to the game and tied the score. Didn't I, Will."

"Right".

Tom said, "Brave old Paul. If this is the same Carol I saw the other day at the restaurant, she did have powerful arms; she was plump. I don't think I'd call her arms little."

Paul said, "She's not plump, she just likes Italian food."

"OK," said Tom, "what happened next?"

"Well, Kathy was my partner. She wasn't very good but we tied Carol and Jeanne and had to play again for the tie breaker. We won then but we lost in the next round. Kathy was glad. All she wanted was to sit down and have another cigarette. Two of Isabelle's grandkids, Sean and Victoria, won."

"First of all half the people there were probably Isabelle's grandkids and my hat off to Kathy, I would have needed a cigarette after that too", said Tom.

"I don't think half the people there were Isabelle's grandkids", said Paul.

"There were a lot of people there? Right Will".

"Right, she only has sixteen grandkids."

"Only sixteen, there's a good Catholic", said Tom. "Will, what are you getting yourself into?"

"Screw you"

"Whoa, I've got a bite," said Tom.

The next few minutes were spent jerking the rod and reeling in the fish. It wasn't a striper it was a flounder and too small. Then Paul got a bite and it was a Blue Fish but it got away. They weren't having much luck. They went back to waiting for bites and Paul went and got three beers for them.

"OK, Paul, so tell me how you and Carol got to go out to lunch? I'm proud of you. It takes courage to ask a woman out", said Tom.

"Well, actually, she asked me out. She gave me a piece of paper with Kathy's phone number on it, because she's staying there this week, and she said to call her after Mass and I did. We went to the British Beer Company. It was great. We had a good time."

Tom said, "I'm surprised you didn't go to Church with her. She sounds just your type. Is that Beer place any good Susan wants to try it?"

"Well worship is a very private thing, she didn't invite me to go with her; and yes that place is good. Susan would like it. It has English stuff like bangers and mash and meat pies", said Paul.

Tom looked over at Will. "So Casanova how was that lecture?"

Will relayed the whole day including the two cousin sleuths and his falling on his face on top of the globe. They all laughed.

They heard a whistle and the captain said "Lunch Time". Paul was glad he had his hand sanitizer with him and was magnanimous enough to allow Tom and Will to use it as well. They all tucked into sandwiches and beer.

After a loud burp, Tom said, "Will, where did you take Isabelle on Sunday"?

Will told them how they went to brunch and took a long walk. Will said he was surprised to see how much Nantasket Beach had changed since Paragon Park closed. It looked different with all the condos and apartment buildings. He said he was happy they kept the carousel.

"O Boy, here we go," said Paul, "I've got something on my line." He pulled and jerked and reeled and swayed; he and the fish both fighting. Paul won. The men looked at the fish like they had just seen the birth of a baby.

"What a beauty", said Will, "a Cod"

"And a keeper too," said Tom.

"How much does he weigh; how long is he," asked Paul.

The captain's mate measured it and said it was a keeper. Will always wondered why fish were measured in length and not weighed by pound. Tom told them that the captain gets to keep what we catch so don't get too attached. The mate took the fish to be filleted.

Tom said, "Where were we, Will, oh yeah, Nantasket Beach."

Will said, "We had a grand day; I asked Isabelle to marry me."

The other two looked at him in silence.

"Well", said Paul, "you didn't tell me that last night"

"You were too busy yapping about Carol"

"What did she say", asked Tom.

"She's thinking about it. Isabelle doesn't want her kids to think I'm the replacement daddy and she doesn't want to live in Louisiana. She thinks we're too old, and she thinks it will be harder on us when we die. She said she's already lost Tim she doesn't want to go through that again with me. I told her we're going to die anyway. We may as well spend whatever time we have left together."

Will stopped talking and jumped to his feet, "I have one".

Tom stood up, "Me too."

The boat rocked. It was getting choppy. Paul said, "Should I get the net ready?"

Will pulled in his fish; it was a striper, not as big as Kevin's but big. He couldn't keep it.

"I should have used mackerel for bait," said Will. "Kevin said he sometimes used mackerel."

"Who's Kevin" asked Tom.

"One of Isabelle's sons, he caught a forty pound striper the other day using mackerel."

Tom reeled in another large Cod and filleting began again.

Paul got three more beers.

"What time are you leaving tomorrow" asked Tom.

Will said, "I have a 4:00 PM flight but I need to get to Logan early to return the car rental and check in. I'm going to Isabelle's in the morning to spend some time with her. Maybe I can turn on enough charm to get her to say Yes."

"I doubt it" said Tom. "It's too soon. As inviting as wife number four may sound to you, Isabelle has more sense than you and she'll want to think it over. Give her time. You only just got back together less than a week ago."

"A week is long time when you're seventy-one", said Will.

"I hear you" said Tom. He lit another cigarette.

The three were quiet as the boat headed in. The clouds had thickened and rain was coming. The captain was trying to see through the drizzle that was on the windshield of the craft. It was pouring. Paul went to his duffle bag and got out three dark colored trash bags and handed one to each of his friends and said, "Here make a rain coat or get wet". They complied. Paul also held out three Snickers bars and they both told Paul they were glad he brought his "stuff". The rain came down hard. For once Paul saved the day.

# CHAPTER EIGHT: GIRLS' DAY OUT

When Isabelle arrived at Kathy's on Monday, the cousins were eager to get going to Plymouth. They drove in Kathy's car; it was the biggest and had a large trunk in case they bought a lot at the Christmas Tree Shop. Kathy not only liked bling she liked nice cars. Hers was a Lincoln Town Car like Isabelle's with lots of extras, like heated seats and leather upholstery. She had worked hard at a bank after her husband died. He left a large insurance policy and she had a good job so she treated herself to a new car every few years, some bling and any black clothes that caught her eye. She figured she deserved it and although you couldn't take a car to bed with you, she wanted something nice to replace her husband. She never re-married. She still loved him. She wasn't morbid, she had lots of friends, and of course the cousins. Kathy read a lot, and liked old black and white movies. She took ballroom dancing lessons, it was nice to be in some guy's arms, most of the time her partners were gay but that was good. They'd be no disappointments for either of them. She took painting lessons too, although she had no talent and she played bingo weekly. She was not lonely. She was driving toward Plymouth with her window open with the hopes that her cigarette smoke wouldn't fill the car. Isabelle sat in the passenger seat and the Vermont girls in the rear.

Isabelle started coughing and asked, "Kathy, when are you going to give up this filthy habit?"

"The day hell freezes over", she said. "I've tried everything, tapes with subliminal messages, patch things, even a hypnotist but I'm addicted to cigarettes. They'll get me in the end. Even my kids preach to me about it. They don't let me smoke in their homes or even in my home if the grandkids are with them. And believe me when that happens, I'm happy to see their back sides go out through the door."

"Isabelle, will you put that lottery ticket in the glove compartment for me", said Kathy. "It's on the dash board. I won ten bucks and

I don't want it to blow out the window. It'll buy me another pack of cigarettes."

Isabelle put the ticket in the glove compartment and said, "Carol I want to hear all about your lunch with Paul."

Kathy said, "I want to hear it again too, Carol, go ahead."

"Oh no, do I have to listen to this again", said Judy. "That's all we talked about last night. Paul almost fell down the front steps when he came to pick Carol up. What a clumsy man he is. He wore those stupid crocks again and one slid right off his foot when he was going down the stairs. I don't know any other man who wears crocks. His foot came down hard on the step and he lost his balance. Carol bent down to pick up the lost crock and he damn near went ass over tea kettle on top of her. It was like a comedy show. When Carol stood up to pass him the shoe, they banged heads and almost knocked each other out. If his head wasn't right from the washer she pitched at him the day before, Carol's hard head did the trick yesterday. I'm amazed he could drive after that."

Isabelle said, "Well I bet the date got better.

"Yes" said Carol. "He did give me quite a clunk on my head. I almost saw stars. After that we got into Paul's car. It's so clean, not like Judy's. There are no empty Dunkin Donut cups all over the floor, or pencils, used napkins, cross work puzzle books or maps. And there are no dusty cutesy figurines on the dash board. I think he must vacuum it all the time. And it doesn't smell. You know Judy has at least three Yankee Candle air fresheners all hanging together from her rear view mirror and none of those scents should ever be mixed together. It often makes me car sick."

"And what was the restaurant like," urged Isabelle.

Carol recalled yesterday's lunch, "Oh, it was like being in Great Britain. There was a red phone booth, and pictures of the Queen. I got in the phone booth for fun and Paul said that he wished he had his camera. There were low ceilings with large wooden beams and a fire place. The walls were painted white stucco. There were signs on the walls and photos of Winston Churchill and a map of England. We got a table near the fire place although it was too warm for it to be lit. The menu was quite extensive and it took me and Paul a long time to order. I think the waitress was annoyed. You know the English eat a lot of greasy food, like fish and chips and sausages. It was hard to decide. Our stomachs aren't what they used to be. I mean I'm sixty-six and he's seventy. Grease can cause gas pains and once I had the runs from eating onion rings so I wanted to play it safe. Paul got Shepherd's Pie and I got Beef with Yorkshire Pudding. Yorkshire Pudding is just a pop over in case you didn't know. I thought it was going to be like a savory flavored custard or something gooey."

She told the girls, "Paul talked about being retired. He doesn't miss his dentist work; forty five years was enough. I told him I still had all my teeth. He was impressed. I told him about my job at the phone company and how my husband died after only three years of marriage".

"He said 'God bless his soul'. Wasn't that nice?"

He told me his house was getting too big for him, now that Marie was gone and the kids had their own places, but he doesn't want to move. I told Paul that my house was too big for me too but I liked to have people come visit and stay with me a lot, so I thought I'd keep it. I told him about the pond and the green house. He said he liked gardening and a green house would be handy. He asked if there were any fish in the pond and told me he was going fishing with Will and Tom today. He's so used to where he lived. He grew up there and Tom still lived nearby. Sometimes in the winter, when Tom and Susan go to Florida, he's lonely. I told him he'd hate the Vermont winters with all that snow. We also tried a hard cider which was sweet; like cider and beer mixed together. The food was hot and pretty good. Paul did have to tell the waitress that the potatoes on the shepherd's pie were dry but he ate it anyway. The waitress seemed put out. He told me that he was a boxer in college. I didn't know that. I can picture it though. He's a wiry looking guy. I told him how Judy and I went to Romania. He said he hadn't traveled much but he always wanted to go to Italy. He likes to read the same things I read, like police mysteries. We like the same music too, show tunes. I had to tell the waitress that my meat was too rare but I waited until after the meal. I didn't want to make her mood any worse then it already was. We had tea and trifle for dessert. They did offer coffee but we figured we'd do the British thing. We were there for quite some time. I wanted to pay the bill, because of the head injury I caused him but he refused and he insisted on paying. He left a good tip too, which I think is a good sign. I hate cheap men. When we were on the way back to Kathy's he asked me to dinner and a movie Tomorrow night. I said "Yes". He dropped me off and we said good bye. He didn't try to kiss me or anything. It was just lunch."

Isabelle said, "It sounds like you both enjoyed yourselves."

"Don't make me puke all over this car", said Judy. "Paul D'Angelo has eaten only Italian food all his life. He probably would have kissed the waitress if she covered his shepherd's pie with tomato sauce and grated cheese. As far as boxing goes, I could take Paul blindfolded and with one hand tied behind my back. I'm amazed he didn't try to examine your teeth and gums. And to tell him you liked show tunes was the silliest thing you could have done. I can just picture Paul breaking into song like "There Ain't Nothing Like a Dame" to win your heart. I'm glad to hear he wasn't cheap. I can only imagine what movie you two are going to tomorrow."

Kathy said, "I think you're just jealous, Judy. It's not everyday an older gentleman asks a nice mature woman out. In fact it's rare. I hope you have a great time tomorrow night."

"Me too," said Isabelle.

"I am not jealous, believe me," said Judy. "I've done my time with two weird bastards, Little Prick and Fat Bastard, and I'm going straight to heaven for it. I don't know why God created men, the poor toads. A huge vat filled with sperm would have been sufficient for all of us girls to dip into if we wanted kids. No messy sex, no arguments, and no lies. From morning until night men are either scratching their asses, picking their noses, filling their faces, re-arranging their balls, farting, burping, rubbing stubble against your face, leaving the toilet seat up, hogging the bed covers, or complaining. They say they never have enough sex. They worship their penises, their egos are too fragile, their minds insensitive and they usually smell like beer."

Kathy said, "Judy, I was a bridesmaid in both your weddings and if I remember correctly you were madly in love with each of them. Try to remember the good things. See if you can tell us some of man's finer attributes."

"I was young and stupid when I met them. I drank a lot in those days. I got some nice kids from them and that's the best thing I can say" said Judy. "Why don't you tell us about your husband?"

"What do you want to know? He was handsome, kind, a good provider, a good lover, a good listener, and my best friend. I miss him everyday. He wasn't perfect but I never wanted for anything and he was a good father to our children. He's been dead a long time. He died too young. I used to blame him for that. Now I don't. I've moved on. We argued like all other couples but the make up sex was great. We had different views on things but we respected each other's opinion. I loved him. He liked my black clothes and my bling. I think that's why I still dress like this. He always thought I'd go first, because of my smoking. You just never know. It's just as well he went first, I was more sensible and that's what was needed when he left me as the single parent. Do I wish he was still alive? Yes. Can I picture him old? No. He'll always be remembered as young. I wonder what he'd think of my maroon hair.

They were all silent for a while. Kathy never mentioned her husband. They all knew him years ago. They liked him. He died at forty-one. He and Kathy always seemed happy and she did a great job raising their two children. She's a strong woman and has always kept her feelings to herself. She always laughed easily and was out going. They never expected her to display such deep feelings to them.

Kathy went on, "I've always been a selfish person, especially selfish with my time and I like to do things my way. I think it was hard for me being married. I had to share and compromise. Now I can eat a bowl of cereal for supper on the sofa with the TV blaring and Entertainment Magazine at my elbow. It must be difficult for women to remarry. You'd have to start being polite again, saying please and thank you all the time. You couldn't stay in sweats all day or burp. The big bonus is having the bathroom all to myself. I like me and I like my cigarettes."

"I hear you sister", said Judy. "My cat, curled up beside me on the couch and my cross work puzzle book give me more pleasure then either of the two creeps I was married to. You have to be maid, nurse, cook, waitress, hooker and mother to those jerks. My cat comes and goes as he pleases and I do too."

They all laughed.

Kathy pulled in at a seven eleven at the next light. "Sorry girls but I'm buying a lottery ticket. Want one?"

The other three ladies said "No".

"Isabelle", said Kathy when she got back in the car, "how was your date with Will on Sunday?"

"The brunch was scrumptious and the walk along Nantasket beach was lovely. He asked me to marry him."

The silence that followed was long.

Finally, Carol said, "Wow. What did you say?"

I said I'd think about it.

"Well, Well, Well, said Kathy. "He's going back to Louisiana tomorrow so you better think fast."

"That's what I won't do", said Isabelle, "I need time."

"How much time do you think you and Will have left? I'll bet Will Benton never had to wait for an answer from any woman", said Judy.

The ladies arrived at Plimouth Plantation and paid their admission, asking for senior discounts. Why not? They walked to the Wampanoag site. It was an outdoor exhibit and real Native Americans portrayed the tribe members. They were dressed in deerskin and were knowledgeable regarding traditions, music and dance. The three women asked a lot of questions and were surprised to get such informative responses. Judy, having been teacher for almost forty years was very impressed.

The seventeenth century English Village was a re-creation of the community built by the Pilgrims and people dressed in clothes of the time and acted out the roles of the early settlers.

Isabelle said, "Remember when Granny made me a pilgrim costume for Halloween and when we went trick or treating everyone thought I was a nurse. It was the same year Carol was Kate Smith. What great costume ideas we had."

The folks playing the roles of these settlers talked to us in their own old style English. It was like traveling back in time. They never slipped into twentieth century language. The ladies viewed their living quarters, saw some of the folks cooking entire meals in fire places, walked into herb and vegetable gardens, viewed the live stock and listened as their stories were told. Other buildings showed us different crafts and occupations. One man demonstrated barrel making, another how wood was milled to build with, and a woman baked bread in a wood oven. They demonstrated how to harness their horses for plowing and how they made butter. It was an enjoyable morning.

The girls hopped back into the car and headed for Plymouth Harbor. They parked the car and walked along the path that took them to Plymouth Rock.

"It has a lot of meaning but it is really an unimpressive looking big stone", said Kathy.

Nearby was the Mayflower but they only looked at it from afar. They had had enough walking for one day and wanted to eat lunch. They went across the street and headed towards Isaac's. They were seated at a window facing the ocean and ordered wonderful sea food meals. Isabelle took two Aleve. Her knees were killing her.

Once back in the car and on the way to Christmas Tree Shops, Kathy lit a cigarette and said, "Let's go shopping."

The Christmas Tree Shop was almost empty. The Fourth of July was over and all items for that holiday were seventy five percent off.

"You should tell Andrea about this for next year", said Carol.

Many people were on vacation and it was Monday. The cousins had the place to themselves. Most of the decorations on sale were sea shell themed or nautical; signs, plates, towels and more; summer stuff. There were aisles full of candles, picture frames, and paper goods, Wrapping paper, ribbon, nail polish and curtains. There was a food department and a toy department. They walked up and down each aisle searching and hunting. The ladies pushed their shopping carts like walkers. The place was a veritable treasure trove.

Kathy spied an old fashioned hook pot holder making kit.

She said, "Look at this. I haven't seen one of these in decades. I used to make hundreds of pot holders. I was good at it too. I could make check patterns, stripes and all kinds of other color combinations. Remember these, Carol?"

"I do", said Carol. "You were better at it than me and faster too, but it was fun to make them. We were busy for hours. I think our mothers just wanted us out of their hair."

"Oh my God, those things" piped in Judy. "I remember those. You two made hundreds of them and they're made of nylon so you'd probably go up in flames if you ever used one."

"I never thought of that," said Kathy. "I'm going to get a kit anyway for me and my granddaughter to do together. I'll just tell her they're decorations and can't be used near the stove. She'll like the weaving part."

The women shopped and some bought silk flowers for arrangements they'd never make, candles they'd never light; and wrapping paper they'd never use. They bought fancy paper napkins in case someone special visited. They loved the food aisle and chose boxes of crackers of all kinds, cans of chowder, spices, very cheap, and paper cups because you could always use them. Isabelle got two toss pillows, red for her TV room and a bag of bird seed. Judy got a few cat toys and a large set of race cars for her grandson. Carol got some pretty drinking glasses saying none at home matched and the price was right. What if Paul came to Vermont she would like the table to look nice. She picked up a plaid table cloth too. She also bought some fancy soaps and two CDs one with show tunes the other dinner music. The other girls all looked at each other. Carol was on the prowl. Kathy got a couple of dish towels and a lamp for her bedroom. They kept piling their wagons full of great stuff. They all checked out and filled the trunk with their goods.

Kathy put on a pot of coffee when they got back. Isabelle said she would not stay; she was tired and wanted to get home. Her knees were killing her. She was old. When she got home she took a shower and went to bed. It was only 6:00 PM.

# CHAPTER NINE: WILL SAYS GOODBYE

Will arrived at Isabelle's house at 11:00 AM on Tuesday. He was dressed casually so he'd be comfortable on the flight. She opened the door and said, "Hey Big Guy". He took her in his arms and kissed her long and hard and passionately. She did not pull away. She returned the kiss. All morning she willed herself to stay in control today but here she was surrendering to his charms.

After a few minutes, he said, "I missed you yesterday."

"I guess you did", was all she said.

They went to the kitchen and she told him to sit wherever he wanted and that she was preparing chicken salad for their lunch. The kitchen was an L shaped room. The large part held a couple of small couches and a big fire place and a big screen TV along with a comfortable kitchen table. The short part of the kitchen is where all the appliances and cabinets were. He liked the set up. It was nicely decorated but not fancy. It was homey, the kind of place to eat and relax. This was the heart of the house. On one wall he saw a large framed family photo of Tim and Isabelle with all the kids, spouses and grandkids. Tim had been a very lucky man. The big bay window at the table looked onto the back yard where Will and Isabelle had sat the first day he came to see her. The bird houses and feeders were strategically placed so they could be viewed from this window. He saw a red cardinal at the bird bath and two yellow finches at the thistle sock. Binoculars and a bird book lay on the window sill. Book cases held a lot of reading material and pillows and throws were at the end of each sofa.

Will said, "This is a great family room; it must be nice looking out at the birds, especially when there's snow out there. I love watching birds"

Isabelle answered, "I do too. Do you like dried cranberries and walnuts in your salad?"

"I never had it that way but I'd like to try it. I'm sure anything you make will be delicious."

"You're such a kiss ass," said Isabelle.

"Paul wouldn't believe those words came from your Catholic mouth, Isabelle," said Will.

"Speaking of him, I think my cousin is after him. You better warn him or maybe not. I have to watch whose side I'm on."

"I say leave them alone. They're old enough to know what they're doing. She's gong back to Vermont tomorrow so let's wait and see. We all have to grab at whatever happiness we can in life, especially at our age. So here goes. Today is Tuesday, Will you marry me Isabelle."

"I'm still thinking about it. I'll let you know," she answered.

She resumed making the salad; she added chopped celery and mayonnaise and mixed it with the chicken, nuts and berries. She got two plates out of the cabinet, washed and placed leaves of lettuce on each and filled them with the salad. Isabelle added grape tomatoes and placed them on the table. She had another dish with cut French bread on it and a pitcher of ice tea. "Come and get it," she said.

He said, "This is a feast".

"Once a kiss ass, always a kiss ass," Isabelle said

They both laughed and they ate and talked. He told her what a great time he had at Gerry's house and how Paul related the whole day and in much detail to Tom. Will told her about the fishing trip. Isabelle said Carol told them about her and Paul at the British Beer Company and that she thought they were getting along splendidly. She relayed their adventures at Plymouth and the Christmas Tree Shop. They talked about when he'd be back and what they might do when he returned. They wanted to get a card game going. She wanted to cook him a nice meal. She said she'd see if any new live shows would be going on next month. Then he looked at the clock and said, "I have to go". She didn't want this time to come; neither did he.

He got up and said, "Can I use the bathroom".

She teased, "You mean may I use the bathroom".

He laughed and went down the hall. She started to clear the table. When he was ready, he went to the front door and she followed him. He held her again and said "I have written down my home phone number, my cell number and my e-mail address for you" and handed her a piece of paper.

"I expect to hear from you", said Will.

She said, "You will, everyday."

He said, "Good".

"We don't have forever Isabelle. If we miss this dance we may never have another one. We may have a many years left, we may only have months, let's dance."

He kissed her again and walked out the door. She walked him to his car and she waved goodbye as he drove down the street.

Isabelle went inside and wept. She didn't even finish clearing off the table.

# CHAPTER TEN: THE MOVIES

Paul picked Carol up at 6:00 PM. She wore a mauve and lilac shapeless dress and white sandals. She had added a purple silk flower to the dress. Paul had on a dark purple polo shirt and chinos. She was surprised to see they both were in a purple state of mind. She mentioned this to him and he laughed, which was rare for Paul. He tended to be serious.

They had decided to go to a local Italian restaurant since they both liked Italian food. Carol wished she had had something red to wear because sauce of any kind usually ended up on the front of her clothes and the tomato sauce would not show on red. She would just have to be careful. She wondered if Paul would mind if she tucked her napkin under her chin. They drove to the next town over, parked the car and entered the restaurant. They were seated and started reading the menus. They ordered a carafe of red wine.

Paul said, "Let's get an appetizer. Do you like arancini?"

She said she never had it but would give it a whirl. The waitress brought the wine and took their order.

"For my meal, said Carol, "I will have meatballs and pasta. Can I have bow ties?"

The waitress said, "Yes, do you want marinara sauce or white sauce on your pasta."

"Oh, marinara," said Carol.

Paul ordered chicken cacciatore with angel hair pasta.

When the waitress left, Paul said, "At least she's more pleasant than that one at the British Beer Company."

"You're right", said Carol.

He proposed a toast. He said, "To many more happy times."

She clinked her glass against his so hard, that it broke and red wine and glass spilled everywhere. The waitress came over and removed everything from the table. It was a great mess. Even the bread basket had bits of glass in it. They apologized to the waitress and she set the table again and brought fresh bread and another wine glass. Carol was mortified. Paul assured her that her first glass probably had a crack in it and wasn't she lucky she didn't get cut or swallow glass. He toasted again. This time Carol was more careful. She barely touched his glass. It was the gentlest ping sound. The waitress brought the arancini. Carol loved them. The food was delicious and they were too full for dessert. They paid the bill and this time Paul left even more of a tip since the poor waitress had to re-set the table. Paul and Carol drove to the cinema and got their tickets. Neither of them wanted a snack. They entered the theater and sat about four rows back from the screen.

"I like to hear and see as best as possible," said Carol.

"Good idea", said Paul.

The movie, "The Exotic Marigold Hotel" was not one that was viewed by many but it starred some famous British actors. It had a plot dealing with senior citizens and their plights, loves and health issues. It was rated a comedy. Paul and Carol related to the movie, and even laughed out loud a few times. When it was over Carol stood up and clapped. Paul told her no standing ovation was required unless it was a live show. She blushed.

On the way back to Kathy's, Paul said he was sorry Will went back to Louisiana but sorrier still that she was going back to Vermont. He did not say he'd miss Judy.

She said she would miss him too and that Vermont was at its best in the summer and she hoped he'd make a trip up to see her.

"You know", she said, "I wish all of you guys would come up. We didn't get to see Susan at all and Tom very little. I know Judy would like to reunite with Susan. They always hit it off when we were young."

He said he'd think about it and asked how long the drive was.

She told him only three and a half hours.

He said if he stopped once, he could probably do it and that they should make plans either by phone or e-mail. "I'm not into texting" he said. "I know that's all the kids do today but I just don't like it."

"I'm with you," said Carol.

When they arrived at Kathy's he walked her to the door. She took the pen and pad of paper from her hand bag and wrote down his e-mail address and phone number and address. She also gave him her information. She put the pad of paper and pen back in her purse and was grateful that for once that she did not spill all her purse's contents all over the ground. He kissed her quickly and gently and said, "Good bye Carol, I hope we see each other soon".

Carol went inside happy but wished the kiss had lasted longer.

Kathy and Judy were waiting behind the living room draperies. They peeked out and saw the kiss. Carol came in and they both looked at her.

Judy said, "That was the most pitiful, shortest kiss I ever saw. If he's like that in bed you're in for a big disappointment."

Carol answered, "Don't say a word, not one more word. He kissed me tonight. Long or short, he kissed me. I invited him to visit me in Vermont and I'm going to be happy. I'd rather have a short kiss than no kiss and I'd rather be looking forward to his visit than just going home to my empty house. End of discussion."

The worm had turned.

Judy said nothing.

Kathy said, "I'm glad you had a nice time."

They all went to bed.

# CHAPTER ELEVEN: GOODBYE COUSINS

Isabelle got up early the next morning. She couldn't believe she slept so long; she went to bed yesterday afternoon. She thought she'd take a walk. She had been eating too much rich food for a week, since that first lunch with the cousins. She needed to lose weight. She made coffee, toasted diet bread and spread it with peanut butter. She turned on her computer. She wanted to send a message to Will.

She had mail. When she opened her e-mail and it read.

"I got home safely around 1:00 AM. Don't ask. I had many plane changes and delays. I am exhausted. I will probably sleep all day. But it is morning so here goes today's proposal, will you marry me? Love Will."

Isabelle typed, "Hey Big Guy, I'm weakening but I still need time. Love Isabelle" she hit reply.

Just hearing from him made her feel good.

She showered and dressed and headed down to Kathy's; she wanted to see Judy and Carol before they left for home. Judy was loading the car when Isabelle arrived.

"Hi Judy", said Isabelle. "You're not going yet are you? I was hoping to have a cup of coffee with you."

"We aren't leaving yet", she said, "I just wanted to get this stuff out of Kathy's way."

They both went inside.

Carol was putting on a fresh pot of coffee and Kathy was taking a hot tray of just baked blueberry muffins out of the oven. "I was going to start a diet today," said Isabelle, "but those look too good to pass up."

"Think of all the women on the Titanic who passed up dessert", said Judy.

Kathy told them to dig in she wasn't going to wait on anybody; especially relatives. They laughed and each took a muffin.

"This is so good" said Isabelle.

"I want the recipe" said Carol.

"It's Granny's recipe, I'm surprised none of you have it", said Kathy.

"I have it" said Carol.

"Can I have some butter to put on mine", said Judy.

"That will ruin the masterpiece," said Kathy but handed her the butter dish from the fridge. They poured the coffee and washed down the best muffins they ever tasted and began to chat.

"How did it go with Will yesterday" said Kathy, lighting another revolting cigarette.

He proposed again and I told him I needed more time. He e-mailed me at 1:00 AM telling me he just arrived home. There were plane changes and delays. Poor Will he must be so tired. He asked me to marry him again in the e-mail. I gave him the same answer. He had a 4:00 PM flight. That's a long time trying to get home.

"Give me a freaking break. Sailors have a girl in every port; Will has a flight attendant in every air port. He probably did it with all the female flight attendants. You know that mile high whichamacallit thing, when you do it up in the air." said Judy.

"Where do you get these ideas", asked Carol.

"How many times do you think a seventy-one year old man could do it in one day", asked Kathy. "He may be Will Benton but he's not superman."

"This is true," said Judy, "even Will must have limitations."

Isabelle changed the subject and asked Carol how her date with Paul went.

"We had a great time," said Carol. "The Italian place was nice and the food was good. I tried arancini for the first time. Paul suggested it. He knows more about Italian food than me.

"He's Italian", said Judy.

Then Carol told them about the wine glass incident. She had not told Judy and Kathy about this. They looked at her in amazement.

"When were you going to tell us about that", said Judy. "You could have put his eye out or something".

"Well she didn't" said Isabelle, "and it sounds like you had a nice dinner."

"We did" Carol answered. "The movie was funny, well in some parts, and he kissed me and I invited him to Vermont and he's going to e-mail me when I get back home."

"Paul D'Angelo kissed you", said Isabelle?

"Yes right on the front door step and right on the lips."

"It was a seven second kiss; Kathy and I were watching through the curtains", said Judy.

"You two should be ashamed of yourselves spying on her and Paul. Good for you Carol, a kiss is a kiss", said Isabelle.

The cousins kissed and hugged each other good bye and Carol invited Isabelle and Kathy to visit her this summer too. She said she had four bedrooms and Judy had two spare rooms at her place.

"Isabelle", Carol said, "Will is invited too".

Judy said, "He's not staying at my house".

"Kathy, Isabelle," said Carol, "think it over"

They looked at each other and said, "Why not." They said they'd look at their calendars and decide on some dates and let them know. Judy got in the driver's seat and they were on their way home before noon.

# CHAPTER TWELVE: AT HOME

In Louisiana it was hot. Will finally got out of bed around 2:00 PM. He couldn't believe he slept that long. He showered and shaved and went to his computer.

There it was, "Hey Big Guy, I'm weakening but I still need time. Love, Isabelle".

His heart beat a little faster. He went back in his bedroom and took his pills. He got dressed and went down for some cereal and coffee. The house was empty; Jack and his wife were at work. The kids hadn't come home from school yet. He opened his mail, made out a deposit ticket and went to the bank. He mailed his checks to the exes and left money on the kitchen counter for Jack. The grandkids came in and were happy to see Papa. They were good kids. The boys looked like Jack which meant they looked like his first wife. He didn't hold that against them. At least Jack and the boys didn't look like Charlie. The little girl looked like her mother. She was a sweet little thing. They hung up their back packs, had a snack, and went into the back yard. Will played catch with the two boys but she wanted to play on the swing. Jack and his wife came in from work and greeted him. Will had made spaghetti sauce from a jar with garlic and onions and ground beef. He had the water boiling and the pasta ready. He usually never cooked but tonight he felt like it. For once his daughter-in-law said, "Hi, good to see you." He asked Jack about his new job. Jack told him it was going well. They made small talk. Will told them about the funeral and how he hooked up with Paul and Tom and some other old friends he knew from the lake. Jack knew who he was talking about; Jack had lived at that same lake as a toddler. He told them he never thought he'd meet his first girl friend again and what a great time they had at her son's party, and how they went to Boston.

Jack said, "I'm glad you had a good time Dad, considering you went there for a funeral. You look happy."

"Of course he's happy", said his wife, "there's a woman involved."

Will said "It's nice to be home." He didn't mean it and longed to be back with Isabelle. Life was back to normal for Will.

In Massachusetts the sky was blue. Kathy was making pot holders with her granddaughter, Lesley. The girl got the hang of it right away. She must take after me thought Kathy.

"Are you having a good summer", asked Kathy?

"Oh yes" said the girl, "we go to swimming lessons every day and sit on the swing seat on the porch at night and have watermelon after supper."

"Do you like swimming?" asked Kathy.

"Yes, but I can't float on my back that good."

"You'll learn", said Kathy.

"Grandma", said the girl, "can we make brownies today"?

"Yes", said Kathy and saw her son's beautiful blue eyes looking at her from the little girls face.

"We're going on vacation soon," said Lesley.

"We're going to my other Grandma's house in Maine."

"That will be nice."

"They have a dog, but he doesn't bite. Mom says we can fish and row a boat. Dad said it's a long ride."

"You'll have a great time", said Kathy.

They finished the pot holders and made the brownies. Her daughter-in-law came to pick the child up just before supper time. Kathy never smoked when the grandkids were there. A rule her children imposed. She was longing for a cigarette. She was dying to light one up.

Her daughter-in-law said, "Thanks so much for watching her, I didn't think it was going to take so long for Ken's braces to be installed."

The boy's teeth were wired and looked uncomfortable. He also had some other circular wire apparatus attached to his face.

"Does it hurt" asked Lesley?

"Not so much," said the boy.

"It's too bad he has my teeth", said the child's mother.

"My grandson will be even more handsome than he already is" said Kathy.

"We're leaving for Maine on Friday, are you sure you wouldn't like to come?"

"Thank you, but No", said Kathy, "I'm planning a vacation too. Isabelle and I are going to see the cousins in Vermont in a few weeks. We haven't set a date yet but half the fun is the planning. I hope you all have a great time. Say hello to your folks for me and tell that son of mine to drive carefully."

She gave the plate of brownies to her daughter-in-law to bring home and kissed the three of them good bye. She had enjoyed the visit and the time she spent with Lesley. The car drove away with small hands waving out the car windows in her direction. She waved back and thought she just might call Isabelle tomorrow and make some plans. Kathy lit up a cigarette, coughed a half dozen times, made a sandwich for supper, read Entertainment and listened to FOX news. Life was back to normal for Kathy.

In Vermont it was raining. The ride had been long because of the weather but once Carol arrived it was good to open the door and feel welcomed. Judy helped her in with her suitcase and all the bags with Christmas Tree Shops printed on them. The sisters parted and Carol went in and opened all the windows. I don't care if it's raining I want some fresh air in here. She saw the blinking light on her answering machine. The first message was from telemarketing. She deleted it. The second was from a lady, nearby who had cancer and needed a ride for treatment next week. Could Carol help her? Carol would and wrote the number down so she could return the call. The Cappellos, her neighbors next door, wanted to know if she was home yet and did she want to play scrabble. She would get back to them. She then went to her computer to check her e-mails. A lot of stores sent her some discount coupons. She printed them. She shopped a lot, even on the net. Amazon reminded her about a new book she had reserved. A former co-worker wrote to say how good it was to see her in Boston on the Odyssey. The food pantry wanted her to change her volunteer day to Wednesday instead of Thursday. She'd get back to them too. Then she saw it. "Hope you got back safe and sound. Paul". Her heart soared, Carol was in love. She read the rest of the e-mails but not with as much enthusiasm. She put on the kettle for a hot cup of tea. She watered her plants, made the call to the cancer patient, and called the food pantry.

It was at that moment that the Cappellos knocked at her door. They were a couple in their late sixties. Jason was a wiry little guy with a salt and pepper beard and moustache and a full head of hair to match. He was a retired truck driver. His wife, Jen, was short, blonde and had twinkling eyes and a great smile. She liked to play scrabble on the internet.

"We were wondering when you were coming home", said Jen. "We saw Judy's car pull away a few minutes ago and thought we'd come over."

Jason handed her a plate. "Here's your supper. It's one of Jen's new recipes and it's great, as usual" he said.

"It's like a taco cup cake," said Carol. "You use the small size soft tacos and put them in a large muffin pan, press a glass down on them and bake for ten minutes. When their hot and crisp; you fill them with the usual taco stuff. You put the lettuce on the bottom. I used ground turkey for the health conscious and I used black beans. I hope you like them."

"Thank you so much, they look delicious", said Carol, "I probably would have had just a bowl of cereal. I have to go grocery shopping tomorrow."

"We'll let you get settled in", said Jen. "I just thought I'd save you from cooking tonight. Jason mowed the grass while you were gone"

"Thank you" said Carol.

"We'll catch up with all your news tomorrow" said Jen. "Have a good night."

They left.

What good neighbors and friends they had been through the years, especially after her husband had died. The four of them had played scrabble every Friday night for the three years Carol was married. They went on many weekend trips too. Jen and Jason were always there for her. She was lucky. The kettle whistled. She made tea. Life was back to normal for Carol.

In Massachusetts Isabelle was pacing the floor. The cousins were gone, the party was over, Will was back in Louisiana and summer was almost gone. She was down in the dumps and restless. She would go for a walk. She did. She had seen all her children since Will had gone home and the kids all looked at her as if she needed to be placed under supervision. None of the boys had said anything to her about Will. They wouldn't, not about something like this. Men are such cowards! The girls were different. Her youngest daughter had always been closer to her than she was to her Dad. She was Mama's baby. But she was being fiercely loyal to her Dad. They were talking just yesterday, while sitting in Tricia's yard watching the kids in their pool.

Her daughter said, "How do you think Dad would feel about this?"

Isabelle responded, "If Dad was alive there would be no "this"; and he'd still be my husband. He's not alive. Now he would want me to be happy as I would him."

"Well what if Will came back here and met you while you were still married?" asked her daughter.

"Look, your father met Will many years ago. He liked Will. He would have shook his hand and said he was glad to see him again. Your father was a very confident man. He knew I loved him and he was sure of himself. Will would never have been a threat to him and I would never have pursued any relationship with any other man as long as Dad was alive," said Isabelle.

"Do you love Will?" asked Tricia.

"Yes, I do", said Isabelle.

"Do you think he loves you?"

"I know he does. He asked me to marry him"

"What did you say"?

"I said I had to think about it."

There was a pause in the conversation.

"I know you kids think he was just a summer romance when I was young. We were close from the time I was thirteen until I was almost nineteen. After he got his driver's license, when I was only fifteen, we saw each other all the time, not just in the summer. I was crazy about him. He loved me and wanted to marry me. We never were intimate if that's what's bothering you. We dated even after I met Dad. When I decided to marry your father, I was nineteen. It broke Will's heart. The parting didn't go well and I never saw him again"

Tricia answered her, "Maybe God sent him here for a reason. I don't know. I know I want you to be happy. I don't want you to be lonely. I just don't want you to rush into anything"?

"How much time do you think I have left?"

There was a long silence and Tricia said, "I hope you know what you're doing."

Isabelle kissed her and walked home.

The next day, Jeanne, her oldest, called her on the phone and said, "Ma we have to freakin' talk. I just spoke with my little sister and she told me about a bizarre conversation you two had yesterday. Are you seriously thinking of getting fucking married?

"Yes" said Isabelle, "and I'm not trying to replace your father. I've known Will for a long time."

"No, you knew Will when you were kids and you're trying to be a kid again. What the hell, Ma. You don't know what he's like now. What do you know about his past fifty years? Has he got an ex-wife? Does he share his retirement check with her? Maybe he's still married. Is he sick? Has he been in jail? How many kids does he have? Does he have any money or is that why he's dating you? I Googled him but I couldn't find anything."

Isabelle began, "Will has been divorced three times. He pays alimony to two of his ex-wives. He doesn't share his retirement checks with any of them because he wasn't married long enough to any of them for them to qualify, but I'm sure part of the alimony settlement takes that into consideration. He is not presently married. As far as I know he's hasn't mentioned any sexually transmitted disease, if that's what you mean. He never mentioned jail. I'll ask him. He has one son, Jack, who is married and lives in Louisiana. Will lives with him and Jack has three children. Will told me he made some profitable investments, he gets a retirement check from the Post Office each month and has some savings from selling his home in Massachusetts. I'm a grown woman and I know what I'm doing. You kids have your lives to live. Let me live what ever I have left of mine. He's in good health, still handsome, polite and respectful to me. He loves me. He wants to marry me."

"That may sound exciting now," said Jeanne, "but in a few years when you both have health issues and have to take care of each other it won't be easy. He may not even stick around. He may want you to live in Louisiana. He has three ex- wives? What kind of man is he? He probably wants someone to take care of him in his old age. How can wife number four even sound appealing to you?"

"None of us knows what the future holds," said Isabelle.

"Death comes to us all", said Jeanne, "and sooner for the two of you."

"Thanks", said Isabelle.

"Do you want to go through burying another husband again?" Jeanne asked.

"I'm grateful for your concern. It has given me much to think about" said Isabelle.

They hung up.

Isabelle thought about how different both girls were and maybe that was good. She would think of what they both said but make her own decision. She looked at all the familiar things around her, the cleared off counters in the kitchen, the once instant coffee jars lined up and filled with candy for the grandkids, the toy room that had once been a bed room. It was a nice house but she wanted more. She vowed to get in touch with the cousins. They needed to make plans. She sat down and began reading a book. Things were back to normal for Isabelle.

In Vermont Judy stepped into her home. She tripped over all the mail that was piled on the floor. She said a bad word a very bad word.

She put her bags down and said "Hello, Cat". You'd think a former school teacher would think of a more imaginative name, but "Cat" she liked and so did he. Judy unpacked her bags, started the washing machine, gave the cat one of its new toys, found places for all the other items she purchased, put out fresh food and water in the cat's two bowls and sat down to have a cold beer. Judy may not be smooth but she was organized. She was glad to be home even if it smelled like litter box. She would get to that in a minute. She just wanted to hold her cat on her lap and stroke his fur. "What a nice time I had" she told the cat. "I missed you. I saw a lot of folks I haven't seen in years and boy did they get old. There was so much grey hair, so many bald heads and fat. Wow did people get fat and they don't hide it. I always wear these jumpers so no one actually knows what my figure looks like. Well I suppose it's not really a figure anymore but at least it's a mystery to onlookers. I went on a luncheon cruise, I saw Dillon, and I went to Plimouth Plantation. The rock did not impress me at all." She got up and took care of the cat poop and urine scented litter. Thank you God for letting someone invent Kitty Litter.

She opened her mail that was lying on the floor beneath the mail slot in the door. "The local paper, advertisements and fucking bills, that's all we ever get, Cat," she said. "What did you do while I was gone," she asked Cat. She didn't wait for a response. She knew he couldn't speak. "Did you catch any mice? Did you stay away from the bird houses? Did you meet any new lady cats?" She looked around her orderly house. She remembered Kathy's was just like it, even to the point of having bill receipts in manila folders the way she did. She liked the way Kathy had her cupboards lined up with all the different types of canned goods grouped together, just like hers, vegetables to the left, soups to the right. Crackers and cookies were on the top shelf and baking needs on the bottom. She thought if she ever needed a roommate she could get along with Kathy. Kathy believed in using the same towel twice and left it hanging over the bathroom door. That's just what Judy did. If you got out of the shower and dried your clean body with the towel why did the towel have to be washed? Why, you could get at least three showers out of it. They had a lot in common and they were related too. Kathy didn't really mind Judy's swearing. She didn't really mind Kathy's black clothes with the bling. Then she remembered Kathy's smoking. Kathy would never stop. Then she remembered Kathy didn't really like Cat. Oh well, at least she had had a nice visit with her.

"Cat," said Judy, "I have big news. Auntie Carol has a boyfriend."

The cat was not impressed.

"Auntie Carol has invited him to Vermont. He might come but I think a trip so far from home could be too much for shy Paul. Maybe you'll meet him. He's a little twerp but he's harmless."

"Isabelle has a boyfriend too. I hope he does not come to Vermont. No woman will be safe."

Judy opened a large can of tuna. She divided it in thirds. One third was placed on a saucer and two thirds went into a bowl. She put mayonnaise in the bowl and mixed. She got her glasses from her hand bag, put the saucer on the floor, and got a fork from the utensil drawer. She opened the newspaper across the kitchen table, sat down on a chair and grabbed another beer. "Come on Cat, let's tuck in." The tuna sure went well with the beer.

She looked at the photos that hung on her wall. The boys when they were young, their high school pictures and their wedding photos as well. She saw the crossword puzzle book by the TV table and sighed. Judy's life was back to normal.

In Massachusetts Paul was having a beer with Tom. They were sitting on Paul's front steps facing the lake.

"Life's quiet without Will and all the excitement of last week," said Paul.

"Will's better off back in Louisiana", said Tom. "In fact, so is Isabelle. I can see how she may have liked him when they were kids but now, well, he's used goods. Why would she ever want him?"

"Maybe she doesn't know about all he's done", said Paul.

"We don't even know all he's done and I'm not sure I want to know", said Tom.

"I'm sure word's gotten around", said Paul.

"Kathy lives the next town over, she hears things and don't think for one minute she hasn't told Isabelle about the ex-wives, if she knows about them".

"Isabelle did eavesdrop at the restaurant that first day", said Paul. "I wonder how much she heard."

Tom replied, "I know Isabelle laughed out loud after she heard Will telling us about the nudist colony. So maybe she doesn't shock that easily. She does have four sons and ten grandsons so she knows boys will be boys."

Susan came over and said, "Hi, Paul. Tom, have you forgotten we're babysitting tonight"?

"Oh yeah, right," said Tom.

Paul said, "Hi, Susan. Carol has asked me to come to Vermont for a visit. She thought it would be nice for all of us to get together to talk about all those years at the lake and play cards and see her neck of the woods. Would you two ever consider going there? She's invited me personally but I don't know if I want to go alone. I mean staying with a woman without being married could be awkward for me. I would like to see her though".

"You know, Tom and I haven't had a trip in a long time", said Susan.

"We just got back from spending the Fourth of July in New Hampshire," said Tom.

"That's family", said Susan. "I mean a trip with friends. It could be nice. I missed out on meeting with all of them when they were here. I always liked Carol and Judy. I'd like to see them again. Carol was a lot younger than me but she was always pleasant. She couldn't water ski for beans. She was a lot like Bob in that department. Judy was funny. Susan liked Isabelle's cousin. She always made me laugh and what a mouth on her. Is she still like that or have the years mellowed her?"

Paul said, "She's even worse now. She scares me a little bit."

"I think it could be fun and just what we all need in our old age. We could stay at a motel or something if you're uncomfortable staying at her house", said Susan.

"Let's think about it, Tom".

"Are Will and Isabelle going too?" asked Tom.

"Oh I don't know. Will is back in Louisiana and Isabelle is Isabelle," Paul said.

The couple walked away to go baby sit.

Susan said, "I think Paul is in love.

"What! No!" said Tom.

"He's shy" said Susan. "We have to help him out. We have to go to Vermont".

"Why aren't women happy just leaving men alone", said Tom.

Tom knew if there was a trip to Vermont in the future he and Susan would go. He never said No to Susan.

Paul sat there pondering what he had just done. Why had he invited them? Was he that desperate to see Carol again? She had only been gone one day. What did Susan think of all this? What would Marie think? He wasn't getting any younger. This house was nice but it was empty. Her house was probably nice but maybe she found it empty. Marie would not want him to be lonely. Marie would want him to be happy. He walked into the house and saw his duffle bag with all his fishing stuff on the hall table. He needed to put that away. He saw the shirt with the red wine stain. He needed to take it to the cleaners. He would tomorrow. He checked his e-mail and there it was, "Miss You, Carol". He put the duffle bag in the closet. He grabbed a cop mystery book and got out the CD entitled "South Pacific". He listened to "There Ain't Nothing like a Dame". Paul's life was back to normal.

# CHAPTER THIRTEEN: LOVE AND DOUBTS

Will sat at his computer browsing the net for air fares to Boston. His mind was wandering. He had heard from Isabelle everyday since they parted and the joy each e-mail gave him made his heart sing. Most of them were iffy answers to his proposals which were sent each morning. All of them said basically the same thing. She needed time. He missed her so much. He wondered why it was taking her so long to decide. Every other woman he had proposed to said "yes" right then and there. Maybe Tom was right and wife number four was not much of an offer. Oh my Isabelle, what is going on? Was she just leading him on? Maybe her children were trying to talk sense into her. Did she think she was breaking their hearts by marrying him? Did she still love Tim? Did she really want to re-marry? She was so friendly and cordial when they met at the restaurant. She called him "Big Guy", just like she had all those years ago. She invited him to meet her family. She went out with him readily. She seemed eager for him to come to Vermont. She returned his kisses. They seemed to be able to converse so easily and about anything. Isabelle didn't really know much about his past. That was probably best.

He had received a few funny cards from her and a love poem she had written. He had started calling her each Wednesday night. He needed to hear her voice even if it was only once a week. Was he behaving like an adolescent school boy? He wasn't what he used to be in looks, in bed or in his financial state. He told her he didn't want any of her and Tim's money. He told her to put it in trust for the kids. She said she had already done so. Will told her he'd never make her leave Massachusetts and her family. Maybe she didn't want to meet Jack or even come to Louisiana. Will felt lonely, sad and old. "Oh God", Will said, "If you listen to sinners, please send me a sign that Isabelle loves me."

The e-mail prompter pinged; he opened it.

It read "Hey Big Guy, I'm crazy about you. Love, Isabelle".

That was the second e-mail he got from her today. Suddenly Will was happy, in love and young at heart.

Isabelle was sitting at her desk paying some bills. She had gone over in her head all the things both her daughters had said to her. She had her own reservations too. What did she know about Will's last fifty years? Why did he marry so many times? Why didn't those marriages last? Would her marriage to him last? Did he just want to get her into bed to settle a score? Was he going to seduce her and then walk away? It was one thing to endure the loss of a man you loved because of his death. It was another to lose a man you loved because he was only playing a game. She had been told he had had many women. Why would he want a seventy year old widow? She certainly didn't have a hard belly or perky tits. Maybe he feels he needs to settle beneath him now, because he's old. He had proposed to her every day since he returned to Louisiana. He had sent her a few cards and once red roses. He had been calling her every Wednesday night. She was so happy when she heard his voice. Was she out of her mind? Was she acting like a silly school girl? Did she have Alzheimer's?

She used her head the first time she married and that marriage worked. She didn't want to use her head. All she could think of was charming, funny, handsome, wonderful, Will. Isabelle felt sad, lonely and old. She said, to hell with all this. She booted the computer. She went on to her e-mail site and typed. "Hey Big Guy, I'm crazy about, you" and then she hit send. Suddenly she felt better; she was in love for the last time in her life.

# CHAPTER FOURTEEN: PLANS

The next two weeks were frantic making plans for the Vermont trip. Carol had to take her anxiety pills three times. Plans and excitement were in the air. Many e-mails, lots of phone calls, some letters were sent and received. The first weekend in August looked good for all. Some could stay four days, some even five.

Will needed to find a cheap flight to Boston anytime after August first but had to arrive before the first weekend so he could join the caravan heading to Vermont. Should he rent a car or use Isabelle's? Would he be staying with Paul again until they left for Vermont? Would Paul be nervous? Should Paul drive up to Vermont with him and Isabelle? He needed to deposit his retirement check, pay bills, pay the exes and leave money for Jack. He needed to pack too. How much money should he bring or maybe just a credit card? What would he need for dress up in rural Vermont? He'd need clothes for his later week with Isabelle. He mustn't forget the aftershave. He thought she liked it last time he was there. Hadn't she mentioned something about a live show she was getting tickets for? He was going to stay at least two weeks this time. Where had he put the condoms and jelly? He was going to persuade Isabelle to marry him. He would have to consult his pharmacist to see if his prescriptions would run out during that time. Would this require another trip to the doctor for a new prescription? He hoped not. He didn't like his doctor, she was a woman. She enjoyed making him bend over and cough while she had her gloved finger up his ass. She'd probably do that even for a new prescription. He'd have to do laundry at Paul's house. What should he bring Carol and or Judy for a house gift? Should he even bring one? He'd ask Isabelle? Maybe he should just take everyone out to eat one night. That's it he'd spring for all on Saturday night. That would impress the hell out of them. Was there even a nice restaurant in rural Vermont? Where did he think he was going, Mars? Of course they'd be restaurants. He'd search the web.

He'd make reservations. Isabelle would be proud of him. He'd wear his new green shirt he thought. It looks good. Will was a vain man.

We're they going to fish at Carol's pond? How many people had their own pond? Was there fish in it? Did she have a boat or would they just cast from shore? Should they bring rods? Carol must have some. He needed to ask Isabelle a lot of questions. He must tell Paul not to bring that big duffle bag with all the fishing stuff in it. What would Tom say about all this? Will thought Tom must not be pleased about going. Tom liked being at home. Did Tom like Carol and Judy. Hell, Tom wasn't even crazy about Isabelle. Susan liked Judy. Susan liked Isabelle. Susan wasn't crazy about him. It would be good for the girls to get together. But Will didn't want the group to separate into men on one side women on the other. No, they'd all have to play nice in the sand box. He'd even have to be nice to Judy. That might be hard. He was staying at Carol's but he'd have meals with Judy and play cards with her and whatever. He hoped this adventure would be fun. Isabelle said something about her and Kathy singing old 60's songs on the drive up. Paul may like it but Paul had said he liked show tunes, whatever they were. Would they sing loud? Kathy tended to have a strong voice. Isabelle was no slouch either. Would he and Paul get headaches? Will wondered if he should bring his light weight jacket. Then he decided No, after all it was August. He hoped his plane wasn't delayed. He hoped getting his luggage wouldn't take too long. He wondered what the traffic in Boston would be like. Then he remembered Isabelle would be there. All was right with the world.

Kathy had outfits laid out all over the bed in her spare bedroom. They were all black. She figured if they were going to be there for five days and maybe went out to eat two nights then she would need seven compete outfits. She wanted to be on the safe side. She always liked a fallback outfit in case her mood changed or she fell in mud. She had the black Capri pants and the black tee shirt with the white sequined star fish on the front. That was one outfit. Number two was black jeans with a black Grateful Dead tee shirt. She'd have to wear that beaded belt with those jeans. It was a little snug but she could pull it off. Then there was the black jersey outfit. She liked that one; it had an elastic waist and two pink flamingos printed on the shirt. Number four was black palazzo pants and a black peasant blouse. The blouse had a few beads at the neckline. Number five was another pair of black Capri pants that had a tiny blue stripe and was to be worn with a solid black v neck tee shirt, there was a v in the front and the back. It was sexy. The sixth outfit was black dress pants with a black and lime green print blouse. This was as daring as Kathy got. She would wear her black beads and earrings with this. The last outfit was a black peasant skirt and a long sleeved silk blouse. It was black. She would bring a couple of pairs of sandals and her black slip-on sneakers. Her night gown and robe were black. Her black bathing suit and cover up would be needed. She should bring her black sweater and maybe a shawl. Vermont got chilly at night. She'd need to pack toiletries of course and underwear. Strangely enough, all her underwear was white. She was going to pack her jewelry in a zip lock bag. She definitely would need the big suitcase. It was a large, red leather one with a strap and one of those pull up handles and wheels at the bottom. She thought Isabelle might bring a king size suit case as well.

Paul and Will may have to put theirs between their legs or between them. They probably didn't bring much anyway, although Paul was a worry wart and probably packed half his closet, just in case. Will was vain, very vain; he may have a lot of clothes too. And the booze, she thought, we need room for that. She couldn't leave that behind. Her trunk was big but not that big. She'd just make it all fit.

The only other thing to worry about was cigarettes. How many should she bring? She decided on a carton, which held ten packs and she'd bring two lighters as well. Tom would thank her if he ran out. Susan was trying to make him quit but he couldn't. Kathy knew the feeling. She lit one up at the thought.

Kathy had made an appointment to have her maroon hair touched up. She thought about having her eye brows shaped. Oh what the hell, she was worth it. She bought a new pair of sun glasses, expensive. Kathy was good to herself.

She also made a trip to the local liquor store and bought a case of beer, two bottles of wine, sangria punch mix, melon martini mix and sprite. She told the clerk to throw in a couple of scratch tickets. She thought the booze would be a nice gesture. Judy would appreciate it. She scratched the lottery tickets. She lost.

Kathy was happy Susan was going. She always liked her. Kathy was the youngest of their crowd and Susan took her under her wing when they were young. Susan was always nice. Even though they lived only one town away they hardly saw each other. Once you got married and have kids you grow apart. You're taking care of business. She did see them when they came to her husband's funeral, but that was twenty years ago. Will and Isabelle had held them all together. Once they split up the friends seemed to lose contact with each other. Will, Paul and Tom still were pals but they never saw the cousins. The cousins were always visiting but they never got together with the men. That was a long time ago. This was going to be fun.

Carol was so excited everyone was coming to Vermont for a visit, especially Paul. She hadn't seen him in two weeks but he had e-mailed her regularly and she responded in kind. Paul was a breath of fresh air, unassuming, kind and good. She hoped he liked her. Carol thought about the sleeping arrangements. She would have to give Bob and Esther the best room; her room. That was OK, they were fussy and he had that sleep apnea thing and needed to plug in the air contraption. Carol planned on baking at least five loaves of Irish bread the day they were all to arrive. She'd have to remember to get lots of butter too. She thought an afternoon tea would be a grand way to start a party. She would get pastries too and make little sandwiches. Men were always hungry. Should she use the real china? Her mother's old stuff was beautiful and would look elegant. But then she'd have to do dishes. Well tea in a Styrofoam cup is nasty. Yes she'd go for china but maybe not Mama's. It could get broken, men are clumsy, and she would feel bad.

She would give one bedroom to Will and one room to Isabelle. Paul would have a fit if he thought they were sleeping together. She was sure they hadn't done so yet and after all they were consenting adults but this was her house. Paul was right, always do the right thing. The last and worst room would be hers. It was a single room, with a single bed but she did not mind. It would only be for a few days. She had aired out the rooms and changed all the sheets. Her mother had crocheted a number of afghans when she was alive and they were all still in good shape. They were the kind with pretty colored squares all sewed together. Should she put one at the bottom of each bed? That might be a good idea. They were colorful and would brighten up the rooms. She did have two bathrooms, old fashioned and plain by today's standards, but they were clean and worked. Old people needed bathrooms, a lot. She'd clean them the day before the company was to arrive and put out those nice soaps she got at Christmas Tree Shops.

She thought she'd serve soup or chowder later or even while they played cards. She had invited her neighbors, the Cappellos, to join them and Jen had offered to do some cooking and baking as well. The three of them, Judy, Carol and Jen, had planned the menus for the five days they would be entertaining. Carol would have to make sure her screens had no holes. Esther would go mad if bugs got in. Would they want to swim? Would they want to fish? She hoped that she and Paul would have some time alone. They could go out in the row boat. Could he still row? Could she? She thought they both could still row. I'm glad Judy agreed to have Paul at her house. She would be too nervous with him sleeping here and he would find it inappropriate. She couldn't wait for their cousins and friends to arrive. There was so much to do. Judy and Carol worked well as a team. Their mother, Edna, was always happy and had so many friends. She invited everyone to Vermont just as they were doing now. Edna knew how to throw a party. She taught her girls well. "Thanks Mom", whispered, Carol. She was excited and felt younger than she had in years.

Tom and Susan were getting ready. Tom told Susan he did not approve of this whole trip. He said "We're all too long in the tooth for a reunion party or whatever. I can't even remember what I did yesterday never mind fifty years ago."

"Oh for heaven's sake Tom, It's just a few days away. I think it was wonderful and generous of Carol and Judy to invite us. Is Carol still the same? She always wore her brown hair long. Does she still have bangs?

Tom said, "What the hell are bangs?"

"You know, short hair along your forehead", said Susan.

"She has a long grey braid down her back; her hair is all pulled back so no bangs, I guess. She looks like a plump Indian squaw," said Tom.

"Oh Tom, not nice." said Susan.

"I hope I can stand it," said Tom.

"You'll be with Will and Paul and Isabelle's brother, Bob, will be there, you always liked him. I'm dying to see what his wife is like. I want to see all the girls. I really want to see if Isabelle and Will are in love."

"They are," said Tom.

"Do you think Carol and Paul are in love or is Paul the only one smitten?" asked Susan.

"I don't know what smitten means but I think Paul likes her. Why I'll never know. I've seen her. I don't know what her feelings are but she should jump at the chance; it may be the only one she gets", said Tom.

Susan said, "Really Tom, you disappoint me, that's a mean thing to say and poor shy Paul."

Susan went on, "I want to catch up with Kathy and Judy. Kathy lives the next town over and I never bump into her. Has she changed?

Tom said, "She has maroon hair now but she still wears black and she still smokes."

"Judy was always my favorite", said Susan. "What a character. She really has a heart of gold, you know. All her sarcasm and dirty language is just a big front. Has she changed much? What does she look like?

"I remember she had a fine figure when we were young. She looked good in a bathing suit then. The day I saw her at the restaurant she had on some ugly loose dress; it didn't show anything. She looked like a pillow in a brown colored dress. When we were kids she had long brown hair. It was nice. Now she has a man's hair cut and it's almost as white as mine. She has false teeth now too. I wonder what Paul thinks of her false teeth. Maybe he could have fixed them. He would love to take a drill to that mouth. He's afraid of her. I remember Will's cousin, Milton, telling me what a good kisser she was. Yeah, Judy's looks have changed but not her mouth."

"Tom Neeley, if I didn't know better I'd think you had a crush on her years ago. And shame on Milton Stanley for kissing and telling", said Susan.

"Wonder what ever happened to Milton?" said Tom.

"We will have fun", she said. "We both like to play cards. We can swim. You can even pollute the great outdoors with those foul cigarettes of yours. I suppose Kathy will be smoking up a storm too. We'll make you two sit far away from us and out doors."

Isabelle was looking forward to the trip to Vermont. She was more excited by the fact that Will would be with her. She decided to just bring a few things, but pretty things, things that were pink and coral. Those colors brightened her sallow old skin. Isabelle was vain. She packed a lot of clean underwear, a swim suit, one really nice outfit, a skirt and blouse and all of it would be comfortable with elastic waists. She'd also need a pretty matching night gown and robe, in case anyone, anyone named Will that is, saw her on the way to the bathroom. At her age she always needed the bathroom. She really didn't care about the rest of them, who were staying at Judy's. Bob was her brother so he didn't count, Esther was too polite to say anything, and Judy, well she was Judy. She would bring more tops than pants because she always got food on her shirts. The boobs were always in the way. She bought a new bottle of perfume. She hoped Will would like it.

She also bought a half dozen nice hand towels for the bath rooms. They were ivory and had satin bands on the edge and some embroidery. They were expensive but she wanted Carol to have them for her bathrooms. She'd include a decorative bottle of nice liquid soap from Williams Sonoma. She wanted to show her appreciation for letting them stay at her home. She would give Judy a book about Plymouth and the colonial days, an Audubon Bird book that identified all the birds of New England and with a pretty little bird house. Isabelle was going to put these items in two gift bags with tissue and maybe add a ribbon. She thought she'd bring a card game called, "Fact or Crap", it might be a change from Scotch Bridge. She would bring one pair of sneakers and one pair of sandals.

She had made appointments to have her facial waxing done, a must. She was getting a manicure and pedicure as well. She would color her hair a few days before and have it cut and styled the day she was to pick up Will at the airport. There were some CD's she wanted to bring for the ride; some with all the big hits from the 60's. She put a couple of the CD's beside the other things she was packing. She thought they could all sing on the way up. They had decided that since Kathy had the newest car, she and Kathy and Paul and Will would ride together. Why have too many cars there? Isabelle planned to go to Kathy's the night before, stay over and be ready early on the day of departure. Paul was grateful since he did not like to take long rides alone. Anyway Will would be staying at Paul's for a couple of weeks and it would be easier if the girls picked them both up at Paul's house nearby. Will would be arriving at Logan, the day before leaving for Vermont. Isabelle said that she'd pick him up and she and Will would go out for a nice supper. Then she'd bring him to Paul's and she'd go right to Kathy's to stay over. She looked through her other CD's and came across a Pat Boone CD and one by the Temptations. The old music could be fun and break up the ride. She and Kathy could still belt them out. Will and Paul would have to deal with it. Isabelle thought she may even bring an audio book for the ride home. She loved it when a plan came together.

Bob and Esther were talking about the trip to Vermont as she and Bob started to pack. Esther was happy to be going and to be with all the cousins and friends. She was not comfortable about staying at either of the cousin's homes. She was reserved. She didn't like staying in anyone's home but her own. She felt like she was putting folks out. She was too polite and a private person. She especially liked having her own bathroom and this would be the case since their bedroom was on the first floor in Carol's house. She liked Isabelle a lot, she was her sister-in-law. Bob adored his sister and it was easy to do so. Isabelle was nice.

Will was another thing. She didn't really know him and heard a lot of stories about the womanizer. Esther did not want to encounter him clad only in a towel coming from the shower while she was waiting at the bathroom door to use the toilet. Will would be sleeping on the second floor, so that was good. Bob was more relaxed. He could be a fuddy duddy too, when he wanted to be, but he usually went along with what ever was going on. Sometimes he was as absentminded as Paul and Carol. He couldn't hear a thing. Esther was pondering how much to bring.

Bob said, "Esther, it's only for two nights. We will only be there, Saturday, Sunday and then we come home on Monday. It's really too bad I can't change my doctor's appointment or else we could go on Friday." Esther was thinking, thank you God you can't.

She answered, "Well we will make the best of the time we have there."

"What? We will bake the rest of the limey half pear? What are you talking about?

"No, No, No We will make the best of the time we have there." she said in a louder voice.

"We will take the nest of the fine calf hair?" he said.

"Look at me when I speak and pay attention. Your hearing is getting worse." she said.

They continued their packing plans. Bob told her he had a separate bag for his pills. He was asthmatic, and had breathing pills. He had high cholesterol and high blood pressure too. He had a prescription for his Barrett's esophagus and antacid for his acid reflux. He took an aspirin everyday and his aerosol mouth spray for the asthma. He also had his sleep apnea stuff to bring. Esther thought it would be a good idea to put all their medications in the one bag. He agreed. She had blood pressure medicine too and her strong migraine headache pills. She also had a rash on her lower stomach that never seemed to really go away. It was caused by sweat. Even though Esther was not a heavy woman, age makes the belly hang over. It was under this overhang that the rash was worst. She didn't want to be continually scratching while she was in Vermont. He told her to make sure they packed something nice for Church on Sunday but he thought just regular clothes for the rest of the trip were fine. Esther knew his term "regular clothes" were outfits that were at least fifteen years old. She said nothing. At her age she knew when to keep your mouth shut. She wanted to look good and would bring whatever she wanted.

"What should we bring for a hostess gift", asked Esther?

"What should we bring for Moses Bift? Who's he?"

"No, she said louder; what should we bring for a hostess gift?"

"Oh, I usually leave money on the dresser of my bedroom."

This was the sort of thing one did at a brothel, thought Esther.

"That's kind of impersonal", said Esther.

"They're my first cousins, they know what I'm like by now and they've never complained before when I've stayed", he replied.

"Well if that's what you want to do", she said.

"I never leave too much and usually less than what a motel would cost", Bob said.

Since he hadn't been to a motel since 1976, Esther didn't think Bob knew what a motel today would cost. They had made a lot of trips to LasVegas but only because he had complimentary hotel rooms. He would die if he knew the cost. Bob was a wonderful, kind guy who would give you the shirt off his back but he was frugal and maybe even cheap. He did leave good tips for waitresses and he bought her nice gifts but he liked to shop the sales and always clipped coupons. Well good for him thought Esther.

Esther asked, "How do you think everyone will get along"?

"How do you stink everyone at a marathon?

Listen to me; how do you think everyone will get along"?

They'd be twelve of them since Carol's neighbors would be joining the group.

"Oh it will be great. Everyone will get along", said Bob.

He was always positive.

"We'll have a lot of laughs', he added.

"Do you think Isabelle will marry Will", asked Esther?

"Do I think Isabelle will carry pills?

"No, do you think Isabelle will marry, Will?

"I don't know", said Bob. "She loved Tim and they had a good life but Will Benton was her first love."

"But they say he has a bad reputation with women."

"Don't believe all you hear. I always liked Will."

That was what made Esther love Bob; he only saw the good in people.

"Do you think there'll be a square dance or bingo up there in Vermont? Should I find a nice plaid shirt to bring or pack our ink dabbers? Maybe I should ask the priest if he needs me to sing on Sunday?" asked Bob.

Oh Lord, why is he socially backward? She didn't answer him but said instead that she thought one big suit case and the medicine bag were enough. She made a mental note to by a couple of Yankee Candles and chocolates to bring as gifts.

Judy was sitting on a chair sorting out sheets and pillow cases. She wanted all the bedding to match in each bedroom. Kathy would be sharing Judy's room. That was alright they were used to each other they could use the old stuff. Judy chose the light blue sheets and matching pillow cases for her room. They were well worn but clean. She would iron the pillow cases. She did not have black sheets although she knew Kathy did. What was this obsession of hers with black? Judy had cleaned, vacuumed, dusted and polished the entire house. Judy was not fancy but Judy was clean. There were still cat hairs everywhere no matter what she did. She knew Kathy didn't like Cat but they were used to each other and had a truce.

Judy would put Tom and Susan in the other big bedroom with the double bed. She hoped they liked floral sheets. It may be a little feminine for Tom but guys usually didn't notice. He'd probably have a few beers and just hit the sack and sleep anyway. The floral ones were newer and better than the light blue. Susan would like them. She didn't know if Tom liked cats. Should she warn him? Was he allergic? Hey they were getting free lodging, screw Tom Neeley. She was sure Susan liked cats. Susan had been her friend at the lake. Judy hadn't seen her in fifty years. She thought Susan was a beauty in those days, tall and willowy. I wonder how the years have treated her.

Then there was Paul. He would go into the only other bedroom. It was medium size, just like Paul? The bed was single, just like Paul. She chose tan sheets for him. Paul was Paul. Should she move the crucifix from her room and hang it in his room? He'd like that but she didn't want to pander to anyone, especially a man. She doubted if he would even notice a cat in the house. Although she thought she'd better move the litter box somewhere way out of the way because Paul would step in it, trip over it, spill it or cause some calamity with it. What did Carol see in him? Was she serious? Paul may drive me crazy but I'd rather have him staying here than Will Benton. I will have to keep my eye on him. I don't trust him. My cousin, Isabelle, must be out of her mind.

Judy was glad Jen was doing a lot of the cooking; she was better at it than Carol and supremely better at it than herself. She had never seen Carol so excited and animated during the past two weeks. She had to admit she was happy too. The first batch, Kathy, Isabelle, Will and Paul were arriving tomorrow. She looked at her pet and said, "Come on Cat get off that quilt, it's going on one of the beds. And Cat, don't forget to remind me to cut some flowers for vases and put them in the bedrooms". She set up the ironing board, smoothed out the wrinkles in the pillow cases and put creases in the folds. She made the beds, put an extra folded blanket on the foot of each bed, moved the crucifix, and stood back and admired her work. She couldn't cook well but she could make a nice bed and clean a bathroom. She then went into the upstairs bathroom. Maybe she should put the crucifix in the bathroom just to get Paul's goat. She decided not to. She still wanted to get to heaven. The toilet was new, out of necessity; the rest was old, charming and typical Vermont. Judy laid out various soaps and shampoo and put a hair dryer on the shelf. She hung her best towels on the rack and stacked a pile of bath towels by the tub. She even up dated the reading material in the book stand near the toilet. She came down stairs and got Kathy and her own room ready. The downstairs bath was much the same as the upstairs except the toilet was older. She spruced it up as best she could; knowing it had already been totally scrubbed. Judy was organized. Judy was clean. Judy was ready.

Jen and Jason were at their house. They were glad Carol invited them to join in this little party that she and Judy were having. They had met the cousins and Esther before. So they knew most of the guests who were coming. Carol had described Will and Paul and Tom and

Susan and said she hadn't seen Susan in many years. She told them of the chance encounter at the restaurant at the end of June. Carol said there was romance in the air between Will and Isabelle and then she told them about Paul. They were pleased to be included.

Jason asked her, "Do you think we'll get all these names straight"?

"We'll try. We already know the cousins so there won't be that many more."

Jason said, "I told Carol I would cut all the grass the day before they arrive. I think I'll even go closer to the pond than she usually does. It will give us more room for chairs".

Jen said, "You know Jason, if it gets too loud, or if you just want to watch the ball game, the beauty of this is we live right next door. I mean you guys may want to watch the Red Sox while we girls have a hen party".

She went on, "I'm so glad they asked me to help with the food. My éclair ring is always a hit and I think they'll love my home made macaroni and cheese."

"Who wouldn't" said Jason? "They will like anything you make. You're a great cook. If you don't need me, I'm going to tidy up my car barn. The guys may want to see what I'm up to. Old cars are interesting".

"You go ahead; I have to feed the goats and ducks. You were so nice to get me this baby lamb. I love him. He's almost ready for another bottle. I want to think up a fitting name for him."

Jen thought how lucky they were to find such a place to retire. Jason and Jen had been married more than forty years. He had been a truck driver and she taught pre school children for years. They had lived in a suburb in Massachusetts most of their lives but moved to Vermont ten years ago. Their children had moved to the mid west and so there was no need to stay in the big house or near the city. Jen always liked animals and Jason always wanted to tinker with old cars but there was no room to do that where they lived. Their house was too big; and their yard too small. On a trip to Burlington to see Lake Champlain they drove on the small routes to see more of Vermont. They spotted a small house with a lot of land for sale. On a whim they stopped and looked at it. They both fell in love with it. They sold their house in Massachusetts and moved to Vermont. She had a goat, farm ducks, a dog, a cat, a rabbit and she had never been so happy. He bought an old pick up truck, a run down, rusty model T, a beat up 1967 Camaro and repaired and refurbished all day long. They're still not done, but what a hobby. They never looked back. They displayed no signs of affection but everyone knew they were a close couple. They attended Church, town meetings and library events. Everyone in town accepted the newcomers. They fit in.

They had one secret; feet. If anyone saw them alone at home you would find them sitting on the long couch, Jen sideways with her legs extended onto Jason's lap and Jason with a tube of cream in his hands rubbing and massaging her feet. This is how they watched television every night. Some folks would find this eccentric but to them it was perfectly normal, like holding hands or putting your arm around another's shoulder. When they had first moved to Vermont, Carol barged in on them one night. She didn't mean to but she's clumsy and she was carrying two heavy bags of clothes for Jen to go through for the church clothing drive. Carol was stronger than most and the door just swung opened due to her weight and the weight of the bags. The scene she beheld, Jen's feet being rubbed and Jason's hand covered with cream didn't faze Carol; she was oblivious to most things like this.

Jason said, "I always loved Jen's legs and now I love her feet too."

Jen smiled.

Carol said, "Oh." Then she went on and said, "I'll leave these bags for you to go through Jen. Anything gross, like underwear, we just throw out. OK?" I'll see you at the church hall tomorrow. I have two bags I'm going through too."

Jason went on massaging and Jen purred like a kitten. That bonded the Cappellos and Carol.

Jen had gone grocery shopping twice and had all that was needed for her contributions to the festivities. She wanted to make the pumpkin bread on Friday so it would be fresh. She agreed with Carol and Judy that the macaroni and cheese would work best with the ham dinner on Sunday.

Paul was in a dither. He was getting ready to pack for Vermont. Paul had e-mailed Carol frequently in the past two weeks and had to admit he missed her. He was glad he was not staying at Carol's house this first visit. He was too nervous. He knew all the cousins gossiped and were probably thinking he and Carol had something going on. He didn't want them thinking he was looking for her bedroom if he got lost in the night going to the bathroom. Of course that meant he was staying at Judy's. Thank God Kathy would be there. Imagine being alone in a house with Judy. Oh God! The first night he would be sleeping with the two women. No, no, he didn't mean that. He would be sleeping in a house with just two other people. They were single women. How far away was their bedroom? He hoped it was on another floor. They were both old and Judy would probably be drunk when she went to bed. Maybe she'd pass out. That would be good. Kathy, he didn't know about her. She never appealed to him and now, even less, with that maroon hair and she smoked. Oh, no, he hoped she wouldn't smoke in the house. He'd keep his door shut. Hopefully there'd be a lock on it. He wouldn't shower on Saturday. He'd risk the body odor. He didn't want to take any unnecessary risks. Thank God Tom and Susan will be there on Saturday. Maybe he should have stayed at Carol's. Maybe he should wait and drive up with Tom and Susan? He told himself to stop thinking about all this now. He had to pack.

What should he bring? He took a deep breath. Just take what is absolutely necessary. Remember how Will and Tom made fun of the duffle bag he took on the fishing boat? They were happy in the end with the plastic "rain coats" and candy bars. Kathy may not have much room in her car. It was big but Isabelle and Kathy would bring a lot. Women were like that. He'd make a list of what he really must have while he was away. He needed his wallet and keys and that's good because his key chain has a tiny flash light and a Swiss Army knife on it. Those were two good things to have. OK, he said to himself, he needed underwear, socks and sneakers. He thought he'd wear a pair and bring an extra pair. He might step in bubble gum or dog mess. He usually did. Why was he such a klutz? He needed under arm deodorant. Oh God, would he need that. He'd need shaving stuff, well maybe not all of it. He'd just bring his razor, extra blades, shaving cream and after shave. Paul did have a heavy beard. Would he need soap and shampoo? He'd just use whatever is there; even Judy must wash.

Paul thought three pair of cargo shorts would be needed and that made him think of the day he and Carol both wore matching cargo shorts to the party. He'd pack one pair of dress pants, navy; Will told him he was taking them all out to a nice restaurant for dinner Saturday night. He included three tee shirts and one dress shirt, white. Should he bring a neck tie? He could wear it to Mass? He could just leave his collar opened. Yes, that's what he would do; leave his collar opened. He would need shoes to go with the dress pants, loafers were easy and a pair of dark socks. He was going to bring a sweater but he didn't want to look like Mr. Rogers. He'd bring a dark colored sweat shirt; Tom and Will always wore those. He had told Carol by e-mail that he was taking everyone to breakfast at a restaurant on Sunday after Church. Will had given him that idea. Will was smooth. Paul wondered if he should bring his crocks. They were comfortable but Tom and Will laughed at them. He decided to leave them at home. What if it rained? Even Judy must have trash bags.

# CHAPTER FIFTEEN: WILL'S SECOND TRIP TO BOSTON

"Jack said goodbye to his father before going to work. "Have a good trip, see you when you get home", he said. He did not hug his dad but shook his hand. Will was OK with that. He knew everyone was not demonstrative and guys especially greeting or biding farewell to one another. His daughter-in-law, Marilyn, said, "Good luck with the lady friend, Studley. I'll want to hear all about it." Will didn't know if she was being sarcastic or making an attempt at humor. He said, "Thanks" and waved good-bye. The couple went off to work. His grandkids kissed him and hugged him and said "Goodbye, Papa". He kissed the three of them on the tops of their heads. He heard the school bus coming to pick up the kids for day camp. He handed them their back packs and out they went. He poured himself another cup of coffee. In about an hour he heard a car horn toot out side. Will went out to the waiting taxi cab which would take him to the airport. It was much too early but it took almost an hour to get to the air port from the house and he needed to be there at least an hour early. There could be traffic. He didn't walk as fast as he used to these days. Will didn't like getting old. He was anxious. He didn't want to miss the flight. He had to get there today.

The flight was uneventful. Will handed his boarding pass to the flight attendant and got to his assigned seat. He had already checked in his large suit case at baggage and so did not have anything to stow above his head. He sat down and thought once again how uncomfortable the plane's seats were. Will looked around and saw a lot of other disgruntled passengers and a few excited ones. He was dying to get to Boston, to see Isabelle and the fastest way was to fly, but what a hassle. The security, although necessary, was a pain. The check in always took long. Standing in line for a while annoyed him and his old legs. The take off was smooth and there had been no turbulence so far.

The flight was about an hour into flight and the "fasten your seat belts sign" shut off. A long flight was no fun for an old man, who needed to take a piss every couple of hours. He climbed over the fellow passenger next to him, teetered down the aisle, went to the rest room on the plane and returned to his seat. He was trying to force himself to take a nap. Flying always made him tired and he was having dinner with Isabelle tonight. He didn't want to fall asleep during the meal.

He thought about the upcoming visit, dinner with Isabelle and the trip to Vermont. He was glad Tom and Paul would be there too. There would be a lot to do and lots of conversation. Will was a sociable person. He liked parties and events. He liked people. He loved Isabelle. Would she have an answer for him? Was she waiting to tell him in person? Maybe they would get married next week. Isabelle said she was going to make some plans for his second week with her. There was going to be something at the library about the Civil War, she'd check it out. She mentioned a show or the Music Circus or something. She said she wanted to cook him a nice dinner too. Whatever she wanted was fine with him, as long as he was with her. He rested his head on the head rest and dozed and dreamt of the woman of his dreams.

When he woke up he heard the pilot announcing, "Please fasten your safety belts as we make our final approach to Logan Airport." He could feel the landing gear move, and the drop in elevation. The landing was perfect and the air craft taxied down the runway to the appropriate terminal. Everyone rushed to the front of the plane the minute the pilot said "Welcome to Boston. It is 4:25 PM. The sky is overcast and the temperature is eighty-two degrees. Hope you had a nice flight and please chose Delta for you next trip." The aisle was full of commotion. Bags were being retrieved from overhead compartments, shoes were being put on; babies were crying, men were looking at the watches, women grabbed their purses. Will just sat and waited for the lull. He had flown enough to know it just takes time to disembark. He was one of the last to leave the plane and the flight attendant was still smiling. She was young and probably thought he was waiting for a wheelchair. How did she smile all day long, he wondered? He was becoming a grumpy old man.

He headed to the baggage claim area and waited for his suit case to come around on the revolving carousel. He grabbed it. Boy it was heavy. He was getting weak in his old age. What had he packed? He checked the name tag. It would be just his luck he'd get to Paul's house and find some old lady's corset, or a long blonde wig or pajamas with cats on them inside. What a vivid imagination he had! It was his bag; the name tag was in place. He yanked the bag off the moving runners and headed for the door. He looked for the sign that said "Live Parking Only", and went to that lane. He didn't have his glasses on; he was a vain man. He was looking for a white Town Car; he was squinting. Then he saw it. He moved as quickly as any seventy-one year old man can while carrying a large suit case. He waved to his darling with his other hand. Isabelle popped the trunk and he put the bag inside. She got out and said, "Do you mind driving? I'm getting too old for the expressway". Those were not the first words he wanted to hear from her but he got into the driver's seat, put on his glasses and she got in the passenger side. He gave her a quick hug and kiss; he heard loud honking behind him and saw a state trooper approaching. He put the car in gear and drove away.

Getting out of the airport was a nightmare. All lanes were bumper to bumper. It was rush hour. They crawled through the tunnel and approached the city.

Isabelle said, "Will, let's have dinner in town. That way we can avoid this traffic. You must be starving."

He agreed.

He got onto Atlantic Ave. and miraculously found a parking meter. Will parked the car and then grabbed Isabelle.

"Come over here you beautiful woman", he said. "He gave her a long hug and kiss and she responded."

"You know what I'm going to say," said Will. "Isabelle will you marry me"?

She said, "Maybe".

Will was hopeful, very hopeful. Will was feeling good. Will still had it.

They got out of the car and Will put coins in the meter. He said, "You're right, I am starving. The last thing I had was a cop of coffee around 10:00 AM".

"You poor baby," said Isabelle. "You should have brought a candy bar or something with you."

"I should have." he said.

They went to American Joe's Bar and Grille. She ordered chicken fingers and salad. He ordered a cheeseburger and fries. She dined and chattered happily. She stole one of his French fries. He tried one of the chicken fingers. He ate the hamburger like a frenzied shark. They talked about the up coming Vermont trip and Isabelle told Will about all plans she and Kathy made for the ride up there. She said Paul was agreeable. Isabelle said Carol and Judy were in a state; they were so happy everyone was coming. Isabelle described Carol's neighbors and told him she liked them and he would too. She asked him what he thought about foot fetishes. Will just shrugged. Isabelle said Bob and Esther would not be coming until Saturday. She said she was surprised that Tom and Susan decided to come but glad since she hasn't seen Susan in years.

Will said "Tom probably doesn't want to go to Vermont but he does whatever Susan wants. He said, "Susan hasn't changed much. She's still tall and thin. Her hair is colored light brown. She wears it different from when she was young. She must be seventy-three. Her hair is kind of straight and ends at her ear lobes."

"I think you call that a bob", said Isabelle.

"Whatever", said Will. "She looks good but not as good as you."

"I think you are trying to win some points tonight," said Isabelle.

"I am", said Will.

They finished their dinner and Isabelle said, "Dieting is out of the question for the next week. Why don't we get a hot fudge sundae for dessert? I mean we could be dead tomorrow."

Will looked at her seriously and said, "Isabelle don't say that."

"OK", said Isabelle, "but let's share a sundae anyway." They did.

When they got back into the car, Will held her against him and kissed her entire face with little kisses. He kissed her neck and then her mouth. She loved it.

Two teenage boys walking down Atlantic Avenue saw them through the windshield.

"Yuck!" One said to his friend, "Did you see that."

"Yeah, two old farts playing suck face. Gross"!

It was just as well Isabelle and Will had not heard.

The traffic had died down considerably. The driving was easy. This was a nice car thought Will. He could get used to driving this car. My pick up truck is good but this is classy. On the way to Paul's house, Will said, "Paul has been e-mailing me every day. He said he'd e-mailed Carol a lot in the past two weeks. Where do you think that's going"?

"I don't know. But she said he kissed her".

"Paul kissed her. Why? He must be a desperate man."

Then he yelled, "Ouch" because Isabelle had pinched him hard.

They made small talk all the way to Paul's. Isabelle told him Frankie Valle and the Four Seasons would be playing at the Music Circus while he was here. Should they get tickets? Also the Drowsy Chaperone was going to be playing at the Norwell Theater. Maybe he'd prefer that. She still didn't have all the information about the Civil War thing at the library, but she would get it. They could always go to the beach, get a card game going or just watch the Red Sox on TV. They could decide these things after the Vermont trip. He agreed and then they rode in silence for a while. She sat close to him like she did when they were teenagers. He had both hands on the steering wheel this time. He was no teenager.

He pulled into Paul's long driveway near the front door. Paul had the outside light on and was waiting and looking out the front window.

Will said, "This is just like when I used to bring you home from dates and your mother was always looking out the window at us."

Isabelle said, "My mother was a good judge of character".

He laughed.

Paul said, "Hi Will, Hi Isabelle."

They said Hello in unison. They both got out of the car. Paul shook Will's hand and gave Isabelle a shy peck on the cheek.

Will said, "Paul, stop kissing my girl".

Paul looked embarrassed. Poor shy Paul. Will got his bag out of the trunk and started walking up the front steps.

"Let me take that", said Paul "as he staggered and almost fell over with its weight."

Will took Isabelle in his arms and kissed her on the mouth for a long time. Paul wished he could be so daring; Will finally let her go.

She said softly, "My charming, funny, handsome, wonderful, Will."

He said, "What?"

She said, "Nothing"

Will was hopeful.

# CHAPTER SIXTEEN: VERMONT FRIDAY

On FRIDAY, Kathy and Isabelle shut the alarm off at 6:00 AM. They took their pills, went to the bathroom, showered, fixed their hair, dressed and finished their final packing. They thought they'd be ready by 6:45. The two old girls moved much slower than they thought. They got all their belongings, the two large suitcases, the two gift bags, and the booze into the trunk. Isabelle pulled her car out of Kathy's drive-way, Kathy pulled her car out, Isabelle moved her car back in. Now everyone would think someone was at home at Kathy's and Isabelle's car would be ready for her upon their return. They headed toward Paul's. They had told the men to be ready at 7:00 AM. It was already 7:30 AM.

The men got up at 6:45 AM showed, shaved and dressed. They put their bags out in the driveway at 7:30 and waited.

"Isabelle has never been on time in her life", said Will. "What takes women so long"?

"I don't know," said Paul.

"I think Carol is a punctual person", said Paul. "She had that big job for the telephone company; you don't get that from being late for work. She also takes cancer patients for chemo and you have to be on time for that. Carol goes to the nine o'clock Mass every Sunday. I think that's why she's on time. Judy never goes."

"I believe that", said Will.

"I think Kathy stopped going to Mass, maybe it's because you can't smoke in there. I hope if she smokes today on the way up to Ver-mont, she has all the windows opened," said Paul.

"Me too," said Will.

"I hope Isabelle hasn't stopped going to church. She used to go to Mass every Sunday. You know old habits are hard to break. I must ask her about this. I'd be surprised if Isabelle is losing her faith. She went to sister school you know. So did Kathy for that matter. Their sainted mothers would be so sad. You haven't tried to influence Isabelle with any of your ideas, have you Will?"

"Are you crazy; Isabelle and I never talk about that holy roller stuff".

"What do you two talk about, sex?" asked Paul.

"No", said Will, "as a matter of fact we don't. Maybe we should."

Kathy's car pulled up and the boys tried to fit their bags into the trunk.

"Stop" said Isabelle. She took the two pretty gift bags out of the trunk and put them on the floor by her feet. "You two will mess up the tissue".

Paul and Will had no idea what she was talking about but said nothing. A CD was roaring in the background "Roses are Red My Love" by Bobby Vinton.

"Oh, No, we're in for a long ride", said Will.

The girls sang with Frankie Avalon to "Venus" and with Connie Frances to "Where the Boys Are". The traffic was bad going through Boston. Kathy was a good driver and it was true, a woman can multi task. She had a hair brush in one hand that she was using as a fake microphone, she had one hand on the steering wheel; she was belting out "Love Me Tender" with Elvis and smoking at the same time. Paul marveled at this. Isabelle pretended to dance and sang at the same time; and not wrinkle any of the pretty tissue paper in the bags at her feet. Will laughed at the two of them and envied their energy. They were in New Hampshire now on Route 93. They headed toward Cracker Barrel for breakfast and a pee stop. The pancakes were good and the girls just had to buy things in the gift shop.

Will and Paul sat outside on two of the rocking chairs that were lined up on the porch of the restaurant.

"I can't understand women," said Paul.

"Don't try", said Will, "it's a waste of time. They're a different species. We just have to love them."

The girls came out with bags, put them in the trunk and said it was a great little gift shop. They were off again. Kathy lit up. Isabelle adjusted the volume and the music began. This time Pat Boone and the girls were singing. Paul and Will just shook their heads. They got onto Route 89 and headed toward White River Junction. They stopped again for gas and the bathroom. The girls told the men what a nice clean restroom the gas station had.  The men were nonplused. One urinal looks like all the rest. They drove on and stopped at Woodstock because it was so quaint and they wanted to stretch their legs and walk around a bit. They parked the car, walked and looked down at the Quechee Gorge. There were a couple of cute shops there too. More bags went into the trunk.

They finally got to Randolph and found Carol's house. They were welcomed with opened arms and introduced to the Cappellos.  Paul's head was spinning but when Carol embraced him he was just fine. Paul was hopeful.

Judy hugged her cousins, and said "Hi" to Paul.

Then she said, "Will Benton, I'll be watching you. This may be a small town but we know a snake in the grass when we see one."

"That's good," said Will, "because there's one right at your feet now."

Judy jumped a foot off the ground. There was no snake. She snarled.

Will said, "Gotchya".

Paul patted Will on the shoulder.

They all looked around at the surroundings. Kathy and Isabelle had been there many times but it still looked serene and lovely. The women could see Will and Paul were impressed.

"What a place", said Will, looking at the grounds, the pond and the quaint house.

"How's the hunting up here? He asked.

Jason answered him, "It's great, every fall I bag a buck and have the meat for the whole winter. What a great stew my wife makes. There are wild turkey and an occasional bear."

"I'd like to try my luck sometime", said Will. "I still have guns from when my dad and I hunted."

"Me too," said Paul, "Maybe we'll come back up in the fall."

The men went on talking about hunting and guns; the women headed inside.

Carol told them she was glad they made good time and hoped the drive was not too much for them.

"No," said Kathy, "We sang the whole time".

"What, Paul and Will too", asked Carol"?

"Well no," said Isabelle, "they were the audience".

The men followed the girls into the dining room. The table had been laid with an old fashioned lace table cloth and set beautifully with china tea cups. It was festooned with plates of homemade scones, with butter and jam on the side. There was sliced date nut bread with cream cheese and pumpkin bread too. Small brownies, cookies and mini cup cakes were on trays lined with fancy paper doilies. Chocolate covered strawberries were lying on a silver dish. The Vermont cooks had gone all out. There were savory dishes as well, with tiny finger roll sandwiches filled with egg salad and thinly sliced French bread spread with butter and sliced cucumbers. Small ham sandwiches on dark bread were sliced diagonally and had the crusts removed. The two large tea pots were at the ready. The kettle was boiling and the cream was being put into the pitcher. There were tiny silver spoons, brown sugar in a sugar bowl, sugar cubes with tiny tongs, a filled honey pot and a small saucer with sliced lemons. It was like a picture taken from a British calendar. The tea pots were brewing, the guests used the facilities and then they all dug in. All the guests complimented the ladies on the feast. Carol took credit for the scones. Jen beamed when they said they loved the pumpkin bread and the strawberries. Judy said thanks when Paul said he liked the egg salad. Maybe Judy wasn't so bad thought Paul. Paul liked egg salad.

After high tea, the girls cleaned up and the men went out and sat in the lawn chairs facing the pond. It was a great spot and the overcast day in Boston had turned into a cool sunny afternoon in Vermont. In the distance they saw the Green Mountains and heard birds, a goat, a baby lamb, ducks and a dog. Jason explained his wife's menagerie. The men said they would like to see it but were so comfortable they wanted to stay right where they were. Jason agreed and they all fell silent and content. After a while, the men discussed what type fish were in the pond, how big they were, how often it's stocked, and what kind of bait is used?

The women joined the guys.

Judy said, "When are we going to play cards"?

"Later" they all answered.

Carol told them there were two row boats, not pretty, but sea worthy and if they wanted to use them they could. Paul asked Carol to go for a row with him. He was dying to see her alone. She said, "Yes". The boats stood up, on their stern side, bottom facing out; they leaned against the shed. The men got two sets of oars from inside the shed and Paul and Will got the two boats to the water's edge. Paul took Carol's hand, helped her into the boat and led her to the aft seat. After Paul was seated, Will gave them a shove off.

Kathy said, "Come on Judy, we haven't rowed in years."

"OK", said Judy, "but I'm rowing."

Kathy and Judy had difficulty getting into the boat. It's not easy to do when you're older than sixty five. Will held the boat for them, Jason helped them in, and Will shoved the second boat out.

Will and Jason were glad they helped with the boarding and launching, since nobody in the group was agile any more. Off the two boats went in different directions. Isabelle, Jason, Jen and Will remained behind. The rowers went out across the water; Paul was showing off a bit for Carol. Judy was popping one oar out of the oar-lock and damn near losing the other completely. The water was calm and like a mirror. Jason and Will talked more about fishing and hunting. Isabelle and Jen were watching the boaters and chatted about recipes, Jen's animals and even Jason's skill at giving foot massages. Isabelle didn't know what to make of Jen's obsession with foot massages and changed the subject when she brought up the fact that Jason always liked her legs and now creams her feet. Isabelle asked Jen what the animals ate. She figured that was safe. Paul took Carol across the pond to the other side and they let the boat drift on its own. Carol pointed out a beautiful dragon fly. Paul showed her a hawk in the sky. A turtle stuck its head up from underneath the water. Carol and Paul talked and laughed. They seemed very happy.

Judy had managed to get to the other end of the pond and saw a fish jump. Kathy thought it was cool to see all the ring impressions it left in the otherwise flat surface. The sun was warm, the breeze just right.

"What a perfect day", said, Kathy as she puffed her cigarette. "I wasn't sure you still remembered how to row anymore."

"Well, weren't you brave to accompany me", said Judy.

"Do you think Paul is saying romantic things to your sister?"

"Paul, please. He likes her alright. You can tell. He's like a puppy dog but I don't think he has a romantic bone in his scrawny body."

"He's not so scrawny", said Kathy. "He's medium built, I'd say, and he was married for forty years to Marie so he must have been romantic a few times."

"Three to be exact", said Judy, "that's how many kids they had. He probably made Marie say a rosary every time they did it".

"Judy, why do you get like that? He takes his faith seriously. You don't have to but you should respect his beliefs," said Kathy.

"I bet Isabelle won't have to say a rosary when she and Will do it", said Judy. "He probably doesn't even know what a rosary is.

"Well why should he? He's not Catholic," said Kathy with the cigarette dangling dangerously from her lips. "Anyway if Isabelle and Will do it thunder will roll and it will be one hundred percent sex."

"You read too many romance novels", said Judy. "They're in their seventies for God's sake. Even if Will gets it up, and I'm not sure he can, Isabelle will have a grand old time trying to keep up with him."

"Oh, I don't know", said Kathy, "She did have six kids you know, she knows stuff. She may be a lady in the living room but a tigress in the bed."

"Are you saying you think Will Benton has met his match?" asked Judy.

"Well he met her fifty years ago, it's just taken a long time to tame these two savage beasts", said Kathy as she flicked the cigarette butt into the pond.

"I'm going to watch him all weekend. I bet he makes a move," said Judy.

"So what, Isabelle can take care of herself," said Kathy.

Judy said, "I don't think so. He's a cad."

I'm still pretty good at this rowing. It took a while to come back to me but I'm good now."

Kathy said, "Let's change places; I want to row."

"OK", said Judy. They moved very gracefully despite their age. Judy crossed the oars, and got up and went to her left, Kathy facing Judy got up and moved to the left just the way it should be done, one on either side of the boat. The boat was rocking dangerously. They took each other's former seat and off they went. Jason and Will, were watching from their chairs; they were impressed. All those years at the lake paid off.

Paul decided to pick a water lily for Carol. He leaned over and got it. Carol told him she wanted to row. Paul got up, crossed his oars and moved to the left. Carol facing Paul got up and moved to the right.

Paul said, "No, Carol, you have to go to the other side."

"Why," she asked?

"Because we're both on the same side of the boat", said Paul.

"What?" she said. She tried to move back when Paul decided he would move instead because she didn't understand. No one knows what happened. Either the two quick movements or too much weight on one side or what, but the boat did capsize.

Carol was splashing and laughing her long braid floating on top of the water. Paul was still under the upside down boat. She dove under to find him and came out pulling him by the back of his neck. His head was under water and his mouth was filled with weeds. Finally he sputtered and grabbed onto the boat. Carol was still laughing. Paul started to laugh too. They were both good swimmers so no one was really worried.

Will and Jason stood up ready to be life guards. Isabelle and Jen wish they had a camera with zoom lenses ready.

Kathy was rowing like an Olympic rower in training, and Judy kept yelling, "Unhand my sister, she gets asthma you know".

This made Carol and Paul laugh all the more. Paul pulled the boat up on land on the other side of the pond; right ended it and helped Carol into the boat. Then he awkwardly got in himself after two tries. The two wet love birds headed the boat away and around the bend.

Carol said, "Paul you have to get me another water lily".

He said, "OK".

Kathy and Judy came to shore, had difficulty disembarking and yelled for help. It's not easy getting in and out of a moving row boat. Kathy had almost fallen in and Will and Jason came to the rescue again. They all came back to where the others were sitting,

"That was fun," said Kathy.

"Where is my sister," said Judy?

Carol just rowed the boat around the bend where she and Paul couldn't be seen. "That dirty little sneak", said Judy. "I thought it was Will I would have to watch this weekend and all the time it's Paul D'Angelo."

"Oh no," said Will, "you have to keep an eye on me too."

Paul did get another lily for Carol and kissed her when he gave it to her. Carol was smart enough to have the boat out of Judy's sight. This kiss was longer than seven seconds this time. She did not move. She didn't want to rock the boat, literally.

Will said "Isabelle want to take a spin in the row boat"?

"No thanks, but I'd like to see Jen's animals", she said, "let's take a walk"

Jason and Jen went with them. They called back, "you guys want to come"?

Judy said she'd seen them a million times.

Kathy said, "Maybe later, I need another smoke and we better stay here in case Carol needs us.

"Or Paul," said Judy "I'm not really sure who the pursuer is. You know when Carol sets her mind on something, or someone, she usually gets her way."

"Lucky Paul," said Kathy, blowing out a perfect smoke ring.

Carol and Paul returned, still wet but glowing. Paul almost fell out on to the lawn getting out of the boat. He remembered how easy it had been when he was a kid. It was tough to get old. Paul helped her out of the boat. She got her short leg caught on the oar lock the first try but then holding both of Paul's hands she managed to get out.

When they all joined up again, they decided to get Will and Isabelle's bags from the car and take them to their rooms.

Will was close to Isabelle and whispered, "Rooms plural, we have separate rooms?"

Isabelle said "Nice try, Big Guy."

Carol accepted her gift bag with the tissue and Judy did too.

"How did it survive a four hour ride without any wrinkles", asked Judy?

"I'm very careful about my wrapping", said Isabelle.

"She has a wrapping room in her house", said Kathy.

"What", said Carol?

"Yes it used to be one of the kid's bedrooms and now that there are so many birthdays, with all the grandkids and Christmas presents, I have a room for that stuff and for me to wrap all in one place."

The other women were impressed.

Kathy asked, "Where do you want the booze?"

Judy said, "My house.

They left Paul's bag and Kathy's suitcase in the car since they would be staying at Judy's.

Will took his bag and Isabelle's bag upstairs and put them in the rooms Carol directed him to.

"Thanks a lot, Carol", said Will, "separate bedrooms. I thought tonight might be the night."

"Sorry, Will, this is a decent establishment. Anyway, it would upset Paul".

Carol and Will went downstairs and they all used the bathroom again before heading to Judy's. It was a short drive about five minutes. Paul carried in his bag in and Judy showed him to his room on second floor. Thank you God, he thought. He was glad he was the only one on the second floor tonight. He changed his wet clothes and hung them on the hook behind the bathroom door.

Will took Kathy's heavy suit case and was grateful she was on the first floor. He could not have made those stairs with this bag.

"What the hell do you have in here, Kathy", asked Will? "It weighs a ton."

"Never you mind, Will Benton, maybe a heavy vibrator or my midget lover" retorted Kathy.

"Good girl, Kathy," said Will, "I didn't think you had it in you."

She laughed.

Judy heated the two chowders, corn and clam and Jen put out the big Caesar salad she had made. Carol sliced French bread and they sat at the table and ate. Coffee and brownies followed. After the meal they moved to the table on the porch. It was a long screened-in porch. It was cool and comfortable. They started a card game. Scotch Bridge was their favorite. Carol had already taught Jen and Jason the game and Jason kept score. The cards were shuffled, the bids made and the games went on. Judy made everyone a drink; beer for the men, wine for Isabelle and Jen; martinis for Judy, Kathy and Carol. Judy was in her glory saying things like, "Uncle Billy always said to get those trumps out" or "Over bid" or "You have another goose egg, or "Under bid." She loved cards and couldn't wait until Bob came. He loved cards as much as she did.

It was so quiet outside. You could hear crickets and no cars, just like it had been all those years ago on the lake. Carol's pond reminded Will of the lake. The row boats and water lily reminded Paul of the lake. The crickets reminded Isabelle of the lake. Kathy and Carol rowed again, just like at the lake. The card game reminded Judy of the lake. What memories they had. They all met at the lake. This was making a lot old people feel young again. The boozed helped too.

A gentle breeze came in and then Cat appeared. Everyone knew Cat except Will and Paul. The animal came over to Paul and purred and rubbed himself against Paul's neck. "He likes you", said Judy. Paul just went up a notch in Judy's score card. Then Cat looked at Will. He arched his back and his fur stood on end. He spat and made a nasty noise. Judy took him off the table and said, "I know sweetie, there's another Tom Cat in the house, but don't worry, he's leaving."

Carol brought her guests, Isabelle and Will, home. Jen and Jason went home. Judy and Kathy went to bed. Paul locked his door. What a day.

# CHAPTER SEVENTEEN: VERMONT SATURDAY

On SATURDAY, they all slept late, well late for old people. By eight o'clock Carol came down for breakfast, put a nice table cloth on the kitchen table. She placed a vase of bright colored dahlias and zinnias in the center. Will poured orange juice from a glass pitcher into glasses and Isabelle poured hot coffee into their cups. A creamer and a sugar bowl with sugar cubes in it stood beside the dish of cream cheese. They ate warmed, buttered Irish soda bread and pumpkin bread on china plates. They had cloth napkins at the ready. They told Carol their rooms were comfortable and that they had a good night's sleep. The truth was Will knocked on Isabelle's door after visiting the bathroom about 3:00 AM.

He asked her if she'd like him to come in.

"Don't even think about it," said Isabelle. "You have colossal balls".

"I do", he said.

Isabelle shut her door. He went back to bed. They both were smiling.

Carol talked with them about their plans for the day. There's a farmer's market in town today, actually every Saturday during the summer. It has a lot of home made food stuff, home grown vegetables and crafts, like sweaters and things. There's also an interesting old library with a lot of exhibits from the Civil War, that's opened too. The fire station has a little museum showing some antique fire engines and photos depicting how they put fires out in the old days. There are some shops in town but they are overpriced. There could be yard sales too. She said she didn't go to them because she had enough junk already but Jen goes. Carol said she would ask her if they were interested. You could go fishing or rowing or swimming if it gets a little warmer.

"I don't expect Bob and Esther to get here before one", said Carol.

"We should wait and see what Paul and the others are doing," said Isabelle.

"That's fine with me," said Carol, "let's go outside and sit in the sun."

They did and it was another gorgeous day. Will and Isabelle decided they would go out for a row. Will insisted on rowing. She didn't mind. It was peaceful out on the water. They too had difficulty getting settled in the boat. Carol held it and then gave them a shove.

At Judy's house, Paul was finishing his morning rituals. He peed, showered and dressed. The bathroom was very clean. Judy can't be all bad. He could smell toast, possibly burned, and coffee. When he went down stairs the table was set with three mugs, one had a cartoon picture of Superman on it, the next had World's Best Teacher printed across the front and the third had a picture of a bright red apple on it. They were clean. A stack of paper plates flanked the two carton containers of juice, one orange and one tomato. A plate of dark, hot toast was covered by an ancient, white, immaculate tea towel. There was a jar of peanut butter standing along side it with a knife standing straight up in the center of the peanut butter. Sliced Irish bread and pumpkin bread were on another plate. The milk carton was there for the coffee and a cracked sugar bowl and spoons were available too. Judy told them that Carol had made the Irish bread and Jen made the pumpkin bread. The only contribution Judy made was the toast. She could not cook like her sister.

"There's plenty of coffee in the pot and butter and cream cheese in the fridge, she said "Help yourselves."

Kathy and Paul did. Judy walked away. Judy was a no nonsense person.

A few minutes later, Judy came back and poured herself a cup and sat down beside Kathy. Cat came in with a mouse in his mouth. "Oh no, you don't," said Judy, "Take your bounty out side. I will pet you later my precious Cat." She opened the screen door and sent the animal out.

Kathy said, "That's the type of thing that really puts me off. How can you stand it? I could never have a cat. What if that mouse got loose?

A mouse loose in the house would drive me insane. I mean, I'd have to call an exterminator. Does this happen often? I need a cigarette."

"Are you finished", said Judy. I'm not afraid of mice."

Judy turned to Paul and said, "I took your clothes off the hook in the bathroom and put them in the washer with my stuff. They should be dry later on. I'll start the dryer before we go to Carol's."

She went and got more milk for their coffee.

"Oh, and Paul I put your pit shit back in your room."

Paul had no idea what she was talking about.

"My what," he said?

"You know, pit shit, anti-perspirant".

"Oh," he said.

"You don't want Tom using it later."

"Thanks"

Paul thought maybe Judy really isn't so bad. She did teach children all those years. She made good egg salad and the bathroom is really clean. She is different though. I hope she never used that foul mouth at school. At least my clothes will be clean and dry and I wouldn't want Tom using my deodorant. She had four sons. She must know stuff. Judy definitely was still a puzzle to him and made him a little scared.

Back at the pond Carol was drinking another cup of coffee and talking to Jen who had just come over. They watched Will and Isabelle out in the boat.

Jen said, "They're in love, you know."

"Oh I know", said Carol. "I knew fifty years ago".

Jen just looked at her.

Carol tried to give her an abbreviated version of the past fifty years and told Jen she liked being out in the boat yesterday and wondered why she hadn't used it a few years.

Jen said, "You didn't have someone nice that you wanted to go row with, and now you do".

She smiled at her friend.

Kathy's car pulled up and out came Judy, Paul and Kathy.

They sat down with Jen and Carol and talked. They all said what a fine day it was.

The clouds skittered by overhead, the willow tree bent its branches lower and there was a frog hopping along the shore line.

Will hadn't rowed in years but got back into the swing of things quickly.

Will said, "Isabelle will you marry me."

She said, "Maybe"

They paddled around for a long time enjoying the pond, and the flies that skated across its glassy top. Isabelle saw a large white swan down at the other end of the pond. It was alone and quite stately. Swans mated for life. Where was its mate? Isabelle felt sad. She didn't want the Swan to be alone. Then from behind some reeds and grass came another one. They glided off together. This made Isabelle happy. She told Will what she just saw. He said he had seen it too but he didn't know they mated for life. That's quite a commitment for a bird. She splashed him with water. He looked at his seventy year old girl and could only see the young kid waterskiing on the lake over fifty years ago. She stared at him and his hair was back, the glasses gone; the wrinkles too. He was just a boy again in her eyes. They headed back to shore.

They heard Paul calling them, he was trying to tell them Tom and Susan arrived. Judy and Kathy were there too. Isabelle and Will returned from their rowing and needed help getting out of the boat. Paul held the boat and Will got out and then helped Isabelle. The three joined the others.

"Boy you guys must have left early", said Will. He kissed Susan's cheek and shook hands with Tom.

Tom said, "When I tell her I'm leaving at 5:00 AM, she knows I mean it, God damn it. We were on the road and no one else was so we made it in good time. I need a smoke."

"Have any trouble finding this place", asked Paul?

"No the directions were good," said Tom, "What a beautiful place".

"Keep your luggage in the car," said Carol, "because you will be staying at Judy's house. You can follow her there later."

"OK", said Tom blowing smoke out of his nostrils."

"There's a cooler in the back of the van with a baked ham and potato salad in it", said Susan. "Where do you want Tom to put it"?

Carol directed Tom into the house and he carried the cooler in. Carol transferred some of the beer and soft drinks into the cooler and put the ham and salad in the refrigerator. Carol said, "We don't want to waste ice. Why don't we just bring the cooler outside and it will be ready for lunch, it still has plenty of ice."

The neighbors next door were introduced. Tom was full of questions about the pond and wildlife. Jason again relayed to Tom the information about hunting and fishing.

Carol invited all of them in again for coffee, muffins and Irish bread. Some brought their food outside others sat at the kitchen table. The cousins were so happy to see Susan. They were all chatting like it was old home week.

"You haven't changed much," said Isabelle.

"I have", said Susan, "luckily, I inherited my lean genes from my father, but I have wrinkles, dentures, and ugly grey hair that I have to color. I wish it was like Tom's beautiful white hair, well not the moustache." They laughed.

"You look pretty fantastic yourself" said Susan.

"Thanks, I have to work at it, especially the weight. I have fat genes and a moustache" said Isabelle.

Kathy came over and hugged Susan and said how she couldn't believe they never run into each other, since they live so close. Susan agreed. Susan told her the maroon hair was becoming and remembered her love for black. Kathy held her cigarette up in a salute to Tom. He returned the gesture.

A little later the gang split up. Jason said he had a something he was working on at home but would join them for lunch.

Isabelle and Will walked off to the library and fire station.

Kathy, Judy, Susan and Jen left in Kathy's car for the farmer's market and a yard sale.

Tom and Paul wanted to go fishing. Carol told them she forgot to get bait. Tom asked her if she had any bacon. She went into the house and gave him some. Paul and Tom took two of the fishing rods from the barn, baited the hooks and off they went in the row boat. Carol wanted to tidy up the kitchen and bathroom before lunch and she also wanted to be there in case Esther and Bob arrived. She washed the bathroom again and put out one set of the nice towels Isabelle had brought. She loaded the dishwasher and made some lemonade and iced tea to go with lunch. She laid out some other things she would need as well, like paper plates and cups. This was going to be a picnic lunch outside. No fuss. Then she went to the barn with some bacon, grabbed a fishing pole and made a splendid cast across the water.

Shortly before 1:00 PM, Esther and Bob arrived. Esther had on denim Capri pants, a lime green tee shirt and white sandals, Bob had on tan shorts, a melon colored polo shirt, suspenders worn on the outside over the shirt, white sox and sandals. Carol put down her fishing pole; she wasn't having much luck anyway, and greeted her cousin and his wife. The usual small talk was made and they took their bags to their usual bedroom. The guests used the bathroom and came out to sit in the sun.

"Where is everybody", said Bob?

"Oh they all went in several directions the farmer's market, the library and fishing out there. She pointed to the boat.

"Is that Tom Neeley", said Bob? "I didn't know he was coming. I haven't seen him for years. This is great."

Bob yelled to the two men and they waved.

Paul rowed in. He and Tom pulled the boat onto the landing and said they had no luck with the fish.

"There are fish in there though", said Bob. "I caught a few bass on another visit. I used to come here frequently when Carol's father was alive. We had a lot of good times".

Bob introduced his wife to Tom.

Esther went to shake his hand and Tom said, "I've been baiting hooks so I'll just say hello."

Paul nodded his head toward her and displayed his hands as well.

Esther smiled and was grateful they didn't touch her.

Isabelle and Will came into the yard hand in hand and told them what a nice library and fire station the town had and that they found the museum in the fire house very interesting. The librarian and the fire chief were very informative on historical facts.

"Being here is like going back in time", said Will.

Isabelle greeted her brother and sister-in-law and asked how the ride up had been. Esther told her there was a lot of traffic until they reached Route 89.

"Getting out of Boston is always difficult on a Saturday morning" she said.

Tom and Paul went inside to wash their hands. Carol was doing the same since it was almost time to get lunch on the table. Will talked with Bob and Jason came over and a lively conversation ensued. The girls arrived home within a few minutes with all sorts of items they had purchased. Kathy found a black beaded purse at the yard sale and a jar of home made jam at the market. Jen got a few old pet bowls at the yard sale for feeding the animals. Susan bought a beautiful hand made quilt. She told them she was going to put it away as a Christmas gift for one of their daughters. Judy bought some fresh fat, tomatoes and a jar of honey at the farmers' market and a 1500 piece jig saw puzzle at the garage sale.

"I hope there are no pieces missing or I'll bring this back to the fuckers", she said.

Susan laughed, "Same old Judy".

Carol and Jen were setting the lunch out. Carol placed a large bowl of home made chicken salad that Jen had prepared, on the table. There was a platter of cold cut deli meats, store bought, and a basket filled with rolls, and several types of different breads, which were Judy's contribution. There was a long dish with sliced tomatoes, pickles and leaves of lettuce on it. The condiments were lined up in a row and the paper plates, napkins and plastic utensils were beside them. Carol had made a giant fruit salad with melons and strawberries and citrus fruit. The two jugs with lemonade and ice tea were waiting to be poured. There was beer and soft drinks in the cooler outside too. Jen called everyone in and said, "Just fill your plates and bring them outside. We're having a picnic today. You can get seconds and thirds if you like."

Will and Jason got more chairs from the barn and Paul helped set them up. Comments about how wonderful the lunch looked were made. Some one said "What a spread" and they all began to eat.

Will, Tom and Paul were sitting in a row eating. Judy sat down on a chair across from them.

"Nice to see the Three Stooges back together again, said Judy. Will, you're definitely Curly, since you have that big, bald head, Ha, Ha."

"She can dish it out but I wonder if she can take it", said Tom

"Oh, I can take it Tom", said Judy.

Susan said, "What's happened in the last fifty years, Judy. I know you have children. There must have been a husband."

"Oh, there was a husband alright," said Judy. "In fact there were two, Little Prick and Fat Bastard. I had a big wedding the first time with the cousins as bridesmaids. I eloped the second time. My first husband had a pretty face, a tiny dick and a nasty temper. I set him straight. One night he hit me. So I punched him in that pretty face, hard, and once he fell down and I hit him over the head with my black iron frying pan. He left and never came back. His brain was probably so damaged he couldn't find his way home but he did give me two nice boys. One of them looks like the son of a bitch. What an asshole number one was.

My second husband was an OK guy. Not much to look at but he never hit me and he was as dumb as the floor so he mostly did what I said. I think he was scared of me. Maybe he heard about number one. He was always at me to be more like his mother. He wanted me to hunt and fish and eat whatever I caught. He wanted me to slaughter a pig once, and make homemade sausages. Did you ever see a real pig intestine? Nasty!! They make sausage in that. It's disgusting. It looks like a long condom and you're supposed to mix the ground meat with spices and shit and fill that thing and then eat it. Gross. He also wanted me to pluck and dress birds, and pull all the messy business out of them. I told him Purdue had them already for me at the supermarket. I said, "Shit we live in Vermont not Appalachia". He got the idea eventually and I bought frozen pre-cooked meals after that. He gave me two boys also. They don't look like either of us. He left me twenty- five years ago for another woman; she was vegetarian. Wonder how that worked out for him? He probably lost weight. He's dead now, the fat bastard!"

Susan almost choked on her food she was laughing so hard. So was everyone else. The old friends finished their picnic lunch. The girls cleaned up and they all relaxed in the sun. The afternoon was slipping by. The conversation was animated.

Stories of the old days were coming out fast and furious. They blurted out memories and instantly were young again. They tossed out old thoughts like Remember when Will did this. Remember that time at the drive in movie. Remember the Pike brothers across the lake, what ever happed to them. They died, too bad. Remember when Isabelle did that. They were all talking over each other. Who did Milton Stanley marry? A girl from Maine I think. He lives there now. Remember when Isabelle crashed Will's boat into the dock? Will's dad was mad. That bass Bob snagged when we were about fifteen was the biggest I ever saw. My grandmother coated it with cornmeal and fried it. It was great. Paul and Marie fell into the lake when the dock collapsed. The friends laughed at the memories. Remember when Judy and Isabelle showed off doing doubles on the water skis. Carol tried water skiing what a disaster. Bob too! Tom got his driver's license first and got that old beat up pick up. All the board games we played. Susan liked monopoly. That's because she always won. Remember when Will took Isabelle to his prom. That was a pretty dress. Remember Cool Aid and making s'mores. Remember Judy doing this. Remember Paul doing that. We were so grateful Isabelle's dad taught us how to play Scotch Bridge. That tape recorder you had, Bob, we had fun with that. That lake was crystal clear. We swam all day some days.

Then they started taking about all their ailments the way old folks do. Bob told them he was on five medications and had trouble hearing. He also told them he had sleep apnea and had to sleep with a mask which was attached to a tube that had air flowing through it to keep him breathing when he slept. Will said he had fluid pills and high blood pressure meds and had to get stronger glasses. Kathy said all her doctor wanted her to do was stop smoking and she hated all the other tests he ran, like chest x-rays and EKG's. Paul's eye doctor told him and could now wear contacts instead of glasses and boy had the bifocals driven him crazy. Paul was pleased with the contacts. Carol told them her asthma had improved a lot with the new nasal inhaler she has and her doctor wanted her to lose some weight.

"Oh all doctors say that", said Isabelle. "My doctor tells me to lose weight every visit and I had the dreaded colonoscopy a week ago".

"Boy what a pain in the ass that test is and I mean it quite literally", said Tom. "That stuff they make you drink before hand makes you want to barf and the doctor seems to enjoy himself."

"But it does save lives", said Susan, "like a pap smear".

The men were all quiet. They didn't really want to talk about that female stuff.

Tom said his doctor yelled at him about smoking and gave him the patch."

"It didn't work," said Tom.

"I tried it too", said Kathy, "I'm hopelessly addicted."

Susan told them she had to wear a brace on her right arm in bed because of carpal tunnel in her wrist. Esther recently had a bone scan which showed that her bones were very weak and a skin check for cancer that went well. She was on a calcium regiment now. She also had a bunion removed.

Judy said, "Well I had a mammogram last week and I know it's important and I'm grateful I don't have breast cancer but a man must have invented it."

"Why" asked Bob.

"Well for one thing it's humiliating to have a technician lift your breast onto a tray".

"How many technicians would it take to lift Isabelle's", asked Tom?

"Ha, Ha", answered Isabelle.

"Hey watch it Tom, that's my girl you're talking about", said Will. "What I want to know is how does someone get such a job? Imagine lifting and placing breasts all day long"?

"Alright, pervert, let's move on", said Judy. "After they have your boob in position they push this huge vice on top of it and squeeze the boob until you almost scream and then they say, hold your breath, and walk a way and then take a picture. They take a couple of views on each breast and repeat the vice and squeezing each time."

Judy continued, "I think a penisgram should be invented and technicians could lift the penis and place it on a tray and squeeze the hell out of it and take its picture." "How would you guys like that" asked Judy.

"Would the technicians be men or women," asked Will?

"Maybe the squeeze would feel good", said Tom?

"What medical information would this test discover" asked Paul

Bob said, "I don't think I'd have that done."

When it was about 4:30 PM Carol suggest that they all take a break and get a nap or shower or both and meet up at 6:30 PM out front because Will was taking them all out for a nice dinner at the White Pony Tavern. Carol's guests adjourned to their rooms. Jen and Jason went home. Kathy drove Judy and Paul back to her house with Tom and Susan following behind in their car.

Some had a short nap, some showered, some just relaxed or read. They all got ready with care for the dinner. Will saw some stubble on his chin and decide to shave again. He wondered why his head was bald and his face still needed shaving every day. He wished it was his face that was bald this would be so much easier. He wore his new green shirt and khaki pants and loafers. He splashed on after shave. Will looked good.

Isabelle looked in the mirror and applied a little make up to brighter herself up a bit. She put on earrings and even wore a strand of pearls. Her blouse was hot pink and her skirt was grey. She sprayed perfume on herself. Isabelle looked beautiful.

Esther wore a lavender sun dress and purple beads around he neck. This was a good look for Esther.

Bob had a shirt that was about twenty years old, still in great shape but outdated. It was like a polo shirt with a wide band at the bottom; it was tan with brown stripes and had dark brown buttons. He wore tan pants and sneakers with Velcro fasteners. This was typical.

Judy looked in her closet and said to all her jumpers lined up on coat hangers, "Which one of you girls wants a night out?" She closed her eyes and grabbed one; it was charcoal grey. She put on her ugly sandals. She was ready.

Kathy was getting all gussied up in a black silk number with a skirt to match. She bedecked her self with several strands of silver chains, a watch full of bling, two bracelets with beads, one wide plain silver bangle type, big silver hoops in her ears. She hoped that cigarette ash that had fallen on her chest and which she tried to brush off was not noticeable. Kathy was Kathy.

Paul had on his navy dress pants, a white dress shirt and loafers. He now wished he had brought a tie. He must keep these clothes clean. He had to wear them to Mass tomorrow. Paul was nervous.

Jen and Jason dressed conservatively and appropriately they had been to the White Pony Tavern before. Jen wore sandals so the sight of her half clad feet would tantalize Jason. Jen was a romantic.

Carol put on a crisp white blouse and a navy blue skirt that covered a lot of sins. She had on smart looking pumps and added a chain with a cross on it. She decided to be daring and tied a navy blue ribbon into a bow at the base of her braid. Carol was on the hunt.

Tom wore his classic chino pants, and a red plaid shirt and a butt sticking out of his mouth and Susan wore a yellow blouse and a tan skirt with a pair of sandals. He didn't give a damn; and she was having fun.

The tavern was large. It was a huge pub style building filled with people. It was situated on a nice lot with a mountain view in the rear. There were outside tables but they chose inside because of bugs. Will was glad he had made reservations because of the crowd and because there were twelve of them. It would be hard sitting a party of twelve without reservations. Isabelle had said to him, confidentially, that she thought the expense of paying for all of them was extravagant. She told him no one expected it.

"Look," he said, "if I went to a resort for five days it would cost a lot more. This is my vacation and I'm happy to do it. Your cousins are gracious hostesses." They were seated at a long table by the picture window. Menus were given out, eye glasses donned and meals chosen. Will and Tom ordered buffalo steak, neither of them ever had it. Five others ordered roasted free range chicken. Paul and Carol ordered the salmon. Two of them ordered roast pork and Isabelle ordered a turkey dinner. They ordered both white and red wine and beers as well.

Judy and Isabelle were the only ones who noticed Paul and Carol had on white and navy tonight. Judy mentioned it to Isabelle on a trip to the ladies room.

"Do you think they synchronize their wardrobes," asked Isabelle?

"No," said Judy "they are just weird, kindred spirits".

Salads came with the meals and they settled in with forks and knives. They finished their main courses and the waitress brought coffee. Judy said I have dessert at home so don't bother with any here. They all agreed they were too full for dessert and it would be more comfortable to have it later at Judy's. Will paid the bill and they all played musical cars and drove safely back to Judy's house. Cat was waiting at the front door with yet another mouse. Judy shooed him away and they all went through to the porch. It was a warm night so it was nice to be in the cool air.

Kathy said she didn't feel like playing cards tonight. Esther said she did not know how to play Scotch Bridge that well and didn't really like cards. Susan said she knew how to play but would rather do something else. Jen said that Part II of Pride and Prejudice was on the BBC channel and she'd like to watch it.

Susan said "Is that the one where Colin Firth is Mr. D'Arcy?"

"Yes," said Jen.

"Then I'm watching that," said Susan.

"Me too," said Esther.

"I don't know what Pride and Prejudice is but I love Colin Firth, so I'm in," said Kathy, "as long as I can smoke".

Judy had all the windows open and the porch was right near the TV area so the air wouldn't be polluted too much. The other ladies agreed that Judy could smoke.

That left eight card players. Fifty two cards divided eight ways is only six cards. They decided there would be two games. Four players at each game and after two or three games the players would switch around. The eight of them fit around the long table, it was snug, but they fit. Bob shuffled one deck of cards and smacked the deck in front of Tom, Tom cut and Bob dealt. Judy shuffled the other deck of cards, Isabelle cut and Judy dealt six cards to each player at her game. There was a lot of shouting and bidding and loser's wining. About an hour later they all took a break, not the Colin Firth lovers, but the others.

Judy put on a pot of coffee and sliced Jen's homemade blueberry pies into slices and placed them on plates. They ate the pie at the dining room table and finished their coffee. The girls watching television ate in front of the TV. Judy stacked the plates and cups in the dishwasher and asked the woman in the TV room how the show was. They all said wonderful in unison. Tom lit up a cigarette, Bob talked about his last hand of cards, Will looked at Isabelle, Carol went to the bathroom. Jason looked lustily at Jen's feet propped up on the couch in front of the TV, Isabelle stared at Will, Paul got blueberries on his shirt, now what would he do for Mass., and Judy petted Cat.

Two players from each table switched and the second set of card games began. All you could hear on the porch was, "Why did you bid diamonds?" "I thought you bid three", "Sorry, that was my fault", "I bid two", "You loser" "Are you sure you have no trumps?" "You didn't follow suit" and of course, "Get the trumps out". The girls watching the television were weeping now because Mr. D'Arcy was at the church getting married. Bob and Judy tied for winning the most games and everyone agreed they were tired. Bob asked Carol what time the Mass would be held tomorrow? She told him there was a 7:30 AM Mass and one at 9:00 AM.

"We should go to the 7:30 AM because Paul is taking us all to breakfast at the Sunny Side Up", said Carol.

"He made a 9:00 AM reservation. That will give the others time to sleep in or get ready."

Bob told Paul they would pick him up at Judy's for Mass at about 7:15 A M. That should give us enough time to get there. They all said good night. Later at Judy's Paul was at the kitchen sink, wearing just his pants and shoes. He had his shirt at the sink and was searching for bleach under the counter. Judy came out of her room to let Cat out for the night. Paul could not see her behind the half closed door. She found Paul talking to the cat. Judy watched from behind the kitchen door and listened.

"How can I get this stain out? Cat" said Paul.

Cat just purred and sidled up against Paul's leg.

"Do you know where Judy keeps the bleach?" asked Paul as he stooped to look in the cabinet under the sink. Cat did not respond but walked up to him and jumped on his shoulder and licked Paul's face. Then Cat jumped down. Paul found the bleach, stood up and put a capful directly on the stain and then filled the sink with water. He closed the bleach bottle, put it away and waited to see if the stain would disappear. Cat jumped up on the counter top near the sink. Paul said, "I think it is working". Cat looked in the sink. Paul started squeezing the shirt. The stain was gone.

Cat was about to lap the water in the sink. Paul gently grabbed him and said, "No, Cat that could hurt you". Paul put the cat on the floor. Paul let the water out of the sink and refilled it with plain cold water. He rinsed the shirt and then tried ringing it out. Cat jumped up again for a drink. Cat was allowed to drink this time.

"Do you think the shirt will dry in time for Mass, Cat?" asked Paul. Cat did not answer. Paul laid the shirt around the back of the old painted kitchen chair and said, "Cat, it's pretty warm tonight. Let's hope for the best." Paul went upstairs to bed.

Judy let Cat out and took the shirt and put it in the dryer. Paul wasn't so bad. The house was silent.

Everyone at Carol's house got ready for bed. Bob had to brush his teeth twice because he missed a couple of teeth the first time and something was caught between his teeth and it was driving him mad in bed. This didn't really matter because they were in Carol's usual room on the first floor and the others were upstairs. Bob got into bed and was asleep in two minutes. Esther forgot to bring her sleeping mask but gratefully it was so dark in Vermont at night it didn't matter. She did hear noise right over her head; floor boards were creaking. What were Isabelle and Will doing in the hall way? She thought about this and fell right to sleep. Carol hit the bed like a sack of bricks and was out cold. She snored loudly.

Will was standing outside Isabelle's room kissing her fervently.

"Did I ask you to marry me today", he said.

"I think so," said Isabelle.

"What did you say," said Will.

"I said maybe".

"That's good. Maybe is good" They kissed again. Will Benton was a good kisser.

He held her a little closer and said, "I think you're weakening".

She said, "Don't count on it".

He kissed her again.

She said, "Maybe; My charming, funny, handsome, wonderful Will."

This time he heard her.

He said, "I love you Isabelle. Good night."

# CHAPTER EIGHTEEN: VERMONT SUNDAY

On SUNDAY, the church goers from Carol's house went outside to get into Bob and Esther's car. When they went outside Will was there all dressed in last night's finery.

"Haven't you been to bed, "asked Carol, "where have you been?"

"Yes, I've been to bed," said Will, "I haven't been anywhere. Where could I go? This is the only nice outfit I brought. I want to look good for church."

"Will Benton, you're going to Mass. You're not even Catholic", said Bob.

"I used to be Baptist" said Will, "a long time ago".

"You haven't been anything for years", said Isabelle.

"Thanks, Isabelle", said Will.

"Well you're welcome to come", said Carol.

"Why are you going to Mass" asked Esther?

"If Isabelle says Yes and marries me, I'll have to get used to it", said Will. "Don't do this Will", said Isabelle.

"Why?" said Will.

"It's not funny", said Isabelle.

"If you don't want me to go, I'll stay here. Maybe in a few weeks we'll be going to Mass together every Sunday for the rest of our lives, Isabelle," he said.

"Religion was never an issue with us, why are you making it one now", said Isabelle.

"Oh let him come. He'd be the only one left here. You don't want him to be all by himself, Isabelle. Do you," asked Bob?

"I'm sure he wouldn't be alone for long," said Isabelle waspishly.

"Ouch" said Will. He thought he'd leave today's proposal until later.

Carol said, "Isabelle he needs all the prayers he can get." They all got in the car and went to pick Paul up.

Everyone at Judy's was still asleep except Paul. He had had a bad night worrying about his shirt drying. The tee shirts he brought with him were not appropriate for Mass and a little wrinkled. He got showered and put on the same dress pants and shoes that he had worn to the restaurant. He went down stairs and saw his shirt on a hanger on the back of the same chair he had left it. It was clean, dry and wrinkle free. He put it on and noticed there was a note in the pocket. It read "Paul, Anyone who talks to Cat is alright in my book. Don't tell anyone I said that or I'll rip your lips off. Judy PS Destroy this once read."

Paul was confused, put on the shirt, and thought Judy wasn't so bad. He balled up the note and made a shot to the trash bucket with it. It went right in. He may play for the Celtics yet. He let Cat in as he went outside to wait for his ride. Paul felt good. When the car pulled up he squeezed in front with Bob and Esther. Carol, Will and Isabelle were in back. Paul was astounded to hear that Will was coming to Mass but said God did work in mysterious ways. They all laughed.

In front of the Sunny Side Up all the heathens were waiting to go in for breakfast. Kathy and Tom were puffing at their cigarettes. Judy and Susan were looking at the menu that was hung in the window. Jen and Jason joined them and asked where the others were. The friends told them that the others would be back from Church any minute and with that Bob's car pulled up. The worshipers and one ex-Baptist got out.

Judy said, "Will Benton, you went to Mass?"

Kathy said, "I didn't hear lightening strike."

"You must really love my cousin", said Judy.

"I do," said Will.

Isabelle was suddenly in a better mood. They all entered the breakfast place. The waitress filled all the coffee cups, eight high tests, three decafs and one tea. Menus were read, pancakes, bacon, sausages, eggs benedict, French toast, and omelets were ordered.

Isabelle said, "I never had banana pancakes before and the maple walnut syrup on them. Yum, Yum, Yum."

"I had the hash omelet," said Tom, "it was great."

"My French toast was superb and the bacon, so crisp," said Susan.

"I love breakfast food," said Carol. "I could eat it for lunch and supper"

"Me too," said Paul.

Kathy said "How were your eggs benedict Esther, mine was very good"?

"Oh mine too," said Esther.

The raves went on and Paul paid the bill. The two cars went to their prospective homes. At Judy's she told her guests they had a day at the pond planned. Swimming, boating and a ham and potato salad dinner around 4:00 PM, compliments of Tom and Susan. There would be a band concert in town around 6:30 PM and then we can catch the end of the Red Sox game and have dessert and a few drinks here. How does that sound?"

Everyone said "Good".

Tom thought swimming, Red Sox, and drinks sounded good. Paul wanted to swim but he hoped he and Carol would go out in the boat again. Susan thought swimming could be fun and the band concert too. Kathy thought all of it was good because it was outside and she could smoke and a martini later would be just the thing. Judy liked ham and potato salad, not so much the band but she'd go along with it and there would be baseball and booze later.

When Carol's guests got back to her house, she told them the day would be filled with swimming and rowing the boats. She asked Will and Bob if they would find the old inner tubes and blow up floats that were in the shed. She knew there were quite a few. Judy's boys had always left them there. She told her pals that Susan and Tom were providing dinner. Susan had baked a ham and made homemade potato salad. Jen was making a special dessert for later. At 6:30 PM there will be a band concert in town and later we can have drinks at Judy's and maybe see the end of the ballgame on TV.

Bob was dying to swim in the lake. Esther wanted to taste Susan's ham and potato salad. Will wanted to go in the pond and so did Isabelle. Carol hoped there would be some show tunes played at the band concert.

They all changed into swim suits; not a pretty sight for twelve sixty and seventy somethings.

Will had on navy swim trunks. He was looking in the mirror and sucking in. It did no good. He was a vain man. What would Isabelle think? At least he had a tan from living down south. He had a pretty face and long legs; that had to count for something.

Bob who was short and tended to be stout, had on a bathing suit that was at least twenty-five years old. He had been short and stout for a long while. It was plaid. It covered everything, it worked.

Esther wore a one piece black and white print swim suit. It had quite a plunging neckline. She was letting it all hang out. Esther had kept her figure but she didn't swim well and knew all the others could. She also lacked confidence and she didn't want to get her hair wet. Esther had a bathing cap on. Esther was in for a long afternoon.

Isabelle had a bright aqua two piece tankini. It hid a lot of sins but not the arm fat that hung from her biceps. She was plump but looked pretty good for a seventy year old. She too was looking in the mirror. Isabelle was vain. She had those big boobs. The men liked them and she supposed they would help her float. She had short stubby legs. Will hadn't seen her in a swim suit in fifty years. Should she wear a jersey over it? She didn't have Susan's lean genes but boy could Isabelle swim. Forget the jersey he may as well get the shock over with.

Carol had a brown bathing suit with a skirt. She thought it was modest and flattering. It had a sash around the middle that added at least ten pounds in an already bad area. She wore ugly rubber swimming shoes and hoped she and Paul would go out in the boat again. The fact that half of her boobs were exposed never occurred to her. How lucky Paul was.

Tom had on a swim suit that was a tropical island print, red, yellow and lime green. He hated it but Susan bought it for him when they were in Hawaii and it was the only one she packed. He was lean and straight. He had no one to impress. Will and Paul might give him crap about it, but he didn't care about them. He looked good and he knew it.

Kathy had on her black swim dress bathing suit and the black cover up. It had a wrap around skirt. It was pretty and it was black. She wore sun glasses adorned with rhinestones and even a bracelet on her ankle. She liked the water and remembered all the times they swam as kids. She looked at her long pointed fake, and expertly polished nails and said, "You girls be careful." She hoped to get an inner tube. How many were there?

Paul had on a red, white and blue geometric design set of trunks. He was of medium build and he looked good except he had a lot of black chest hair and a lot of black hair on his back too. He was Italian. He had a set of small swimming goggles to protect his eyes, he wore contact lenses. He was probably the best swimmer of the lot. He was happy to be going in the pond.

Susan had a long, lean body. This did not mean she should be envied. Susan had a flat chest. The wonder bra worked miracles for her in clothes but in a swim suit forget it. She was on her own. She had tried many false boob things but none worked or stayed in place. So Susan would have to just go with it. She didn't want to get her hair wet either.

Judy came in bike shorts and a tankini top. She didn't want anyone seeing her butt cheeks. Bathing suits never covered them and she thought the crotches on bathing suits were never wide enough. So she always wore bike shorts for the bottom. Her top was similar to Isabelle's but Judy's had a deep v neck. Evidently sixty- nine year old boobs were OK to expose; just not the butt cheeks. The top was brown. The shorts were black. She did not care.

Jen was plump and wore a black and royal blue swim dress. She had a cover up on top of it; a big bright blue dress shirt. She was modest and stylish. She had no shoes on, the little temptress. God only knew how Jason would react. She liked to swim.

Jason had on an animal print bathing suit. What was he thinking? It was brown and black. It came down below his knees because he was so short. He also had on a tan tee shirt. He thought he looked good. He kept looking at Jen's feet. She was driving him wild.

Nonetheless, everyone's nasty parts were covered and swimming was on the agenda.

Bob and Will were looking in the shed.

"See any inner tubes?" Will asked Bob.

"What," said Bob, "See any thinner boobs?"

"No," Will said "Inner tubes."

The men found eight inner tubes; six good to go but covered in dust and spiders' webs. One they could inflate, there were no holes. The other could be repaired but they had no time. They found the pump and started inflating. They also found two plastic inflatable rafts. These could be blown up too. There were two Styrofoam surf-boards one was five feet tall, the other had been five feet but now was about four feet tall; a piece had broken off. They both could still be used. There were several of those bright colored pool noodles too. "What fun", said Isabelle! Sometimes she was like a child. The water toys were repaired and cleaned off and everyone grabbed one and headed for the pond.

Before they went in, mother hen, Carol, said "Everybody line up and get sprayed with sun screen. I drive too many cancer patients for treatments to allow you all to neglect your skin". One by one they came in front of her and she sprayed away.

"This is water proof," she said, "so it will last."

"Will, make sure we get that bald head of yours"

They all complied and were allowed to swim.

Kathy was glad she got a tube; Judy too. They swam out with their tubes and they climbed up as gracefully as any two out of shape senior citizens could and sat in the holes of the tubes. It took them quite a few tries to do this. They floated in the water for the rest of the afternoon.

"Do you think we'll be able to pry our behinds out of these later asked Kathy.

"It will be difficult. Who cares", said Judy, "let's have some fun" and then splashed Kathy's jewel bedecked sun glasses.

They frolicked in the water for hours. All of them forgot how old they were. Paul tried to swim across the pond but got tired half way across. He said "I ain't what I used to be." Carol picked him up in the row boat. It was fun watching Paul get into the boat. Carol was pulling him in and holding on to the oars at the same time. He was bouncing the boat to his side, trying to gain momentum. "This used to be so easy when I was young", he said. "Carol, don't come to my side of the boat or it will tip again like yesterday. After several attempts, Paul got one leg over and Carol finally let go of the oars, crossed them in front of her and reached over and hoisted him in. They decided to go for a row again. They went to their special place around the bend. Carol thought he looked very sexy with all that body hair. Carol was glad he wore the goggles to protect his contact lenses. Carol was a practical woman. Paul saw her shoes and thought, what good, practical ideas she has. Then he saw Carol's bosom peeking out of the swim suit and he thought, my God, hers are almost as big as Isabelle's. Why hadn't he noticed these wonderful attributes? Paul was a sexy man.

Will and Isabelle jumped on the two inflated rafts face first and then paddled out to the middle of the pond. Will actually bounced and almost fell off. Isabelle had noticed when Will jumped on the raft and the leg of his swim trunks moved up that she saw a tattoo high on his thigh. When they reached the middle of the pond and were just relaxing and floating, she told him she thought she saw something on his thigh. He told her he got a tattoo when he was in the Army a long time ago. She asked him what it was. He told her it said "Isabelle". Isabelle asked him how his wives felt about it. He told her his first wife was only seventeen and she thought it was cool; she had one that said "Joe" on one of her butt cheeks. "Nice", said Isabelle. My second wife wanted me to get it removed but I told her I had been drunk when I got it and I still felt those needles; there was no way I was going to be stuck with those needles again sober. It caused a lot of fights and I was made to wear a band aid over it a lot. "You are such a chicken", said Isabelle. My third wife didn't notice I had it until about six months after we were married. She was into some weird voodoo stuff and said having a person's name on me guaranteed me that person's protection or something. "Interesting", said Isabelle. Isabelle moved her hand over to him and raised the leg of his swim suit. There it was "Isabelle" and beside it a broken heart. She was picturing him fifty years ago, away from home and feeling lonely and unloved. Tears immediately filled her eyes and she said, "Will I'm sorry". He took her hand and said it was a long time ago. Then he said, "Now may be a good time to propose again". She said, "Not fair Will" and with that he dumped her raft. Into the pond she went. "Race you in", said Isabelle.

Tom and Susan were in the other boat and although Tom was actually teaching Susan to row, it looked like he was embracing her from behind and their heads were very close. Tom, who was now dying for a smoke, was telling her that the flat part of the oars should not be spanking the water, they needed to be turned the other way. She told him he looked young in the Hawaiian swim trunks. He told her to pay attention and to dip the oars in and pull. She leaned against him and said, "You are a sexy man, and kissed his neck. Then she said, "I expect a response." He said, "Susan, what do you think a seventy-three year old guy can do standing up in a row boat?" Then he added, "How about, later?"

Jen had a wide grin on her face. She was sitting in one inner tube and Jason was sitting in another. He was rubbing her feet. Something about being out on the water was making their foot game very pleasurable. His hands were strong; her feet were soft. They needed to be home, and soon. Perhaps they should head in and see if the macaroni and cheese needed tending.

Esther had fallen off the Styrofoam surfboard five times. She had had enough. She said, "This is not fun".

Bob said, What, Misses Hot Bun!!?"

"Oh God" said Esther.

Bob helped her up. His arms were around her and it looked like another embrace of some kind. They headed toward shore. He noticed the low cut top of her swim suit and said, "Esther do you know, I think this swim suit of yours is immodest. I think you need to sew it in the front. It could lead men to sinful bad thoughts." He began covering her front with a towel.

She said, "I wish you'd get some sinful thoughts".

He said "What? And then he got it. He laughed.

Judy said to Kathy, "Look at all those perverts we're hanging with. Are we at a fucking senior's orgy or what? Do Carol and Paul think we can't see them swapping spit behind those reeds? I think Will is talking dirty to Isabelle and she likes it. If Isabelle and Will don't stop looking into each other's eyes and holding hands they are going to crash right into Tom and Susan's boat. What in the world are Tom and Susan doing? She must like it from behind or something. The foot fetishes are at it again in public. I think feet are freaking ugly. This is their foreplay and we're watching. And Esther and Bob; who knew? He never seemed to be a touchy feely kind of guy. What the hell is going on? My sister is a slut in a boat with the Italian Stallion. My cousin is listening to an x rated proposition from a world renowned seducer. Tom is actually making indecent advances on his wife, from behind, and in front of everyone. The neighbors are playing erotic tootsies. I think he's sucking her big toe. My other cousin is manhandling his wife while she's half naked. Are there always these open displays of affection when people go swimming? Shit Kathy what are we doing?"

"Not getting any", she replied. "I need a cigarette."

Using their hands as paddles, Judy and Kathy glided their inner tubes back to shore. The tubes did stick to their asses when they tried to stand. After much pushing they came off with a loud, popping sound. They came up on the lawn; Esther and Bob did too. The others were still acting like kids doing handstands under water, seeing who could float the longest and Paul even tried to do a cannon ball off the dock. It wasn't bad for an old man. Will wanted to try a shallow dive. It was the biggest belly flop ever. It hurt but Will's pride prevented him from saying so. Tom was showing off his back stroke and Isabelle her breast stroke.

Tom said, "Isabelle can still do a good breast stroke"

"She does have good breasts" Will said to Tom.

No one else heard. They laughed.

They all started swimming laps and the men were challenging each other to races. No one their age was still any good. Isabelle beat them all except Paul.

Jen and Jason said they were going home to change and check on the macaroni but everyone knew what they were going home for.

Judy, Carol and Esther started to get the food ready for Sunday dinner. Since everyone was wet they would eat outside at the picnic tables. A huge pan of cold potato salad and a big tray sliced baked ham were put on the tables, with cloth covers on them. Esther made a nice garden salad, covered it with plastic wrap and took it outside. Judy brought out a tray filled with the paper goods, utensils, salt and pepper and a few bottles of salad dressing. Susan took out the rolls and butter. Kathy carried cans of beer, some wine and soft drinks in a cooler with wheels. The guys came out of the pond when they saw all the food being laid out. It was almost four in the after noon. They all showed off today in the water; they would be sore tonight. Jen and Jason came back, dressed in casual shorts and tee shirts. Jen carried a large pan of hot macaroni and cheese. Carol brought out another pan with hot buttered corn on the cob. They all served themselves and sat down to a feast. They took their time eating and after dinner they rested for a few minutes.

"We should clean up this mess and get ready for the band concert", said Judy. The men even put the water toys away. They all helped and everyone went to their appropriate home to change. They met at the park in town where the bandstand was. Carol and Judy had plenty of extra blankets for everyone to sit on.

Promptly at 6:30 PM the band began. First the musicians played a medley of John Phillips Sousa's marches, then songs from the forties and fifties; then they went to patriotic songs. Carol joined in with "God Bless America"; she never forgot that Kate Smith costume. Next came a few tunes from the fifties and sixties. Bob was singing "Love Me Tender" and thought it was a good Elvis impersonation. A medley of Beatles' music was heard and they all sang, "She loves you, Yeah, Yeah, and Yeah" Then some country and western songs followed. Kathy and Judy did a duet singing "....Country Road take me home, to the place where I was born, West Virginia, mountain mama take me home....". They saved the best for last, show tunes. Paul and Carol belted out "There's No Business Like Show Business", "Sunrise Sunset" and "Some Enchanted Evening". They were in their glory. They were singing along with the crowd. They knew every song. Will wondered if they all should have lighters to sway in the dark; Kathy and Tom would be ready.

He held Isabelle. They were sitting on a blanket, her back to his chest. They just enjoyed being there, in the park, with their friends, but most of all with each other. He kissed her head as she leaned back and pressed her cheek against him. This reminded him of one night long ago when they watched fireworks and she sat against him this way. Her hair always smelled great. Was it the shampoo or was it just her. What a couple of old fools they were thought Will. Isabelle relaxed and Will crossed his arms around the front of her. Will kissed her again. Isabelle thought of another kiss one Fourth of July when they sat on a blanket under the stars many years ago. Isabelle loved the kisses on her head but she was more practical. She thought "How will I ever stand up?"

When the concert was over they all had trouble getting up off the ground. Some had to get on all fours first. It was better if you had someone to help you. Isabelle had bad knees, swam too much today and had difficulty getting off the grass. She was glad she had Will's help and a bottle of Aleve.

At Judy's house they all waited in line for the bathrooms. A delicious éclair ring that Jen made was sliced and eaten. It looked impressive and tasted divine. It was éclair dough shaped into a huge donut shaped circle with a hole in the center to make a ring; then the ring was sliced crosswise, like making cake layers and filled with a vanilla cream filling and the top was put back on and then melted chocolate was drizzled back and forth over the top. Jen had brought it from home, put and put it in Judy's fridge before going to the concert. It was yummy. Judy let Cat in and they all watched the last two innings of the Red Sox game. Watching the game reminded them all of the trips the all made together to Fenway Park, when Ted Williams still played.

Later, Judy and Kathy served drinks, martinis, beers, Coke and rum drinks and wine. They talked and laughed about the nice breakfast place they went to, the swimming, the concert, the dinner they had at the White Pony, the card games the night before and all the day's events. It was good to be with old friends. Jen and Jason reminded everyone that they were invited to breakfast at their home in the morning. "How does 9:00 AM sound", asked Jason? All nodded and agreed they would be there. They all said how tired they were. They decided to sleep in tomorrow. All went to bed and slept soundly. Even Will didn't prowl he left that to Cat.

# CHAPTER NINETEEN: VERMONT MONDAY

On MONDAY it was glorious; the sky was blue and not a cloud in sight. All had slept well and long. Bob and Esther rose first to pack and load up their car before eating. The cousins and their friends were all heading to the Cappellos for breakfast. Jen had made three huge cheese and mushroom quiches. These were accompanied by a heaping pan of breakfast sausages. She also made a large Danish ring with fruit in the center and white frosting and slivered almonds on top. Jason poured everyone hot coffee and cups of juice were available too. The food was all laid out buffet style on the counter. Plates were filled and bodies moved either to the kitchen table or the picnic table in the yard.

Judy and Kathy were eating together. Kathy was eating a piece of the Danish ring.

She said, "Judy you have to try this, I think I'm having an orgasm. It is soooo good."

Judy said, I'm eating the quiche right now but I have some of that on my plate. Wait a minute". Judy finished what she was eating and took a bite out of the piece of Danish. "Oh yeah, I see what you mean", she said.

Kathy said, "If she'd make me one of these to bring home, I think I'd suck her big toe."

Judy said, "Oh, God". The two of them began laughing hysterically.

Isabelle had heard the entire conversation but did not understand the meaning. Isabelle raised one eyebrow. She was good at that. Judy and Kathy immediately stopped.

Isabelle said, "Behave". There was silence.

"See that's why God gave her six kids. He knew she had that eyebrow thing going for her," said Judy.

"I thought you didn't believe in God", said Kathy.

"I do, I just don't want others to know, especially Bob or Paul; they'd be dragging me to church."

"I hear you sister."

The men meandered outside in the sunshine and ate like it was the last time they ever would. Men are like that. They talked about sports teams, fishing and manly things. The women sat at the kitchen table and chatted about clothes, movie stars and womanly things. When the meal was finished, Bob and Esther said they were going to head back to Boston. Every one followed them to their car and hugs and kisses were given and farewells made. Off they went.

The others turned back to the Cappello's yard and this time the women sat outside sunning themselves and having a second cup of coffee. Jason invited the men to his barn to see his hobby, antique cars. Tom was ecstatic.

He said, "Wow I had an old pick up fifty years ago similar to that one. It was my first car. You're doing a great job restoring it."

"What about the Model T," asked Will, "are you going to start on that next?" "Well, No", said Jason, "the parts are too hard to find and expensive. I think I'll work on the Camaro".

"That's a classic. Will you build dual exhaust pipes," asked Paul?

"Maybe", said Jason.

"Where do you get parts for these things", asked Tom? "Do you belong to a club?"

"I have subscriptions to auto magazines. They run ads and you can find things on the internet."

"Are you going to appear at shows and parades asked Will.

"When I get them done, I will."

"Look at that running board on the T", said Paul.

"The wood on the back of the truck is beautiful. It looks so shiny like spar varnish", said Tom.

"It's not it's a special seal they make just for the older cars with wood," said Jason. "Remember those Woody station wagons?"

"Isabelle's grandfather had one of those", said Will.

They went on and on talking about cars and what a great hobby Jason had. Jason told them he found a lot of parts in people's yards.

"The winters are harsh up here", he said, "I'm glad I have the barn to protect them. I have a propane heater for the real cold weather. It's interesting and it keeps me out of trouble."

The guys went out and joined the girls. Carol asked them all if they'd like to go back to her yard and have a horse shoe tournament.

"Count us out", said the Jen, "I want to tidy up and get ready for tonight. We have a dinner engagement in Woodstock. I don't even know what I'm wearing. I have the animals to feed and laundry to do and Jason has gardening too."

Isabelle told them she would sit this game out and Susan told them she didn't even like horse shoes.

"We'd like to help you clean up" said Isabelle and Susan. They got up and went in with Jen to help her.

"That leaves six of us", said Paul, "so we will only have three on each team."

"We can't play that way. It has to be an even number" said Tom.
"We need Isabelle and Susan," said Will

"Have you ever seen Susan play?" asked Tom.

"That bad?" asked Paul

"Yeah" said Tom.

"Tom you take one team and Paul you lead the other. Just pick three players and let's get this game started," said Will.

Isabelle and Susan came back to the gang and Isabelle said "We'll be the spectators what are the teams?"

"You're on my team, honey", Tom said to Susan.

"Me?" said Susan, "You're joking. I stink at this"

"I think you may be better now that you're older", said Tom. "I mean you look stronger than usual today. No, I mean I'm going to teach you some new tricks"

"Shut mouth Tom," said Will. "You're digging a very deep hole."

"You're on my team, honey", said Paul to Carol.

"Thank you, Paul", said Carol.

Judy said, "Remember washer toss, Paul, she split your head open"

"That was an accident" said Paul.

"Right," said Kathy.

"It was", said Carol.

"Your turn Tom", said Judy.

"I pick Will"

Paul said, "I pick, Judy." Carol was amazed.

Tom said, "Come on over her my fellow smoker and let's see how good you are."

Kathy joined Tom, Susan and Will.

That left Isabelle.

"Thanks guys, I'm the last kid in the school yard to get picked. Looks like you won me Paul."

"Poor baby", said Will.

"Lucky me" said Paul with sarcasm.

The boys set up the stakes and hammered them into the ground, measuring out the appropriate distance by walking one foot after another. They got the horse shoes out of the shed. Paul went first and got a leaner. Will was next and knocked Paul's leaner around the stake along with his own. Tom was best at the game. He got a ringer almost every time he threw a horse shoe. Will was a close second. Paul was good too. The men were far superior to the women. Susan and Isabelle didn't give a damn and that was good because the two of them could have played until the cows came home and they'd still never be good. They knew this and they were good sports. To give her credit, Kathy was an OK player. She had a nice, straight, strong graceful throw. The points were racking up and Tom's team was winning hands down. Paul said it was because Tom's team had two men and he had only girls. Will told him to be careful. Three angry women could be nasty.

"You should know", said Judy.

Will looked at her with a scowl.

Isabelle said, "You asked for that one, Big Guy."

Every time Carol got up for her turn, the other players moved back. Paul did not. He was loyal and hoped his old reflexes would react in time if necessary. Carol did have that strong little arm. So far she landed a horse shoe on the picnic table and one almost went in the pond. Most of them were on the ground near where the game was taking place. She did get a few points for nearness and one leaner.

Judy was the dark horse of the day. At first she was a mediocre player as the game progressed she was getting points. She even threw a couple of ringers. Yes, Judy could be trained. Judy could be good at this. Judy could be one of the guys.

They played three games of twenty-one. That was enough for old folks. They all needed a break, for cigarettes, bathroom, beer or all.

Tom and Susan packed up and made their farewells. Tom, honest to a fault, said, "You know, I really didn't want to come to Vermont. Susan talked me into it. But what fun I've had. It was good to see all of you". He kissed the women and shook hands with Will and Paul and said, "I'll see you boys back at home."

"Thanks for having us, said Susan, who ever had this idea was is a genius. I feel so much younger. The memories do that." She kissed them all goodbye.

Everyone waved to the departing car then went back in the yard for another drink.

They talked for a while and then Carol asked Paul to fire up the grille.

"It will be a small group for supper, just six," she said.

The women went inside to help with the preparations. Judy marched them all over to the sink to wash their hands. She was weird about things like that. Judy had already made a pot of baked beans with sliced cooked hot dogs in it for a side dish. It just needed reheating. She put it on the back burner of Carol's stove on medium low. Carol got out the ground beef and Kathy and Judy made hamburger patties placed them on a cookie sheet and covered them with foil. Isabelle was making a tossed salad. Carol had a small bowl of coleslaw, a jar of pickles, sliced onions, sliced cheese, and other condiments on a tray. Carol popped a pan of corn bread batter into the oven. When the burger patties were ready Kathy brought them out to Paul, who would be cooking, and handed him a spatula. Judy took the tray of condiments and accompaniments and the paper goods to the picnic table. Isabelle joined them with the salad, the salad dressing, a bowl of olives and butter on a small plate.

The late afternoon sun was starting to fall in sky. The breeze picked up. The sound of frogs croaking, bees buzzing and ducks quaking filled the air. In the distance on the other side of the pond, cows were grazing. The pond itself, had ripples running across its surface and its color was a dark blue. Vermont with its mountains in the background was heavenly.

Carol and Judy came out with more food and asked Will to carry the pot of beans from the stove. Judy and Kathy went in and got more beer and wine from the fridge. Paul cooked the burgers to perfection and the barbeque began. After they had stuffed themselves they grabbed lawn chairs, lined them in a row facing the pond and sat back and digested the food. They were silent and they were at peace. They almost dozed off when Isabelle said, "Look!" A huge mother turkey crossed in front of them with nine baby chicks. The turkey was beautiful and wasn't the least bit afraid. The chicks had fuzzy furry hair, brown in color and soft looking. They were trying to keep up with their parent and one fell over on its side trying to get up. The family scurried away to the bushes and some other hidden place where they lived. "What a nice surprise", said Isabelle.

They played cards at Carols that night and enjoyed it a lot. They went to there respective homes and set in for the night.

Carol was back on the first floor in her own bed now that Esther and Bob had gone and wondered if Will would behave himself upstairs.

Outside Isabelle's bedroom, Will said, "Isabelle will you marry me?"

She said "Maybe".

# CHAPTER TWENTY: VERMONT TUESDAY

On TUESDAY, Carol got up early and made blueberry muffins and scones for breakfast. Her boarders got up at different times and joined her in the kitchen. It smelled wonderfully of fresh baking. The coffee was hot, the juice chilled. The muffins and scones were on the table with butter and jam along side them. She had a bowl of strawberries there as well. Will was not looking forward to the long ride home especially if Kathy and Isabelle sang the whole time. Isabelle joined them. She told Will he did not have to worry she had brought an audio book for all of them to listen to on the way back. It was a mystery by Robert Crais who wrote a series about a Los Angles detective named Elvis Cole. She said she knew he'd like it. Will told her he had read a few of them and asked which one she brought. I don't remember the title but it's his newest. Will assured her he would look forward to it. He turned to her and said Carol can be the witness today, "Isabelle, Will you marry me?" She said, "Maybe." Carol was teary eyed. Isabelle loved the muffins and ate two with tons of butter. Will had two scones with jam and one muffin plain.

Judy came in the back door with Paul and Kathy. They all sat down and ate. Paul said it smells so good in here just like a bakery. He put cream in his coffee and smiled at Carol. After breakfast they made final preparations to go and Will told Isabelle he'd get her bag into the car if it was ready. She said it was and he went to get it. Kathy was outside arranging things in the trunk. Isabelle kicked Judy under the table and nodded to the door. Judy said, "What the hell, Isabelle"? Isabelle raised one eyebrow and got out of her seat. Judy followed her. Will was stumbling down with the suit cases and went out to the car.

Carol and Paul were alone in the kitchen.

He said, "Carol I had a wonderful time. You and Judy are good hostesses. The food, the entertainment, everything was great, but especially you. I'm glad I came and I will miss you when I get back to my lonely house."

She said, "Oh Paul, I'm so glad you came. It made me so happy to see you again."

"Will you e-mail me", he asked?

"Everyday" she said.

Paul moved closer, took her in his arms, and gave her a warm embrace and a very long kiss. She responded. Then he headed toward the door. She followed him. The men got in the back seat and the two girls in front. Carol walked over to Paul's widow; stuck her head in and kissed him again right in front of everyone. "Good bye" she said and almost got her head stuck pulling it out of the window.

Judy and her sister waved until the car was out of sight. The cousins and friends all had a great vacation. The sisters sat down and had another cup of coffee. For once Judy said nothing.

The ride home went smoothly. They made a couple of stops for the bathroom and gassed the car up. They enjoyed listening to the mystery story on the CD player. They got take out at McDonalds and ate in the car so they didn't have to interrupt the book. The ride went faster than they expected and by early afternoon they were at Paul's house. Will and Paul took their bags into the house and they came back out to say good bye. Will told Isabelle he would call her later to firm up some plans they discussed for the week. Kathy and Isabelle said goodbye to Will and Paul and the girls left. The boys went in the house and Will said, "Want a beer"? Paul said, "Yes".

Kathy managed to get all her luggage and bags of items she had purchased into her house and Isabelle transferred her things to her own car. Kathy left her car parked on the street so Isabelle could back out of the driveway. Kathy had asked Isabelle to come in for a drink or coffee and Isabelle said no she wanted to get home. The cousins hugged and Isabelle drove off. She came home to a mailbox full of mail, a house with no oxygen and a hot muggy day. Her sandals were the first things she took off. She opened her suitcase and took out the big plastic trash bag she always packed that was full of her dirty clothes. Isabelle went straight to the laundry room. Whites first Isabelle said to herself reaching for Tide and Clorox. The rest will have to wait. This made the suit case much lighter to carry upstairs.

# CHAPTER TWENTY-ONE: WILL PLEADS HIS CASE

The rest of Will's visit to Massachusetts went smoothly. He and Isabelle went for walks along the beach during the day, they saw a show at a community theater one night, and they did get tickets for the Music Circus for another. They also attended a lecture and exhibition on the Civil War. He asked her to marry him. She said Maybe. Will went fishing with Kevin one morning and played washer toss at Joe's when they went for supper one night and he helped Isabelle baby sit so Tricia and Dennis could go out for lobster. He asked Isabelle to marry him again. She said, "Maybe". He and Isabelle played cards at Jeanne's with all her boys and Dan. Gerry invited them for a cook out and they swam at his pool. Billy even took Will for a beer at the Sand Trap. Will got to throw the dice, a weekly event that can win you a lot of money. Will lost.

On his last night in Boston, Isabelle cooked him a nice romantic dinner. She was a good cook and she made a homemade chicken pot pie, salad and they had ice cream for dessert. After dinner, they did the dishes together. Isabelle was sad he was leaving.

Will looked at Isabelle with a serious expression, he said, "This is going to be my last pitch for marriage since I'm leaving for home soon. I want to spend whatever life I have left with you. I want to grab at whatever happiness I can and hold onto it with both hands. You are that happiness."

"Will, I know what you are saying", said Isabelle, "but if we marry, we will become so attached that it will be unbearable when one of us dies and some day one of us will die and the other will be left alone and devastated. I don't want to be the one standing beside a coffin, with tears streaming down my face saying goodbye. I can't even think about it. If we just go our separate ways now we can say we had a lot of fun and a nice little reunion."

"That's not enough for me Isabelle", said Will, "I want you to be my wife and while I'm on that subject we should talk about sex.

"Really what do you want to know", said Isabelle.

"Ha, Ha", he replied, "very funny" Then he went on to say he hoped she'd say yes and then they could make love.

"Listen Isabelle," said Will, "I don't want you to be disappointed, I am seventy-one years young but that doesn't mean I can still make love like a teenager. I've had a lot of experience with women and Tom and Paul make me out to be a Don Juan but I'm not what I used to be. I like to take things slower now. I've never made love that often. I've had a lot of sex but making love is having sex with someone you love. I had three wives. I think I loved two of them and I had one wife I didn't love. All the rest were slam bam thank you Mam; one night stands, and meaningless encounters. I was younger then. I'm not as sexy as I was in my prime. Sometimes it takes a while for me to get"... silence, I don't always"... silence, "you know. Do you understand? I can't always ... silence".

"Get it up?" said Isabelle, "For heavens sake Will, I was married for forty-nine years. I know what you're talking about. I've had young, ardent, spontaneous, sex. Sometimes we exhausted ourselves. I had six kids. I remember what a night of full of youthful passion is. If I had to go through that now, at my age, it would probably kill me. I think slow is good. You're the one who should have concerns. I'll bet you've never made love to a grandmother or even someone who's gone through menopause. Age plays cruel tricks on all of us. I'm less responsive; I'm dry, I take longer to climax. You may tire out trying to get me there. It's OK women don't always need to climax. Women sometimes just like men making love to them, holding them, caressing them. Men don't understand that. Men love with their bodies, women love with their hearts. Sex is wasted on young people. They don't appreciate it. They just do it. But we had our turn at being young and sexy and I'm glad neither of us wasted it. The sad thing is women my age desire sex more than when they're young. They're more comfortable with it. I think it's because they know they won't get pregnant."

Isabelle went on, "Whatever we have together will be an expression of our love, Will. It may be better than we think".

Will responded "I'm glad your positive about this and I'm glad we can still talk about anything. I love you and cherish you. Any love making we do will be our private pleasure. No right or wrong. No negative feelings about performances. No great expectations. Some nights may be spectacular; some nights it may work, other nights will just be a lot of hugging."

"Oh, are we limiting ourselves to nights only", asked Isabelle? "I think at our age whenever the mood comes we should go with it."

They both laughed out loud.

Then he said, "I know you've heard songs that say I hope you take a chance and dance. The songs are true. We are both going to die. Everyone does. We may have six months or six years left. I don't know and neither do you. If we don't spend them together we will have missed out on so much happiness. If we just go on the way we're going now, we'll die with regrets and the one left behind will have regrets too. We are going to die someday that's a fact and the one left will be sad. Would you rather be sad with wonderful memories or sad with regrets? Would you rather just sit this one out or dance? I hope you'll decide soon. Our time is running out.

Isabelle looked at him and said she would give him her final answer before the week was over.

# CHAPTER TWENTY-TWO: WILL AND ISABELLE

The trip back to Louisiana was long and sad. Will wasn't sure if he could keep all this traveling up. Maybe if he stayed home longer this time Isabelle would miss him and acquiesce to his persistent proposals. That would mean he would be away from her but perhaps that was what was needed. He'd continue his e-mails and hoped for a better reply than "Maybe"

A couple of days had passed. He played with his grandchildren and told Marilyn and Jack how beautiful Vermont had been and of all the fun they had. Jack said he looked years younger. Will didn't feel it. He felt old and alone. Marilyn asked how his pursuit of Isabelle was going and he told her Isabelle was still in the maybe stage. His family went to work and school and he was left by himself to ponder his plight. Why did she have doubts about getting married? Maybe she had heard too much about his past. Maybe she didn't want to start something in her senior years. What if she just didn't want to hurt his feelings?

The mail man walked up the walkway and put some envelopes in the mail box. Will went out and greeted him and made small talk about the weather and sports. The mail man continued his route and Will took the mail inside. He separated it on the kitchen counter as he always did. There was a credit card bill, a cable bill and an ad for seal coating the drive way addressed to Jack; and another credit card bill for Marilyn. Will's retirement check, and add for life insurance for senior citizens and a plain white envelope with no return address. His address had been computer printed on the envelope. The post mark read Boston. He knew it was from Isabelle. Paul and Tom used e-mail when writing to him. He wasn't sure they even knew his address. No one else had his address. She must be sending him a joke or cartoon. He slit it open and a single sheet of paper floated to the floor it smelled like her perfume. He picked it up and all it had on it in large letters was "LET'S DANCE".

His heart was racing; he called the air port and booked the next flight to Boston. It was for 4:00 PM that afternoon. He knew that was too soon and he had so much to do but he didn't care. He went to the bank made his deposit. He mailed the alimony checks. Came home packed his clothes. He left a note for Jack. Luckily he had Jack's name on his bank account. Jack could take care of sending him money or even take care of depositing his next retirement check. He would have to make a note to have his checks sent to a Massachusetts bank when he got settled. Jack would assist him. He couldn't think of that stuff now. He packed his bags, two large ones this time. He also brought a framed photo of Jack and his family. He could have other things sent to Boston later. He was confused. He was anxious. He was happy. He remembered to bring a snack for the flight just as Isabelle had told him. He then called Isabelle. The phone rang four times and the answer machine kicked in, then it stopped and Isabelle said, "Hello". Will said, "Thanks for the note, and yes I want to dance too." He told her he was booked on a direct flight to Logan Airport leaving at 4:00 PM. He would take a taxi cab to her home and then he could have Paul pick him up at her house. She said don't make any plans with Paul yet they're could be delays. Make sure you bring a snack.

He asked "Did you know you can get a marriage license in Maine and get married the same day?

"I didn't know that", she said.

"I want to drive to Maine tomorrow and get married, said Will.

"Aren't you getting ahead of yourself," Isabelle said.

"No Mam", he replied, "I've waited long enough."

She said "OK." They hung up.

His flight was on time, his luggage the first to arrive on the baggage claim train and there was a cab ready and waiting at the curb out side the terminal. He and the driver deposited the bags one in the trunk and one on the back seat with him. Will sat back and willed himself to calm down. The ride on the expressway was a breeze, at 8:30 at night.

The traffic was over.

He arrived at Isabelle's feeling pretty rested since he had napped on the plane. He paid the driver, got his bags and was greeted by Isabelle's opened arms. They stood at the doorway embracing for a long time. He took the bags inside and she said, "Go wash up I made us some sandwiches." They had sandwiches and cookies and milk

They talked about tomorrow's trip to Maine and said they would bring a few things and drive along the coast after their vows were exchanged and make it a little honeymoon trip. They had nothing definite in mind they would fly by the seats of their pants.

She said, "You must be tired".

He said, "I'm really not. I slept on the flight and I'm too excited to be tired. I should call Paul."

"No" she said, "don't call Paul. I want you to stay here tonight. Tonight's the night Will Benton. I want you in my bed."

Suddenly Will was nervous and excited all at once. This he did not expect. He would never turn it down. Did he still have the KY Jelly and the condoms handy? Will wanted her more than anything.

Will said, "Oh yes".

Isabelle was in the bathroom showering every part of her that could possibly smell like old woman. She had many thoughts. Should I have gotten some bikini waxing done, would have been too painful. Should I have bought a thong; it might get caught somewhere nasty. Should I perfume my whole body? But Will's in the bedroom. I can't just saunter in naked and start spraying my self in front of him. He may not like the smell. He may be allergic. What do I really know about him? I can't let him see me naked. I must make sure the lights are low, very low. I must come into the bedroom with at least a towel around me. What if he's not undressed when I get there? Do I tell him to get naked. What if he wants to take a shower? I'm going to need a lubricant. At what point does one apply this and how will he react? Do I say "Stop the music I need to put some jelly in there first"? I never had one night stands. How do these young girls do it?

At least Tim had fifty years to get used to the deterioration of my body. It didn't happen over night. One year the boobs dropped, the next year the fanny. After each baby the belly flesh was more like skin wrapped Jell-O. The upper arm overhangs are like fat bat wings.

My thighs rub together when I walk. Gravity is a powerful force. All the cup cakes and potato chips add to it as well. Thank God for nice clothes to cover up all this messy business. Now I must be naked in bed with a man who hasn't even seen me in a bathing suit since 1963 let alone nude. That's not true he saw me in Vermont. I was in my prime 1963. It was one thing to hold a slim, firm teenage girl in your arms in the moonlight fifty years ago but now he'll be holding a huge, sagging, soft, flesh covered, one hundred and fifty pound marshmallow. Poor Will, you don't know what you're getting into and I do mean into. He'll be in shock. What if he has a heart attack and dies either from fright or activity? How does one explain that? What if the sight of me, the feel of me, diminishes his hard on, that is if he can get one at his age. Will I inspire him to have an erection or will I have to manually assist.

Oh God. Just be patient, just let love take over. He is seventy-one. What does a seventy-one year old erection look like; probably like half a young one. The blood flow is not the same in older people. Will the fat marshmallow flesh get in the way of the half erection? Is my pubic hair grey? Will he care? Why didn't I think of this stuff before deciding to go to bed with him. Why am I so impetuous? I'm running out of time. This may be my last chance to seduce a man. Well seduce is not the right word. This may be my last chance to have sex. They say any sex is better than none. So here goes. Isabelle grabbed the towel and left the bathroom. Just be patient, let love take over.

Will was in the bedroom. He liked the king size bed turned down with the top sheet folded over invitingly. He's nervous. He's never been nervous with a woman in his life. The last time he was with Isabelle they were young and hard and fully dressed. He did try to keep fit but he always had clothes to cover the blemishes. Now he had those man boobs, and all his chest hairs were white. He had a tire around his middle that resembled a flesh colored bicycle tire inner tube. He had a lot of large age spots and sun damage marks on his skin. He resembled a leopard without fur. His jowls looked more like a turkey's wattle every day. Maybe he shouldn't bend over her so the jowls won't hang down in her face. We should do it on our sides; that eliminates the gravity problem. In bed there's no gravity to show all our sagging parts, right. The flesh just lays there like vanilla pudding on a platter. He had a lot of creaking joints. Will they make noise while he's performing? What if he burps or worse farts? The stomach ain't what it used to be. The noises could be awful. It's all that acid.

What if she tries to run her fingers though his hair only to find the bald head. She knows I'm bald but she may like men with hair on their heads. Will wants to take a shower but if he asks does that mean he thinks he's dirty, he's noisy and wants to see her bath room, or he's just prolonging the encounter. What will she think? Why was he so tense? If he kept this up, and he hoped he could keep something up, he'd be the two minute wonder. He must calm himself. He had been with many women, many, many women. Why was he upset? Will the womanizer, Will the lady killer, Will of the nudist colony what has happened to you? And he didn't know what she liked. She had been with the same man for fifty years. Tim knew her wants and desires. She was used to that. Will knew diddly squat. What if the one move he made was exactly what she hated? She had a lot of kids, she must know stuff but he didn't know what stuff. Who thought sex could be so complicated. What about foreplay. Do I kiss her a lot? Do I feel her up? I like boobs. Does she want me to start with them? Oh God what am I doing? She's the one I've wanted my whole life and now in my seventies I don't know where to begin. Just be gentle, women like gentle. When do I whip out the condom? Does she want to use a condom? We are too old for babies. Will she think, that I think she has some disease? She knows I've played around she may think I have something? I don't. Should I say this? Just be gentle, women like gentle. Remember you're not having sex; you're making love for the first time in your life. I never did it with the love of my life. Just be gentle.

Isabelle comes into the bedroom covered by a large bath towel. Will says he'd like a quick shower. She says of course and off he goes. Isabelle is grateful he's in the other room. Now she can spray perfume all over her and especially in all the nooks and crannies that will be involved in this adventure. She decides to insert the KY jelly before he returns so as not to embarrass anyone by its application later. What will he think of her? She's had six children. He may think her vagina is the Ted Williams Tunnel. His penis could get lost there. There's only one lane. Let's hope he's an eighteen wheeler and not a Volkswagen. Oh my God, the faucet just shut off. What do I do at foreplay? Do I touch him? Do I just lay back and enjoy it? What if he talks dirty or sticks his tongue in my ear? Is he kinky? He's coming. Hopefully he'll be coming again in a little while.

Will dries himself off and decides to return to the bedroom with a towel around him. He looks down at his privates and says, "Come on start your engine." Maybe I should have gotten a Viagra prescription. He gets a bright idea; and unwraps the condom in readiness and places it in his hand. I'll just leave it on the headboard and it will be ready when I need it. I won't have to fumble with the embarrassment of unwrapping it. Besides if I take my mind off what I'm doing to unwrap it, whatever hard on I have, may just collapse. I've waited for this moment my whole life. Come on guys he says to his balls don't let me down. I don't wan to be limp. I wonder where her special place is. Will she want my fingers in her? Should I mention the KY jelly at that point? Should I try that before the boobs? Maybe she moans when she has an orgasm. Just be gentle.

The Lord hates a coward so Will enters the bedroom. Isabelle is already in bed with the top sheet pulled up to her ears. He slides in beside her as gracefully as any seventy-one year old man can and removes the towel. He reaches over to touch her. She is naked. This is good. It's dark but not totally. This is good. He looks into her eyes, gently caresses her cheek with the back of his hand and moves a piece of hair back from her face. He places tiny kisses on her eyes, her lips, and her neck. Then he moves his hand to her breast. He likes what he's feeling. He gently squeezes them. Her breasts are real and spectacular and bigger than he thought. His hands have never been full before. He kisses each breast gently. He feels her nipples responding. She slides closer towards him. Their bodies touch. There's nothing like nakedness. He likes the softness of her nude body. She likes the furry chest hair against her breasts. They kiss; a lot. His hands move down her side, along her hip over to center stage. His fingers explore and find her secret place. She does moan. She even quivers. He's ready, well as ready as any man his age can be. He slides inside, kissing her all the while. Not an easy trick. His motions at first are gentle and slow. Then a little faster, then fast, then fire works explode.

They lie in each other's arms. She was smiling, actually down right grinning. He said, "Finally, I made love to the girl of my dreams. Shit, I forgot all about the condom."

Isabelle's heart was full of love she was in her bed with Will Benton. She had just made love with him. They did it. They were seventy and seventy-one years old and they did it. Oh, Will, my charming, funny, handsome, wonderful, Will.

# CHAPTER TWENTY-THREE: WILL AND ISABELLE MARRY

The next morning Will woke up and saw her sleeping naked beside him. He was filled with joy. He looked up at the sky lights above the bed and saw heavy rain. It didn't matter. He thought of their love making last night and was delighted. She opened her eyes and said, "Hey Big Guy". He kissed the top of each breast and then her mouth and said, "Good Morning, Sweetheart." They smiled at each other. Then he said, "Nature's calling". Will got up and went into the bathroom. Isabelle took the opportunity to get up and find a robe, she didn't want Will to see her naked in broad daylight. She heard the toilet flush and then the shower door open. She made the bed, and took her pills and brushed her hair. She got a medium size suit case from the closet in the wrapping room to pack for Maine. She was getting some underwear out of her bureau drawer and putting it into the bag when Will returned to the bedroom. He had a towel wrapped around him. He didn't want Isabelle to see him totally naked just yet. How vain they both were.

Will said, "Have you seen the weather"?

"Yes", she said "happy the bride the rain falls on today".

They laughed. She pointed to two tall chests of drawers. These are empty she told him. They had been Tim's. There was no need for her to mention that. She told him he could fill them with his stuff if he liked and put the empty luggage in the wrapping room closet. He teased her by saying he was finally going to see the holy of holies, the wrapping room. She laughed and said that they should pack for Maine. She had a frilly nightgown in her hand and he told her that she wouldn't need it. It was pretty she told him and he may need encouragement. He told her to pack it.

"I think we should take as little as possible and all comfortable, casual clothes." said Isabelle. "What do you think?"

"That sounds good. Do you think we should bring bathing suits? The hotels may have pools or we may see a nice beach. It might be better to have them", said Will.

She agreed.

He opened one large bag and took out a pile of clothes still on hangers. A navy pin stripe suit, a navy blazer, four dress shirts various colors, three pair of dress pants, two pair of chinos, one pair of jeans, six polo shirts, short sleeved, of bright bold colors, four polo shirts, long sleeved of darker winter colors. He hung all of these immediately in the closet. That was easy, thought Isabelle. Men do have good ideas once in a while. She must tell Judy. He put a couple of pairs of shoes in there and the two folded sweaters on the closet shelf. Will closed the empty suitcase and asked where the wrapping room was. Just next door. Will carried the bag into the next room and was amazed at what he saw.

The closet was to the left of the entrance. He slid the mirrored door open and put his suitcase inside. He looked just to the right and saw shelves lined with rectangle storage baskets all labeled and holding things like tissue paper, white, colored or printed. Another basket had gift bags flattened and folded. Others had had ribbons and bows. There was a variety of craft items too in a large basket. One basket held a glue gun with glue sticks, bags with feathers, bags of magic markers, test tubes filled with glitter and other similar items. On the wall across from the entrance stood two wing back chairs with a small table between them which held a lamp and a small CD player. There was a stack of Christmas CD's nearby. Isabelle saw him looking in that direction and told him she liked to listen to Christmas music while she wrapped. On the right hand wall was an enormous box in the corner that held tan boxes that were from Amazon.com or American Girl and other places. Isabelle saw that he noticed this and said, "That's where I keep Christmas gifts. I shop all year long usually on the internet. Since the family is so big, it saves time. There was a table along the right hand wall as well and on it was a huge box cover, upside down and spray painted white holding two train tracks, trains a couple of small buildings and little statues of people. Will pointed to it with a questioned look in his face.

"Oh, that's part of my Christmas village. It needed work and I wanted to redesign the tracks. You'll see in December", answered Isabelle.

Beside that was a scary black and orange centerpiece half way finished.

"That's for the Halloween Party. It's not finished yet".

He had no idea of the magnitude with which Isabelle decorated for holidays.

Will stared at her and said, "What am I getting into"?

"Fun" she said.

On the last wall was another long table with a container holding scissors, tape dispensers, and pens. The rest of the table was empty with room for wrapping. In front of the table was a straight backed chair. At the right hand of the table stood a kitchen type trash bucket filled with rolls of wrapping paper of all kinds each standing on end.

Isabelle and Will went back into the bedroom and he began unpacking his second bag.

He took out his shaving kit and said, "I'll need this for later, I haven't shaved yet, then I'll pack it for Maine."

He put it on the bed. She finished putting tee shirts and Capri pants and a pair of slacks into the suitcase. He put most of his other things into the chest of draws, underwear, socks, tee shirts, and shorts. He put a few pair of shorts and tee shirts in the suit case along with his swim trunks and said he'd wear the outfit he had on yesterday to get married in. He had a framed photo of Jack and his family. He placed it on the chest of drawers. He had emptied the second bag.

Isabelle said, "I'm going to take a shower. Feel free to go downstairs and make coffee when you're ready. There's cereal in the cabinet over the stove and bread for toast. Help yourself. I'll be down in a few minutes".

Will knew a few minutes to Isabelle meant about twenty.

He said, "I'll just put my pants on now and come up and shave later. I can bring the packed suitcase down then."

He took his pills and headed down stairs.

Isabelle showered; she heard him shout, "Do you want me to make you a cup of coffee?

"You'd better, or you'll have one grouchy girl on your hands", she said.

He laughed and went downstairs. Isabelle used the blow dryer and curing iron and put on a long full skirt with an elastic waist and a nice jersey top. She put on earrings and perfume and figured she'd pack the blow dryer and curling iron when they cooled off. She looked at the photo of Jack and his family and took it down stairs with her. He had coffee and toast ready. He told her he was slow getting it ready because he was watching the birds outside and there was a crow on a tree branch and some sparrows at one of the feeders.

Isabelle looked in the direction of the yard, and said, "Oh there's the red cardinal." She took a sip of coffee and a bite of toast."

She said, "Will, I'd like to put this photo in the living room over where I have some family photos. We are one big family now. Is that alright?"

He was happy and said, "Yes".

They finished eating and packing. Will brought the bag down and put it in the trunk of the car. He told Isabelle she might need identification so she went and got her birth certificate and pass port. He had his ID's in the suitcase already. Isabelle called her daughter, Tricia.

She said, "Will is back and we are going to Maine for a few days. We should be back by Friday. I'll call you when we get back. Don't worry about me. I'm happy."

She didn't wait for a reply, which was good since Tricia was speechless.

The rain was still coming down but she always kept an umbrella in the back seat. Will was by her side. Life was good. They drove through the city without a hitch except for the rain. They stopped for a rest room and coffee in Kittery.

They drove to Portland, found a nice jewelry store and bought two plain medium width gold bands. Will told her to get whatever she wanted and she said, "This is what I want". They found the City Hall; parked in the lot at the rear of the building and found the marriage license office. They filled out the necessary forms, displayed their ID's and paid the fee. Will asked when there would be someone available to perform the ceremony. They were told to go upstairs to the Clerk's office and wait for the Justice of the Peace who usually arrived around 1:00 PM. There were other couples waiting as well. They waited chatting about where they'd go to lunch afterward. The Justice of the Peace, who officiated, turned out to be a woman. She was pleasant and conducted the ceremony with dignity. The Clerk and lady typist in the office were witnesses. About 3:00 PM Will and Isabelle exchanged vows and rings. "You may kiss the bride" was said with glee and the license signed with ink. Will and Isabelle came down the steps, Isabelle looking at the ring on her finger and Will was looking at where he was going and holding on to her. It would be just their luck to fall down the steps of the City Hall.

It was now a little after four. They had a sumptuous lobster meal at Milos which was a restaurant in Portland out on a pier. They had been hungry but took their time and basked in love and joy. They left Portland two hours later, it was still raining. They headed north to Booth Bay Harbor. It was only 8:30 PM when they arrived. They each got an ice cream cone; that was supper. They got a room at the Tug Boat Inn. They went to bed. This time to sleep they had done enough today. They were glad they had their "wedding night" the night before.

In the morning they took a walk. The rain had stopped but it was a grey and misty day. Boothbay was a great place to walk around, lots of things to see. They poked into Gimbles, and other shops and Isabelle bought an ornament to put on her Christmas tree to remind them of their wedding. They saw the rail road village, the Carousel Theater, and many other sites. It was a pretty sea shore town. Around noon they headed for Bar Harbor. They stopped half way at a little diner and had sandwiches and used the bathroom. Then they went on to their destination and checked into a hotel overlooking the ocean. They walked around a bit and bought sweat shirts that said "Bar Harbor". They would need these, since they planned to take a harbor cruise in the morning. That night they feasted on a clam bake with lobster, potatoes, steamed clams and corn on the cob.

They were in bed and Will teased her by saying I wonder what your Sister Superior would have said about you having pre-marital sex the night before our marriage. Isabelle smiled and told him that Sister would have said to the other nuns, "Poor sinful Isabelle. We must pray for her. She has succumbed to the temptations of lust which led to sins of impure thoughts, acts and fornication. Let's hope Isabelle will go to confession, perform much penance and repent. She must stay out of harms way and the occasion of sin, namely Will Benton." They both laughed.

They slept naked in each other's arms. Will had never been so happy. He finally had his Isabelle. The next day was bright and beautiful. Once again they woke up happy to see each other's face. She said "Hey Big Guy" and he kissed each breast and her lips. She reached over and put her hand on his cheek. Breakfast was complimentary and continental. It was good. They went out on the cruise in a Nova Scotia style boat. The group was small and the narrator knew his stuff. They learned about the history of the community, the endangered species, the rules of lobster fishing and much more. There was a strong wind at sea. It was chilly and they were glad to have the sweatshirts. When they got back to the dock they took the car to Cadillac Mountain and saw a spectacular view. They drove around Acadia National park for a while and headed back to the hotel. They dined on fish and chips and went to their room early. They made love that night. They had been too tired the other two nights but tonight was wonderful. It was slow, and sweet and gentle and very passionate all the same.

Isabelle and Will rose early and checked out. They were on the road by 7:30 AM and decided to head south and stop somewhere for breakfast. They drove as far as Bath and found a cute little place and ate bacon and eggs. The got back in the car and drove another two hours. She had remembered to bring an audio tape and they were listening to a humorous legal mystery, one of a series, whose main characters are Andy Carpenter and his dog. It made the ride enjoyable and the time went by fast. When they reached Ogunquit, they found a room at the Anchorage Inn. Will asked at the front desk about sites to see and things to do. The woman advised them on a few ideas and mentioned the Playhouse where "My Fair Lady" was playing. She said she could call and try to get tickets if they liked. They nodded and she made the call.

The woman said, "The seats are on the right of the stage and half way back, would that be alright?" It was last minute so what did they expect. They said, "Yes" and they were told to pick them up at the box office. They had lunch at Barnacle Billy's, lobster rolls and ice tea, and walked around Perkins Cove. Around 2:00 PM they went back to the hotel, took a swim in the pool and decided to walk some of the Marginal Way, which was in front of the hotel. This is a path that runs along the rocky beach and has wonderful views. It's about two miles long but has benches along the way for resting. They tired easily; they did not get very far. They came back and collapsed in chairs facing the beautiful rocky Maine shore. A flock of bright, white, sea gulls flew in front of a mass of dark green trees on the left making a wonderful contrast in color. Their noises were loud and constant but some how soothing. They watched these sea gulls gliding back and forth and the movement made them fall asleep outside in the chairs. When they woke from their outdoor nap, they went to a little place up the street for a salad supper and then onto the Theater. They enjoyed it immensely and said it was Broadway quality.

"What a great show", Will said when they were heading back to the hotel.

"I loved it said Isabelle." She was still humming "I'm Getting Married in the Morning"

"We should mention this to the cousins and friends. We could make plans and come up here for a long weekend. It's not a long ride and we could get tickets to a show in advance", said Will.

Isabelle said, "What a great idea. I'll make some calls when we get back".

They were asleep for the night about five minutes after returning to the Anchorage Inn. They next day was sunny and hot. They had free coffee and cereal in the community breakfast area. Isabelle said she had eaten so much the past three days and would have to diet when she got back home. Will agreed that he would too. The two of them packed up and once again hit the road with their audio book making the journey interesting.

They arrived home, safe and sound, before noon. They had been gone five days and the mail was jammed into the mail box. Isabelle retrieved it, opened the door and put the mail on the hall table. Will brought the suitcase in. She opened it and took the plastic bag with dirty clothes out of the suitcase and went into the cellar/laundry room to start a wash. The cellar was the exact opposite of the wrapping room. It was a disaster. Tools, filing cabinets, shelves with cans of paint, duct tape and other hardware store items were everywhere. An old fan, an enormous Christmas wreath, a beat up picnic cooler and much more were all living together helter skelter. There was a clear path on the floor to the washer and dryer and on top of the dryer stood bottles of bleach, Tide and Downy in a neat row. Isabelle was sorting the clothes, putting the whites in first. She noticed the look on Will's face. Isabelle knew Will was a bit of a neat freak. She said, "Tim was an excellent attorney, all his files were organized and he knew where each brief and document was; but household things, that was different. He was a bit of a hoarder and even retrieved things from the trash that I would throw out. He liked "his stuff". He just never had places for "his stuff." He used some of the filing cabinets for former client's files and office supplies. The office was tidy, the rest of the house was tidy, the cellar not so much. I did mention it to him, many times through the years and he would tell me that he knew where everything was. I gave up. I left this mess to him. In marriage you have to pick your battles."

"When Tim died the cellar was the last thing on my mind, said Isabelle. "I've asked the kids to take anything they want. They don't want anything. I tried sorting things out but it's overwhelming. And now I'm so used to it, I just leave it. I only come in here to do the laundry. I want to enjoy life now. The kids don't want to help, and why should they? It's their father's mess. I don't blame the kids. They can deal with it when I die. I'm too old for dealing with this by myself. I don't even keep the house as neat as I used to. I've learned people are more important. I refuse to be a slave to housework for the rest of my life. I want to have fun while I can".

Will said, "Your wrapping room is so organized and the kitchen cabinets too. The rest of the house looks great. This must drive you crazy."

"I can see it's already driving you crazy", said Isabelle. "We will make this one of our first projects together. I can do this if I have someone to help me. We can do one part at a time. We will organize the cellar and purge it of its junk and memories".

"We will need a dumpster", Will said sarcastically, "but I'm up for the challenge."

"Oh come on", said Isabelle and they headed to the kitchen. She called Jeanne first.

She said, "Jeanne, I want you to call your siblings and tell them Will and I got married four days ago in Maine. We had a nice honeymoon staying at spots along the shore. We are very happy and hope you are too." She waited for a reply.

Jeanne said, "Tricia told me you and Will were going to Maine for a few days. I knew something was up. Well I will call my brothers and Tricia. Practice safe sex. You two are something else. Tell Will I love his persistence." They both hung up.

She handed the phone to Will and said, "You should call Jack, Paul and Tom."

Isabelle opened a can of soup and put it in a sauce pan to heat.

Will said "Jack was surprised and happy".

Paul was shocked and said to give you his best.

Tom said "It's about time you did something right in your life".

They laughed.

Isabelle served Will a cup of soup and handed him a sleeve of Ritz crackers to go with it. They would have to go grocery shopping later and gets lots of salad stuff.

Isabelle picked up the receiver and called Kathy, Judy and Carol. They were all delighted and ooing and ahhing. Kathy wished them well. Carol said "God bless you both". Judy wanted all the details. Isabelle said she would talk to them in length when she saw them again.

Will asked her, "You aren't going to talk about our love making to them are you."

"What a silly man you are", said Isabelle, "of course not. That is our private business."

"That's good", said Will. He sipped some soup.

"They just want to hear about the Maine trip and the wedding ceremony", said Isabelle as she crushed crackers into her soup.

"Not Judy, she'll want to hear all", said Will.

"Well she won't", said Isabelle, "I promise."

# CHAPTER TWENTY-FOUR: PAUL AND CAROL IN LOVE

A few weeks later, Carol and Judy made another visit to Kathy's. Kathy invited Isabelle for lunch. They got together and Will spent the time with Tom and Paul. Everyone got caught up on each other's news. Carol's friends, the Cappellos had gone to Montreal for a week; one of Carol's cancer patients had passed away, God bless her soul, and an old friend from the telephone company spent a week with her. One of Judy's sons and his wife had a new baby girl, Gretchen, Cat had to go to the vet twice; he was getting old like her, and her refrigerator died and she had to break down and buy a new one; she got one that made its own ice. Kathy's daughter was pregnant again, Kathy's doctor was still screaming at her to quit smoking, she went to see "The Music Man" revival with some girls she had worked with at the bank and she had a new driveway installed. Of course they listened to Isabelle tell about the Maine wedding and honeymoon and though Judy did press her for sexual details. Isabelle said that was none of her business.

"That means either Will sucks in bed or he's so kinky she can't talk about it", said Judy.

Kathy asked her, "How did the kids take it?"

"Pretty well, they seem to like him."

"Are you happy you married him?" asked Carol

"I am. We do everything together. He goes to church with me every Sunday. I never asked him to, but he does. He helped me clean out the cellar which was no easy task. We had a huge yard sale. We bought corn stalks and chrysanthemums and he helped me put the fall decorations and lights outside already." Isabelle replied.

"Isabelle has tamed Will Benton. That's quite a feather in your cap, Isabelle", said Judy.

Carol was impressed he went to church. She couldn't wait to tell Paul.

Kathy asked, "What does he think of the wrapping room and all of your decorating?"

"He likes it", said Susan. "He found the wrapping room to be neat and organized. I don't think he anticipated the extent of my decorating but when he saw all the Rubbermaid tubs with their holiday labels lined up in the craw space he had no choice but to accept it. He's a tidy orderly person; bordering anal."

They all laughed and Kathy put on another pot of coffee.

Will and the boys caught up with their news. They were sitting on Paul's back steps that faced the lake, having a beer. Tom, took a swig from the bottle and told them Susan had picked out some green paint for him to re-do the dining room walls, and wasn't he lucky to have a project like that he said sarcastically. Tom said he had caught a large big mouth bass in the lake, and his youngest daughter brought the grandkids over to swim almost every day during August.

Paul said he was now going to the later Mass on Sundays at church so he could meet Esther and Bob and that Bob really should get a hearing aid. He bumped into Kathy at the supermarket in the frozen food aisle one day and his son and daughter-in-law came for a weekend with the kids last week. He also told them that he had e-mailed Carol everyday since the Vermont trip and that he was taking her to dinner tonight.

"Well that is news" said Will, "maybe you and Carol should get hitched like me and Isabelle."

"Yeah," said Tom "then all three of us could be miserable". He lit a cigarette.

"That's not true and you know it", said Will. "You and Susan have been married for fifty some odd years and you are both very happy."

"Fifty-two", said Tom, "and yes, you're right I still love the old girl but I'm not crazy about a green dining room or getting up and down on the ladder with a roller and brush. She wants a green dining room and she will get one, my poor knees."

"Carol has been returning my e-mails too", said Paul. "I know more about her now than I ever did. She is such a caring person. What a great time I had in Vermont. I think of it a lot."

"So where are you taking her?" asked Will.

"The Monponsett Inn then maybe back here for a glass of wine and some show tunes."

"You sly dog, did you buy condoms and KY Jelly?" asked Tom.

Will laughed out loud.

Paul said, "I find that distasteful, Tom. My intentions are strictly honorable. I am a gentleman."

Tom said, "Come on Paul I was just having a little fun."

Paul said, "I have never said a disparaging word about Susan and you can keep a civil tongue in your head when referring to me and Carol."

"I guess he told you, Tom. For once I'm not the bad guy. See the influence Isabelle has had on me," said Will.

"Sorry, Paul", said Tom. "I hope you and Carol have a nice time tonight, she is a good person."

Paul said, "I hope she feels the same way about me as I do about her."

Will got up to leave and said, "Well, I have to pick up my beautiful wife at Kathy's. Nice talking to you guys."

Will pulled away and Tom said, "Look at him driving her Lincoln Town Car. He always comes out on top."

Paul said, "He is the happiest I have ever seen him."

That night Carol wanted to dress with care she asked Isabelle for some pointers during lunch. Isabelle thought none of the outfits Carol brought were glamorous but Paul liked Carol the way she was. Isabelle said this to her, "Carol, Paul likes you the way you are, just be yourself."

Isabelle continued, "You have pretty brown eyes and green goes well with that. Why don't you wear the dark green jumper with a jersey under it?"

Carol said she had a long sleeve yellow jersey but never would have put them together".

"Maybe Kathy has a scarf we could attach at the skirt pocket for color", said Isabelle.

Kathy said she had just the thing, a pale yellow, with black and green spots on it. She went and got it. Isabelle tied it into a fancy knot and let the rest hang down and pinned it to the pocket. She placed the jersey on a hanger under the jumper. The outfit looked better than any of them thought it would.

Kathy said she had a pale yellow hair ribbon that her grand-daughter had left behind and Carol could tie it in a bow at the base of her braid.

"What about shoes" asked Isabelle?

"I have clogs they're brown", answered Carol.

"Oh well, comfort is good", said Isabelle, trying to be positive.

Judy came in and saw the outfit they were getting ready for Carol and said "That really looks nice. I have just the thing".

Kathy and Isabelle exchanged grimaces but Judy came in with a pair of jade looking earrings and a green beaded elastic bracelet. They did go well.

"Perfect" said Carol.

"I have a shawl that is black you could carry it or wear it around your shoulders. Black goes with everything."

Isabelle thought the shawl and the braid might be too Native American but said nothing.

"I did buy new perfume, Channel #5", said Carol. "It was expensive but I know a lot of girls from work used it; they called it classic".

"Today is a lucky day. I bought a lottery ticket and won five bucks" said Kathy. "I am giving all that luck to Carol, so she can have a nice night with Paul."

"Thank you", said Carol.

"What about the five bucks," said Judy "who are you giving that to?"

"The American Tobacco growers", Kathy answered.

Will pulled up and went inside. He gave Isabelle a long kiss on the lips and dipped her in his arms for effect. The cousins sighed. Well not Judy. He hugged the rest of them even Judy. Isabelle told him she was ready to go. Carol congratulated him on his marriage and said she hoped it was his last and that she was very happy he was going to church.

Kathy said, "We all knew you two would end up together some day. Good luck." Judy said, "Are you behaving Will Benton?

Will said "Yes" and then he added, "Don't you all know how much I love this woman pointing to Isabelle?"

Judy said, "You fucking well better".

Will and Isabelle left.

Paul had on a grey suit, a pale yellow shirt and a green print tie. He didn't know it, but once again, he and Carol were on the same color wave length. He had showered, shaved and added men's cologne. Paul called the local florist and asked what would be an appropriate flower to bring on a special date for an older couple. The florist told him a small nosegay would be nice. He selected baby yellow roses. He had his car cleaned and shined at the car wash. He shined his own shoes and was very nervous. He picked up the flowers and drove to Kathy's. He felt like a boy going to his first prom. He hoped she was ready and he didn't have to spend any time with Judy. That could ruin the night. When he arrived Kathy's car was gone; a good sign. Carol opened the door and looked fabulous in her green and yellow ensemble. Paul handed her the flowers and she blushed. She locked the door and they went out. Paul said she looked lovely. She said he did too. He asked where the other girls were. She said they went to play BINGO at a VFW Post.

She said "I told them not to wait up for me".

He said he had brought some wine and he had a new show tune CD he wanted her to hear and perhaps she'd come back to his house to hear it after dinner.

She said she'd be delighted.

The restaurant was dimly lit; a man was at the piano playing soft music. They ordered their meals and enjoyed the scenery. They were seated by a window overlooking the pond. There were many small trees here and there on the lawn; each had been lit with tiny white lights. It was enchanting. Paul and Carol ate salad to "Moon River" and their main course was enjoyed by the sight of the green eyes of a raccoon looking in the window at them from the lawn outside. Paul held her hand while they waited for coffee and dessert. Carol told him how handsome he looked and wasn't it so funny that they both had yellow and green on.

"We must think alike" she said.

"We're kindred spirits", he replied.

They had not spilled anything, or broken anything and no one had stepped in anything. Paul took this as a good sign. They drove back to his house and he escorted her to the living room. She had never seen Paul's home. It was lovely. It reminded her of a log cabin even though it wasn't. I was rustic; maybe because it was right on the lake. It had an overstuffed sofa and chairs, end tables with lamps and a built in stereo system. She saw the view of the lake and thought it was breathtaking even at night. He asked her if she wanted to freshen up and she did. His bathroom was much more modern than hers and very clean. She was dying to see the kitchen but waited to be asked. He asked her if she'd like some wine and she said she would. She followed him to the kitchen where there was a big table in the center, and cabinets and appliances all around. It was a comfortable kitchen. The kind she liked. Carol took the glass from him and he led her back to the living room.

In the hallway she stopped to look at some framed photographs. She had met his first wife, Marie, many times. She was a nice person. There was a picture of Marie and photos of his mother and others of his children and grandchildren. The photos were hung in a neat row on the wall. He identified anyone in the pictures she didn't know and they went into the living room to sip their wine.

He turned on the show tunes and they started singing together. Afterward he put on soft music and asked her to dance. They had each had a couple of glasses of wine and Carol was on her third. They danced to "Strangers in the Night" and she tripped and fell on the floor knocking him on top of her. She said that she was alright and started having a laughing fit. He did too. They lay there, Paul on top of Carol, laughing until the music stopped and so did they. Paul stayed where he was, looked into her eyes and kissed her passionately. Carol responded and they were embracing right there on the living room rug where the eyes of Marie, his mother and the children and grandchildren could see from the hanging photographs. After several moments, Paul came to his senses and got up. He helped Carol up and she sat on the sofa. He turned on another CD. They resumed their kissing. No one knows what else happened that night but it was the turning point in their relationship. They both received Holy Communion at Mass the next morning, so no big sins had been committed.

The Vermont cousins stayed until Friday. They had to get back. Kathy and Judy hung around together, shopping, playing scrabble, watching Red Sox games on TV. They went shopping at a Good Will store and Ocean State Job Lot one day. They met Esther and Bob for lunch. They did a jig saw puzzle and drank martinis. Mostly they just talked and had a good time together. Paul and Carol were out and about every day. They went to a movie matinee and out for tacos on Sunday. They had a picnic in the park and danced to show tunes at his house all night on Monday. Paul took her to see a show at the Music Circus Tuesday night. They had lunch with Will and Isabelle on Wednesday. Carol finally got to see Tom and Susan's home when they were invited for dinner on Thursday night. She especially loved the pale green color of the dining room walls.

Paul told Carol he would come over to say good bye on Friday morning. Will and Isabelle joined them bringing a box of Joe from Dunkin Donuts and a dozen muffins. When Paul entered he gave Carol a wrapped gift. It looked like a ring box. It was.

There was a diamond ring inside and Paul said, right in front of everyone, "Will you marry me?"

Carol said, "Yes, Yes, Yes."

# CHAPTER TWENTY-FIVE: ISABELLE AND WILL SETTLING IN

The first several months of their marriage were enchantment. Will and Isabelle were madly in love like two star struck teenagers. They loved being in each other's arms. They loved having each other's faces being the first sight they saw each morning. The hugs and kisses were many. The couple got ready for the fall; they put more bird feeders out, added another bird house to the back yard and finished the cellar clean up. The yard sale was a big success. Fall decorations went up. They planted lots of tulip bulbs for a spring showing and weeded and pruned in the garden. Toast with peanut butter was eaten daily; Will was getting used to this. Kids and grandkids came and went unexpectedly. He sometimes felt like he lived in Grand Central Station. Will didn't mind this he knew when everyone went home he would be alone with Isabelle and in her bed. His dearest girl would be in his arms for the night.

Some days he and Isabelle would just sit out back alone and bird watch and doze and even nap in the sun. Will went to Mass every Sunday and out to breakfast with her church friends. They did the grocery shopping together. Went to the library and sometimes even went swimming at the town indoor pool. It was a happy time for them both. They took walks and played cards with some friends. They enjoyed a movie now and then either on television or at the cinema. Football season meant lots of games, grandkids were playing or the NFL was. They went to some of the grandkids soccer games as well. They picked apples and bought pumpkins. Isabelle and Will were having fun. Isabelle marveled at how Will adjusted to this ready made family and embraced his role of being her husband.

Isabelle had a long narrow living room /dining room with vaulted ceilings that are about twenty feet high. Two palladium windows flanked the front and side of the room. One October morning

Will woke up and saw Isabelle was not in bed. He was worried; he got up and called to her. She answered, "I'm in the living room". He went to the balcony, adjacent to their bedroom and looked down to see her standing on top of a large buffet attempting to hang a ring of fish lines over a hook that was about six feet over her head and about fifteen feet off the ground. She used her broom, her mop or any long stick she could find to do this. Will stared at her in amazement.

"What on earth are you doing", he asked?

"Oh, I'm hanging bats! I have to move when the artistic mood hits me".

"Don't fall, I'm coming right down", he said.

"For heavens sake, Will, I do stuff like this all the time. If you must come down put some clothes on" said Isabelle.

She had a huge pile of black bats, cut out of construction paper in all shapes and sizes nearby. She had scotch tape and a spool of thread at hand. Once the lines were set on the hook she attached bats to threads and taped them to each line with no rhyme or reason, big bats, long threads, small bats medium length threads, medium bats, short threads, whatever. When one line was filled with hanging bats she got down and brought the line across the room, up the stairs to where Will still stood naked, and tied the end of the line to the banister of the balcony. After this was repeated ten times, and Will did help her, the effect was marvelous. It was as if hundreds of bats were suspended in air. She then turned on the overhead fan and they swayed in the breeze. Her husband saw her looking at this. She was like a little girl looking at something magical for the first time. He told her it was wonderful.

"How did you ever think of doing this?" asked Will.

"I wake up at night with ideas", she said, "and I go with it".

He kissed her head but said nothing.

She said, "Let's go have breakfast". They did.

Other Halloween decorations went up, invitations were mailed, creepy food was prepared, and arrangements for a magician were made. Will dressed like Daddy Warbucks and Isabelle was Orphan Annie. The mysterious black and orange arrangement with feathers and sprayed twigs, that had been in the wrapping room had been finished and now was the table's centerpiece. Costumes were donned, donuts were eaten from strings with hands behind backs, family and friends joined them and the Halloween party came and went. Seventeen Tubs of Halloween decorations went back to the crawl space and up came three Thanksgiving tubs. Thank God for the help of strong and eager grandsons.

In November Isabelle and Will prepared for turkey day. They brought another table into the dining room and put folding chairs around it. Matching cloths covered each table; the good china came out, wine glasses, serving dishes, and silverware that hardly ever get used. Many trips were made to the grocery store and liquor store. They baked pies together, sampling them as they went. There were pumpkins outside and in, and figurines of pilgrims and Indians placed here and there. A cornucopia filled with orange leaves adorned the fireplace in the living room. Gourds and leaves and pumpkins were on the fire place in the TV room with orange and gold candles standing guard at each end. Garlands of bright colored leaves looped along the stair banister bedecked with ribbon and a large paper turkey was taped to the mirror in the dining room. The stuffing was made, the potatoes were mashed, the turkey roasted and the gravy had no lumps. Folks arrived, Bob and Esther too. Each bowed their head, grace was said, and everyone was fed. Football games were watched. The cleanup began and guests started going home. The next day was busy. Put the Thanksgiving tubs away. Bring up twenty-three Christmas tubs and pig out on leftovers. "That was the best part", thought Will.

This was all new to Will. He liked the continuity of these family traditions. He knew it kept the family strong. He admired Isabelle for initiating these celebrations and continuing them. He knew the amount of work it entailed did tire his old girl but she loved it and lived for it. He would help her all he could and he wasn't shy about asking some of the older grandkids to help.

Will in his younger years, when his parents were alive, did sometimes visit them for Thanksgiving and Christmas. During his marriages there was a visit one year to an in-laws' home, a Christmas at home with Jack as a baby, a visit to his parents another Thanksgiving, some holidays he was allowed to have Jack; some his ex wife had Jack, his second wife did not always want Jack for the holidays. Some holidays were spent with Jill's folks, some with Alice's. Then Jill moved out of state and he hardly saw Jack. His second wife also had children from another marriage and they would have to stay around for her ex to pick up and drop off the twins when it was his holiday to have them. There were years when he was not married and he'd either go to his parents or later when they died he'd go to a bar. His third wife didn't care about holidays, certainly not Christmas, since she was into other beliefs. She did spend one Thanksgiving with Will at Jack's house. She was no help and did not eat turkey.

Will asked Isabelle if Tim was as enthusiastic about all the holidays.

"No", she said. "When we were first married, he told me I had tinsel for a brain. Tim found Christmas to be too commercial. He was probably right since it is a religious holiday. He was not impressed with the wrapping room. It was wasteful. That stuff would be in the trash tomorrow was his idea. He told me if I died first, he would never shop and buy presents. He would give the kids and grandkids each twenty dollars and a hearty handshake for Christmas. But he'd be the one with the camera at the Christmas party taking shots of the babies on Santa's lap making sure the big brightly lit tree was in the background. After everything was wrapped and looked beautiful under the tree he'd say something like. Did you get everyone enough? This would be about five minutes before the gift exchanging would begin".

"It took many, many years of urging to get him to put on a Halloween costume", said Isabelle. "Tim was a serious man. He didn't like silly. But Thanksgiving he loved. No gifts, no commercialism; just food and family. He got used to the decorating and the holiday festivities. He knew how I felt about the cellar so he had to compromise. So he got used to my silliness. He had to; he loved me."

"Well I love you too" said Will, "and I think all this decorating and celebrating is the glue that keeps a family together."

He told Isabelle what his holidays had been like for the past fifty years. Will said he had never been so happy and he was glad to help her with all of this.

She kissed him and said, "Thank you, Will for loving the holidays and for loving me."

The big Christmas wreath went up on the same hook that had held the lines of bats. A huge red bow was attached to the wreath. Tables were set up for the village. It took a few days for the village to be completed but then all the little houses lit up. The part that was being repaired in the wrapping room was done and the two trains went in a circle, in opposite directions and into tunnels and back out again. Some animated features in the village needed batteries and they were replaced. Will was fascinated with the village and not unduly impressed with Isabelle's engineering skills.  The huge live tree was delivered and set up. Jeanne's boys helped Will put the lights on it and the star, and ornaments on the high part. Isabelle did the rest. Shopping and wrapping was completed. The party went on as usual. Santa came to the house. Kids sat on his lap and Will took pictures. Will and Isabelle mailed gifts to Louisiana, an American Girl doll for his granddaughter, and two very big Leggo sets for the boys. There was a small gift and a large check for Jack and Marilyn as well.  The Saturday before Christmas all the girls in the family held a cookie swap in Isabelle's kitchen and dining room. Hundreds of cookies were made; at least twenty different kind. The girls brought over their goods and divided them onto trays, wrapped them with plastic and left carrying their treasures with them. On Christmas Eve everyone sat around the big tree and opened and gave gifts. On Christmas Day Will and Isabelle made the rounds to all of Isabelle's children's homes to see what Santa had brought.

On New Year's Eve Isabelle and Will got take out Chinese food, sipped champagne, and watched the ball drop at Times Square right in front of their television. They went directly to bed.  The tree was undecorated, dismantled and sawed into pieces. As usual, it took four guys to get it out at the street for the trash collectors. The next week was busy clearing up and putting away all the Christmas paraphernalia. Will and Isabelle went to bed every night for the past week very tired. They were old. Will was starting to think maybe Tim had the right idea and where on earth, he wondered did Isabelle get her energy. I hope next year is as good as this one. I finally have the girl of my dreams.

# CHAPTER TWENTY-SIX: WEDDING PLANS

Carol and Paul were floating on cloud nine. They were trying to set a date for their wedding. They choose the end of April. They talked more on the phone now but made most of their plans by e-mail. Paul was pleased that Carol had decided to get married at his church instead of hers in Vermont. She told him that all of the cousins and most of their friends lived in his neck of the woods. It will just make it easier. They had talked to the priest at each of their churches and arranged for the wedding date.

Since the wedding was small they decided the expense of the Monponset Inn would not be too great for the reception. Paul contacted the function manager at that establishment and gave her the date for the wedding. They then went on line to view prospective menus. Paul wanted something Italian. Carol did not want a traditional wedding cake. They decided on boneless chicken dinner for the entree, and a pasta dish with marinara sauce for a starter. There would be a large antipasto at each table to begin the meal and coffee and strawberry shortcake for desert. The bar would be cash not open. They were eliminating all the old fashioned rituals of garters, wedding cakes and throwing of bouquets. They were too old for that nonsense. They made all the reception plans by e-mail.

She told Paul she was going to make their invitations herself, she was pretty computer savvy.

He said, "What a remarkable woman I'm marring and thrifty too".

She asked him for a list of the names and addresses of everyone he wanted to come. He e-mailed it back to her the same day and she thought, "What a reliable man, he is so prompt".

Carol was only having one attendant, Judy, and Paul chose Bob for his best man. Although he was closer to Tom and Will, they were truly heathens and Bob was in good standing in the Catholic faith. Paul had thought of asking his eldest son to be best man but didn't want to hurt the younger one's feelings. So he chose Bob. Carol suggested that Paul's children take part in the ceremony. Paul's eldest son was to do a reading and his daughter and youngest son would bring up the gifts. That made Paul very happy. What a kind hearted person she was. Paul told her he would just wear his grey suit and Bob could just wear a suit as well. Carol thought that was wise and said she thought white shirts were best and hoped the neck ties were not too flashy. He said he didn't own a flashy tie. So they were all set in that department. Carol said she and the cousins were going to pick out appropriate dresses for herself and Judy. She really meant that Isabelle and Kathy had more fashion sense, but didn't say this.

She asked Paul if he'd mind if she didn't wear a braid at the wedding.

He said, "No. I remember you with all sorts of hair dos when we were young. It's your hair have it done any way you like. You'll still be my girl."

"What a romantic man he was," thought Carol.

She thought she would go back to her eye doctor and get contacts as well. If Paul didn't have trouble putting them in every day, surely she could get the hang of it. Carol begged the cousins not to give her a shower. She and Paul needed nothing and wanted nothing. They had two houses full of everything.

Paul told Bob not to listen to Will and Tom if they suggested a bachelor party.

"We're all too long in the tooth for that sort of thing", said Paul.

Bob agreed and said, "I didn't have one when he got married. You can get into trouble, even arrested".

"I know," said Paul, remembering two of Will's bachelor parties.

They needed a florist too said Carol. What was the name of the one he used when he bought her that beautiful nosegay? She wanted some flowers at the church and one flower each for Bob and Paul. Two small bouquets would be needed for her and Judy and centerpieces for the tables. She'd have to figure out how many tables after they made the invitation list. They wouldn't get the license until a month prior to the wedding date. They marked their calendars for that. Really thought Carol, Isabelle and Will had the right idea, just elope and no fuss. But were they really married in the eyes of God. The church did not always recognize a Justice of the Peace. Well one mustn't judge.

The only thing left to plan was the honeymoon. Paul surprised her by saying I really want to go to Italy. "Oh yes" said Carol "how wonderful"! They agreed to do some research and compare notes at the end of the week. They both looked on line for air fare deals, tours, and called travel agents.

Then Carol thought of clothes for her honeymoon. She and Paul liked to dress casually, and often alike, and so she didn't want to be something she wasn't. She decided she would use a few of the outfits she had and get a few extra. She may even get her and Paul a couple of matching shirts. She would talk to Kathy. She also wanted beautiful lingerie. Perhaps Isabelle could give her some direction. Isabelle did have that good bra that hoisted the girls up. Carol thought she'd buy a couple of those and some panties. Someone at work was always mentioning Victoria's Secret. Was she too old for that kind of underwear? After all it was a honeymoon. A couple of lacy night gowns would be nice too. She would definitely have a talk with Isabelle. She did not want to go shopping for these things with Judy and Kathy. They would make rude remarks.

Paul wanted to pick out the wedding rings and have them ordered in plenty of time. The next time Carol came down to Boston, they would shop for these.

Carol and Judy came to Boston in mid January to go shopping for clothes for the wedding. It was good to have something to do after the let down of the holidays. They went to the South Shore Plaza and tried their luck at Lord and Taylor and Macys. Isabelle found a lovely cream colored dress with a sweetheart neckline, heavy lace trim in the shape of a v at the bodice and a soft handkerchief type skirt for Carol. It needed alterations since the sleeves were long but that was the only adjustment. Carol looked great in it. Carol loved it. Carol said she'd bring it to her tailor in Vermont.

Isabelle said, "No, when you come down again in March, have the alterations done then and down here. This dress is beautiful. Don't take any chances with all that traveling back and forth; the dress could get stained or something. You will be getting dressed at Kathy's house anyway. So leave it at Kathy's and have it altered in March. Who knows you may lose a few pounds before then." Carol agreed.

Judy's dress was more difficult to find. She said she only liked jumper style dresses.

She said, "I don't want to look like some twenty year old freaking bridesmaid". Carol said, "Look we all wore screaming yellow and bright aqua at your first wedding. It's payback time".

Judy laughed and said, "OK, I'll wear whatever you like."

Kathy saw a sheath style dress, royal purple and made of a taffeta type material. It had three quarter sleeves and was on the rack labeled "Mother of the Bride." She got the biggest size, the bigger size and one in the big size and dragged Judy to the dressing room.

Judy said, "Oh you've got to be kidding".

Carol said, "Kathy, you actually picked a dress that's not black, way to go."

"If it came in black, I would have picked the black", answered Kathy.

Isabelle said, "Get in the dressing room right now, Judy, there are three of us and only one of you."

Judy tried it on. Judy had a waist. Judy looked good. She only needed the bigger size to cover those voluptuous hips.

Isabelle asked Kathy and Judy where they could find head gear, flowers; and ribbons, head bands something to go with the dresses.

"Be creative", said Isabelle, "we can always attach tulle".

They gave her a pained look.

Kathy said, "There's an accessory store upstairs".

"Ok" said Isabelle, "you two go there and see what you can find in cream and purple and then meet us at the Cheesecake Factory in a half hour".

Judy said to Kathy, "I have a man's hair cut how creative can I be".

"Yeah", said Kathy "and Carol's braid, really, what can you do with that?"

Isabelle said, "Carol and I are buying new bras. Judy what size do you wear."

"I'll get my own fucking bra if you don't mind", said Judy. She and Kathy headed up stairs.

Isabelle and Carol went to the lingerie department in search of bras and then they had a date with Victoria.

Isabelle did not mention the panties or night gowns to the other ladies, instead she had Carol try lingerie on and now Carol knows Victoria's Secret.

The girls had a lovely lunch. Isabelle bought a slice of cheese cake to bring home as a surprise for Will later.

On the way home they stopped at a retail shoe store and got plain, sensible satin pumps with wide heels. Carol gave the woman at the counter a swatch of cloth from her dress and left a deposit. Judy did the same. Kathy ran in the corner store and got a couple of scratch tickets. She got a free one. She went back and turned it in and scratched the new one and lost. She lit up a cigarette.

They all went back to Kathy's with dresses on hangers covered with plastic, accessories in a small bag and underwear in a larger one. Isabelle had placed the Victoria Secret bag inside the large Macy's one so Judy and Kathy would not see it and tease Carol. Carol was pleased at all they had accomplished. She took out her note book and wrote, "Pick up shoes in March, get alterations done in March" They were all sitting around talking when in came Will and Paul. They had been ice fishing but had not luck. Tom got a big mouth bass and he was cooking it for supper. They told the girls Susan had fed them a hot lunch. Since Susan was babysitting their granddaughter, Will and Paul got to meet one of the grandkids, a pretty little girl. Carol dashed into one of the bedrooms and hid the dresses and other things. Will bent over Isabelle's chair and kissed her head.

She looked up and said, "Hey, Big Guy I got you a piece of cheese cake for later". He said, "Oh, sweetheart, you're my piece of cheesecake for later".

"I think I just threw up in my mouth a little bit", said Judy. "Will if that's one of your best lines I don't know why Isabelle ever married you."

Will said, "Judy everyone here knows you're all talk. Why do you waste your time trying to get everyone's goat"?

"I'm freaking good at it", she said, "That's why."

Will shook his head.

Carol joined the group and gave Paul a hug.

"We were so lucky today", said Carol. "Isabelle found me a beautiful dress for the wedding and Kathy found one for Judy. We ordered shoes to match and had a great shopping spree."

Isabelle stood and put on her coat to go.

She said, "Will and I are leaving for Louisiana tomorrow so I'll say good bye to you girls now and see you when you come down in March. Kathy, I'll call when I get back. Have fun with the plans".

Carol thanked her for all her help. She and Will hugged them all good bye and when Will got to Judy he growled at her. She laughed out loud. He shook hands with Paul and off they went.

Judy said, "I need a drink".

Kathy said, "I need a cigarette. Want to play Scrabble?"

"You must love to lose", said Judy.

"Shut up," said Kathy.

Paul said, "Carol, I hope you're not too tired, because we are going to pick out our wedding rings right now."

"OK," she said and off they went.

They looked at many wedding bands. They tried some on and finally found the rings they wanted.

Paul said, "Let's just buy them now. I'll put them in my safe at home. It will be one less thing to do later".

"Good idea" said Carol, "How marvelous that you think of everything."

Paul almost blushed.

Paul said, "You know the florist is just up the street. Why don't we just stop by and see if they have some ideas for you?"

Carol was delighted and they went to the florist. Carol explained that they were old and didn't want any showy floral displays. She told the woman the exact things she needed and the woman let them look in a photo book of floral arrangements for a few minutes. Remember to only look at the arrangements listed for your month. The flowers may be out of season if you pick something else. They opened the book to April and saw many beautiful things. Carol asked for the florist's recommendations.

She said, "Well first, the two men only need a cream colored rose for their lapels."

Paul said that sounded good.

"I would have a basket arrangement for the church holding all kinds of spring flowers of many colors but especially with cream and purple, like this", said the woman. She pointed to a photo. That looked gorgeous thought Carol.

"For you and your attendant I would suggest tulips, cream for you with lots of cream ribbon and a couple of tiny violets to bring out the purple color and I would do just purple tulips with cream ribbon for your sister."

She showed Paul and Carol a photo of a similar bouquet done in coral tulips with ribbon wound all around the stems and streamers of ribbon hanging. They loved it.

"Do you want anything for your heads", asked the woman?

"I think my cousin is going to try to make me a cream fascinator hat and my sister a purple one".

"I see", said the florist.

"My sister has no hair," said Carol.

"Oh dear", said the florist.

"Oh, no, she really has hair but it's very, very short."

"Well I hope your cousin is a very clever girl," said the florist.

"She is" said Paul "you should see her bats".

The florist was getting a little confused but a sale was a sale and the customer is always right.

She told Carol that her only other concern was the centerpieces for the tables at the reception.

"How about small round bowls with cream and purple tulips, just plain and simple", asked Carol?

"We can do that", said the woman, "and I think that's a nice choice. How many do you need?

"I don't know yet; can I get back to you?" asked Carol.

"Of course", said the lady.

Carol asked her for prices and she listed them on a sheet of paper. She figured the total price out as if there were ten tables. The total can be refigured when we know the exact number by either adding or subtracting the number of table vases. This is not the final bill but it is pretty accurate except for the centerpieces. Paul and Carol reviewed it and thought it was reasonable. The florist said she usually got ten percent down when an order was placed. Carol wanted to give her a deposit toward the flowers to hold the order and Paul agreed and wrote out a check.

The florist said, "Call me any time with any questions or additions, but you must call me by the first of April to let me know how many centerpieces I'm making."

She shook their hands and showed them to the door.

Paul and Carol did a high five outside and Paul said, "One more thing to cross off our list."

They went and got a pizza and beer for supper then returned to his house to listen to music. Paul and Carol discussed finances. He thought they should go to the social security office to discuss the change of their marital status and see what that would do to their monthly income. They agreed to go tomorrow to the social security office. She told him she had put a deposit on the Monponset Inn for the reception. He wanted to share that expense. Paul thought they should keep both cars. They would have to discuss car insurance, which state was the least expensive and how did that work. Which house would be their legal residence for voting and income tax purposes. Maybe they should ask a lawyer or their accountant. They both agreed to live in Massachusetts for the winters and Vermont for the summers. They could see how that worked during the first year.

They sang along with the show tunes and kissed to the soft music. At 11:00 PM Paul brought Carol back to Kathy's. They had accomplished a lot today. Life was good.

# CHAPTER TWENTY-SEVEN: NEW ORLEANS AND MEET THE FAMILY

It was Sunday, Isabelle and Will had packed their bags. They had a direct flight to New Orleans that departed at 2:00 P.M. She was excited because she was going to meet Will's family and see a city she had never been to. They got to Logan Airport in plenty of time. At the ticket desk they relinquished their luggage to the baggage attendant and took the claim ticket. Their tickets were in order so they proceed through air port security. They both removed their shoes, not easy to do for two old timers, with no chairs. They leaned on each other. Isabelle went through the metal detector and was frisked by a female security person and Will beeped the metal detector and reached in his pocket and found his keys and then went through again. This time he passed. He was frisked by a male security person and had the wand waved all around him. Now they had to put the shoes back on, leaning on each other again. Flying wasn't easy anymore but hopefully it was safe.

They boarded and settled into small talk while the pilot took off, and soared to a higher altitude. She teased Will saying she did not want to go to that nudist colony while they were there. He teased right back saying she might like it. He held her hand and she rested her head on his shoulder. They both slept for most of the trip. They both needed the rest room so off they went up the aisle in search of the toilet in the air. By the time they returned to their seats it was time to fasten their belts and the plane landed safely in New Orleans' Louis Armstrong airport and slowly taxied to the assigned terminal.

This was a whole new experience for Isabelle. She was happy. They got their bags from the baggage claim area and headed outside the terminal. The day was gone by now but not quite dark. Jack was waiting in the line for live passenger pick up and Will and he put the luggage into the rear of his SUV. Will introduced Jack to Isabelle, he gave her a quick hug and said hello. The three of them got into the vehicle and sped off northeast to small town just south of Slidell where Jack lived, about forty-five minutes away. At first he made small talk asking how cold it was in Boston and how hot it was here. Then he thanked them for all the wonderful Christmas gifts and said the boys were really enjoying the Leggos and his daughter, Nina, loved the American Girl Doll.

He said Marilyn was cooking them a hot meal so he hoped they had appetites. They said they did since the air lines don't feed passengers any more. Will asked him if he had taken care of selling his truck. Jack said he was working on it and two prospective buyers were literally having a bidding war for it in fifty dollar increments. Will laughed and said, "Sell it to the highest bidder." Isabelle was looking at this young man about the same age as her Kevin. He was tall like his dad but had dark brown eyes and no huge smile with the dimple and no big hands. Jack had hair, lots of hair and dark brown hair. Will's had been light brown almost blonde when he had hair. Jack definitely looked like his mother but he had his father's charm. He was turning it off and on especially when talking to her. She suspected Jack had a reputation with the girls similar to Wills' reputation during his wild years between marriages. The men talked about neighbors, and changes that happened while Will was gone. Will told him that Paul was getting married. Jack was surprised. "Good for him", he said. "I thought he looked lonely the last time I saw him". Will said that Tom was still the same grumpy, smoking, cowboy he has always been. Jack laughed at that. Jack heard his father tell more tales of the Vermont vacation and told his dad that it must have been fun for all of the old timers to get together. "Hey, watch that old timer stuff" said Will. Isabelle chuckled in the back seat. Jack asked Isabelle how she enjoyed Vermont and she told him about the rowing and swimming and how bad she was at horse shoes. Jack said he thought you needed upper body strength to be good at it.

Will told him how beautiful Maine was on their honeymoon and said he hoped Jack and the family would visit New England some day soon. Isabelle said she would love to have them. The ride went smoothly and they arrived home just as dinner was ready.

Marilyn hugged Will and Isabelle. She said it was nice for the kids to have some grandparents. Since her folks lived in Florida, the children missed out seeing them too. Marilyn called the children to the table. Nina looked just like her mom, lean and wispy with fair hair and blue eyes. Both boys resembled their dad with dark brown hair and dark brown eyes. Marilyn proved to be a good cook. She had made meatloaf, mashed potatoes and green beans. They were eating in the dining room, it was nicely decorated. The home was modest but pretty and comfortable.

There was peach cobbler with whipped cream for dessert.

"We usually don't have sweets with our meals", said Marilyn, "but tonight is special". The kids were pleased.

"There's hot coffee", said Jack, "regular or decaf for those who want to sleep". Isabelle insisted on helping with the dishes.

The boys wanted Papa to play checkers with them. He did. Nina helped in the kitchen too. She asked Isabelle if she had any granddaughters.

Isabelle said, "I have six".

"Wow" Nina said.

"What are their names, how old are they, do they live near you"?

Her mother said, "slow down Nina, one questions at a time".

Isabelle laughed. Nina waited. Isabelle said, "All the girls live near me. Victoria is seventeen, Veronica is fifteen, Isabelle is ten, Fiona is eight, Lily is eight and Eileen is five."

"So you have grandsons too", asked Nina.

"Yes, but there are ten of them and I don't feel like reciting all of that right now." "That's OK", said Nina, "I hate boys anyway."

Isabelle said, "Your dad is a boy and Papa is a boy and you don't hate them". "Well", said Nina, "they used to be boys now their men. There's a difference". Isabelle wanted to say, "No there isn't" but only said "I see."

The checker games were over. The boys came into the kitchen and asked Isabelle what sports her grandsons played.

She told them and one of them said "How many grandsons do you have?

She said, "Ten".

One boy said "Wow".

The other said, "No, way".

They asked her if they played computer games and she said she wasn't sure but she knew they played XBox games.

Their mother told them to take their showers, finish their homework and get ready for bed.

The oldest said, "I have the shower first, my homework is done".

The second went to an opened book and sheet of paper on the kitchen table and said "I hate times tables".

Isabelle said "We all hated times tables but we get through them eventually".

He just looked at her.

Marilyn poured another cup of coffee for herself and raised the pot toward Isabelle. Isabelle thanked her but told her she'd never sleep if she had any more. Isabelle told her it was a delicious meal and the kind of thing they eat at home. She said she was afraid she was going to be given grits and gumbo just because she was from up north. Marilyn laughed and said she didn't even like grits.

They left the boy to his homework and joined the others in the living room. Nina was sweet talking Will. She told him she had missed him and she was doing well in school. Then she asked him to read her a bed time story. He read and she listened leaning her head on his chest. The older boy came into the room wearing sweats and put his back pack near the front door.

"Is everything in that", asked Marilyn, "like your finished homework".

"Yes mom it is".

"Let me look at it" she said.

He gave a couple of sheets of paper to his mother.

She said, "Jack Jr., this book report is a mess. You don't write with a ball point pen that's leaking. Where's the pen? Is it in the bag? It will get all over everything."

"No", he said, "I threw it away".

"Well your math is alright but this report has to be done over. March right in the kitchen and get another pen and copy this over", said Marilyn.

With that the second son ran past them with his back pack and she grabbed him and said "Not so fast, show me that sheet you were working on at the table".

He gave her the times table sheet and she said, "Good job".

He put it in his book and put the back pack on the bench near the front door.

"Go take your shower and get ready for bed, son," said Jack.

The boy ran upstairs.

Nina was now telling Will about a dance recital she had been in.

She described her costume. "It's upstairs, she said, "and maybe tomorrow I'll put it on and show you the dance. Would you like to see that, Isabelle?"

Isabelle said that she would.

The younger boy came back down stairs with sweats on and said, "Nina the bathroom is all yours".

She said "What did you put there, something to scare me?"

"No", he said.

"I don't believe you," said Nina.

"Papa do you think he put something in the bathroom to scare me?"

"No, and if he did I'll get even with him".

The boy looked at Will. Nina smiled a smug girly smile.

Will said "Go take your shower, Nina, and get into your pajamas.

She came down stairs a little later in pink pajamas with flowers printed all over them.

Marilyn said "Get a drink of milk you three and then off to bed. Don't forget to say good night to Papa and Isabelle".

They did as they were told and then as they raced up stairs their father said, "Brush your teeth, I'm sick of supporting the dentist".

The next three days passed just about the same as the first night. They were all becoming familiar with one another. Jack and Marilyn seemed to like Isabelle. They could see that Will adored her. They thought Isabelle had somehow tamed him. The children really took a shine to Isabelle as well. After school Will and Isabelle took them for a walk to the park, Will tossed a football back and forth to both boys and Isabelle watched Nina at the playground. Usually the kids had a babysitter watch them after school so this was a treat for them. Isabelle found Jack and Marilyn to be a loving, devoted couple. She thought they were good parents too. Will and Isabelle helped with the chores and cooking while they stayed there. Jack and Marilyn told them to stop doing so much, guests aren't supposed to work.

Isabelle said, "We're not guests; we're family."

On the weekend, they all went to a movie, it was a comedy and PG rated. Jack was stunned when Will drove him and Isabelle to Mass on Sunday. He had never seen his father at church except at funerals. The truck still drove well. Will liked that truck. "Well keep bidding boys", Will said, it goes to the highest bidder". On Sunday afternoon they went to a pond and the guys, young and old fished, the ladies chatted and Nina roller bladed around them on the paved path. Nina had also brought a few small dolls, a sticker book and a soccer ball to practice her kicking. When the men had enough fishing they kicked the soccer ball around. They were too fast for Will, he almost fell down a couple of times trying to return the kick. They had a picnic on a blanket, with sandwiches and lemonade. The sky was a medium blue dotted with small white clouds. The trees were not like the ones in New England and they had Spanish moss hanging from their branches. The trees were beautiful and their site was a little eerie giving Isabelle ideas for next Halloween. Will told Jack and Marilyn that he wanted to take Isabelle to see New Orleans for a few days. He said they would use the truck and they would be back on Friday.

After everyone was gone off to work and school on Monday, Will and Isabelle loaded a suitcase into the back of the truck and headed south. The drive was peaceful and Will pointed out some of the sites. That huge body of water is Lake Pontchartrain. You know there's a lot of history in this city. There was an historical battle here in 1815, the Battle of New Orleans. Andrew Jackson, with his somewhat irregular group of men, defeated British troops here. It was during the last part War of 1812.

It took less than an hour to get to New Orleans. The weather was fair and the roads well paved. Because they left around 9:30 AM there was not much traffic. Isabelle was taking in all the sites. Will told her they were too early for Mardi Gras this year but maybe another year they would experience that. As they approached the city proper, Will pointed out several of the tall buildings, including the Shell Building, and other places of interest in the skyline and of course the Mississippi River. He showed her Loyola University and Tulaine. He found the Windsor Court Hotel, checked in and the valet took his truck to park. Their luggage was sent to their room and they went outside. The door man gave them directions to the booth that sold tickets for the narrated tour of the city. Will and Isabelle walked up the block, purchased the tickets and boarded the bus. They drove by the French Quarter, some of the famous cemeteries, and learned some nicknames for the city, like "Nawlins" and "The Big Easy". The narrator told them about the French population that arrived around 1718. New Orleans played an important part in the Revolutionary War. In 1779 New Orleans was under Spanish control that lasted until 1801. The city has been a principal port on the Mississippi River throughout history. They were told about what a melting pot of culture New Orleans was with the French, Creole, Cajun, Irish and German populations co-existing and mingling. The narrator spoke about Jazz, Louis Armstrong, and how the music of the city was influenced by Acadian and African music. Local foods were mentioned like beignets, square shaped pastry like donuts; Po'boy sandwiches; jambalaya; and Praline candy. The tour guide briefly talked about sports naming the Louisiana Superdome home of the Sugar Bowl and the New Orleans Saints. The man pointed out St Louis Catholic Cathedral and mentioned that Catholicism was still the prominent religion, however there were many varieties of Voodoo practiced. The City Hall was pointed to as they passed and the narrator said the City was run by a mayor and a city council. The devastation of Hurricane Katrina was talked about followed by a discussion on levees and floods. The tour ended, and Isabelle and Will finally came back to their first stop and got off the bus.

Isabelle knew she'd never remember all this, but she was trying to. Isabelle loved to learn. They walked along famous Bourbon Street, had lunch at a sidewalk café, visited the cathedral and shopped on Magazine Street. They sat on a bench and just watched the tankers; shrimp boats, cruise ships and other vessels go by.

Their days were filled with adventure their nights were full of love. They visited cemeteries, rode a street car on the Riverfront line. They went on a Dinner Jazz Cruise aboard the Steamboat Natchez. The people were friendly, the shrimp the freshest and the flowers all in bloom even in February. Will and Isabelle were happy. He asked her if she wanted him to find out if the nudist colony was still around. She looked at him with one raised eyebrow. He was silent. Their hotel was beautiful, the city amazing and the trip wonderful. By Friday morning they were ready to go back to Jack and Marilyn and the children.

On Friday night they got pizza for everyone and told them about their trip. This started a lot of conversation since Jack and his family had been to the city many times. On Saturday they all attended the boys' basketball game. Their team won. Upon returning home the women made lunch and the men shot hoops in the driveway. The afternoon was spent doing laundry, grocery shopping, ironing and watching television and all the other normal family Saturday chores. The boys played computer games and Nina was in her room with her dolls. Will and Isabelle offered to baby sit so the younger couple could go out for a date. Jack and Marilyn were delighted; they hadn't been out in a while. Will and Isabelle played monopoly at the kitchen table with the kids, made pop corn and had fun.

On Sunday Will and Isabelle went to Mass. When they got home Jack was standing with a young man in the drive way. He was the highest bidder. The truck was sold.

Isabelle asked Marilyn if she would be using the dining table during the next few days.

She said, "No, why?"

"Will and I want to start a brand new jig saw puzzle on it and let the kids work on it after we leave to go home. That way they will think we're still here finishing it with them" she said.

Marilyn said "That is a great idea."

On Monday Isabelle and Will said they would leave on Tuesday. They discussed this with Jack and Marilyn and the kids. Marilyn said, "You are welcome to stay as long as you like and I'm sure it's a treat not to be standing in snow. School vacation is next week and Jack and I and the kids are driving to Destin, Florida to stay with my folks for a week. It's in the pan handle so it's not too far. You two can have the house to yourselves if you chose to stay."

"Will said, "Thank you, but I think we want to head north, even if there's snow. We've had a wonderful time and I can't thank you enough for letting us spend it here with my grandchildren"

Marilyn was touched. She had not liked Will at first, she thought he was ladies' man and not reliable, and she still had the bad memory of Yvonne. But now that he was married to Isabelle he was a different man. He and Isabelle were truly in love. Marilyn thought to herself, they should have married all those years ago and then she thought, no way, because then there would be no Jack.

Jack said, "We really enjoyed your visit, Dad, and if you and Isabelle are ready to go home, that's fine". "You know you can come back whenever you like."

The kids protested their leaving with grumbles.

Isabelle said, "You guys are going to see your other grandparents next week. You have a lot of planning to do. What will you bring with you? What will you do? Will you swim in the ocean and have fun at the beach?"

The boys looked hopeful and Jack Jr. said to their parents, "Did Grandma and Grandpa get new diving masks or shall we bring ours".

"What about pails and shovels", said Nina, "I want to make a princess castle in the sand."

The youngest son, Dave, said, "Isabelle I like you a lot; I hope you visit us again." "I'm looking forward to it", said Isabelle.

"Papa" said Nina, "my other Grandpa has hair".

Will said, "Good for him".

They all laughed.

There was snow on the ground when Isabelle and Will returned on Tuesday.

They didn't care and they longed for their own bed. The car had been cleaned off and the drive way shoveled; either Kevin or Jeanne's boys did that thought Will. The mail was stacked on the table in the front hall one of the kids brought it in thought Isabelle. It was good to be home.

# CHAPTER TWENTY-EIGHT: CAROL AND PAUL'S WEDDING

About forty-two people would be attending the wedding. They would only need the small function room at the Monponsett Inn. Carol finished the seating plan and there would be three tables with eight at each and four tables with six at each. She liked a lot of room for moving around. There would be no head table. Carol and Paul would be sitting with Bob and Esther and Judy and Kathy. All other guests were at assigned seats as well. The final florist arrangements were made. Church music was selected. Bob helped her with that and had arranged for one of the choir members to sing a solo of "Ave Maria" at the Mass. The ceremony would take place at 6:30 PM on Saturday night.

The license was obtained, the dresses altered, the shoes picked up and Isabelle had made two lovely head pieces for the bride and attendant to wear. All the plans were in place. Will was going to bring the girls to the Church in the Town Car. Judy threatened to buy him a limo driver's hat. Their passports were ready for Italy. Their bags packed. Their plane tickets at the ready.

Carol and Judy decided to get their hair done on Saturday morning, the day of the wedding. Isabelle wanted Carol to go to her hairdresser so Carol came to Weymouth and headed to the salon to get a make over. Judy went with Kathy to "Mildred's House of Beauty" to have wonders done for her.

She told Kathy, "Under no circumstances am I getting maroon hair. I don't like it."

"Well I do," said Kathy, "besides it would clash with your royal purple dress."

Carol had her eyebrows waxed but did not need any other facial hair removed. Isabelle asked, "Why do I have the moustache." as the hot wax and hair filled cloth strip was being ripped from her upper lip. "Ouch", she said.

"You must take after your father's side", said Carol.

The hairdresser wanted to tackle Carol's hair first. It was the biggest challenge. She asked Carol if she would consider a color treatment. Isabelle was surprised when Carol said "Yes". They decided on a warm brown and the color was applied. While they waited for the color to set, the hairdresser washed, cut and blew dried Isabelle's hair in ten minutes. The hairdresser was used to Isabelle's unruly cow licks and knew exactly what looked best on her. Isabelle always colored her own hair so it didn't take long to do the rest. Carol was looking at make-up, that the other stylist was showing her. She was going to have her make-up put on professionally today; and was gong to buy some of the products as well. Carol wanted to look good. She was the bride. When the color was rinsed Carol looked ten years younger. The brown hair made her eyes sparkle and since she now wore contacts her whole face lit up. The hair dresser suggested a trim. Isabelle was hoping Carol would agree but didn't think she'd part with the trademark braid.

Carol said, "I don't want to wear a braid anymore. I want a new look with bangs and a long bob."

Isabelle was staring at her in amazement. "I'm so proud of you Carol, this is the first time in thirty years, that you have changed your hair do."

"It's about time," Carol said. "I want Paul to be proud of me".

"Well he already is but he'll be pleased to see how well you look".

The hairdresser worked her magic with the scissors, blow dryer and curling iron on Carol's hair. A brand new Carol appeared in the mirror. She looked great. She felt great. She was the bride.

"Let's get our nails done too, but just clear shiny polish", said Carol. "It doesn't show so much when it chips."

Isabelle agreed. How practical she was thought Isabelle.

Back at Mildred's House of Beauty" Kathy sat reading a magazine with her head covered in maroon goop and foil. She was getting highlights as well this time. She would be a two toned maroon headed woman. Judy was discussing a hair cut with the lady in the pink smock. Judy was undecided about what to do.

She told the woman, "I haven't had my hair cut since December for Christmas. That was four months ago. It is now longer than it has been in decades. I don't think I want to go back to that masculine look I was wearing. What do you think?"

"Well your hair is still short but we could make it much more feminine with a good shaping and layering. I think a pixie style cut and then a few spikes with gel will do the trick."

"I'm in my sixty-six year old sister's wedding today; I'm not going to a freaking rock concert", said Judy.

The woman and Kathy both laughed.

"What about color", the hairdresser asked.

"What about it" said Judy?

"Do you like the grey"?

"Yes", said Judy.

"What if we perk it up with a rinse to lighten it a little? It wouldn't turn it yellow if that's what you're thinking".

"I wasn't thinking that at all" said Judy, "I don't want to look like a blue headed old lady."

"Oh, my", said the hairdresser, "No one's used that stuff for years."

"In Vermont they do".

Judy's hair was rinsed, shaped and styled. It was now a pale grey very pretty, almost white. The style was short but feminine. There were little wisps framing her face and the hair on the back was left long at the neck base curling upward. What a marvelous tool that curling iron was thought Judy.

She told the woman to spray the hell out of this so it would last. Kathy's hair was finished and looked the same only with subtle stripes.

"Judy let's get our nails done", urged Kathy.

"Why not", said Judy.

So she decided to get fake nails like Kathy's. They got the nails put on and polished, Kathy's red, Judy's white and then paid their bills and went home.

In the car Judy said, "Does it always smell that bad having your nails done"?

"Yes", answered Kathy.

"Between that smell and the cigarettes you'll get lung cancer. You better stop all this" said Judy.

Kathy said "Take care of yourself, Judy".

"In other words Fuck Off," said Judy.

"Yes" said Kathy.

Then Kathy said "I always do my own make up I'm not paying for that". "Let me put some make up on you today", she said to Judy.

"What are we eleven years old again and playing fashion games?"

"No but you really look good and I thought a little eye mascara and blush could go a long way," said Kathy.

"Alright but if I look like some cheap hooker, Bob and Paul will faint and Will might think I'm trying to make him feel at home".

"Be nice" said Kathy.

Judy said "You sound just like Auntie Chickie. "How many hookers do you think he's been with, thousands?"

"My God, Judy", Kathy said, "What an imagination you have."

Carol, Judy and Kathy arrived at Kathy's within minutes of each other. They were all amazed at the transformation of both sisters. Wait until Isabelle sees you Judy. She will be so proud of you.

Judy said, "Carol do you think Will has been with thousands of hookers?"

"What, even Will Benton isn't that good or stupid" said Carol.

Isabelle arrived about two hours before the wedding to help the girls get dressed.

She was astounded by Judy's hair. She told Judy how great she looked and Kathy what a good job she had done.

Judy said, "Yeah now if I could just grow a moustache I'd look like Tom."

Will had on his best suit and looked handsome. He read the newspaper and watched TV while the girls got ready. He could hear them as they cackled and laughed. He liked women but when a few of them got together it was bedlam.

Isabelle was wearing a light blue lace dress with a low cut neckline. It was straight and simple. It was on a rare days like this that she wore heels; they were low but heels nonetheless. Her hair was perfect.

Her make up was perfect. She looked great. Isabelle was old but still a beautiful woman.

Kathy was already dressed in an elegant black chiffon wide legged pant suit. Her new two toned hair color actually complimented it. Kathy had on a long strand of red beads, red and black beaded earrings and two red bangle bracelets. She carried the black beaded bag she had bought at that yard sale in Vermont. She actually looked very retro and chic.

Isabelle was shocked to see Judy's fake nails.

"Kathy, you've made her into a beauty", said Isabelle.

"I really had nothing to do with it, well maybe the nails", replied Kathy.

Judy and Carol had both dieted when they went home in January. Carol also walked a lot too, although it was difficult in all the snow. Judy had lost twenty pounds and Carol had lost twenty- five. They were telling their cousins about their diet ideas. Isabelle was praising them and Kathy told them they just should have taken up smoking.

"That's what keeps my weight off.", she said.

They all looked at her. She was not thin.

Judy said "I'm glad I skipped all that exercise it wouldn't have been worth the stinking five extra pounds."

The dresses fitted perfectly, the head gear was place on their heads and out of the bedrooms they went for Will's inspection. Isabelle had warned him to be on his best behavior and to compliment the ladies on their appearance. Since none of these so called girls were lookers when they were young, it was hard to think they'd be pretty today. But he promised Isabelle he would be a gentleman and compliment them. Isabelle had already said to him earlier, "You tell them they look pretty; even if you are lying through your teeth".

Will stood up when the bride and her attendant entered the room. He said, "My God, who are these two beauties. I'm blown away. You both look lovely; you too Kathy."

Kathy said, "Thanks"

Carol blushed and said, "Oh, Will thank you".

Judy said, "Keep it in your pants, Will."

When they arrived at the church, Tom was standing outside without Susan. Will got out of the car and opened the doors for the women. Isabelle took Kathy's arm and they walked down the aisle and sat on the groom's since his had fewer guests. Bob and Paul were standing at the altar waiting. Tom complimented Judy as she walked by.

He said, "Wow, You look very nice. Yeah, now you have hair like me. I must tell Milton Stanley."

"Thanks Tom, you know what you and Milton Stanley can do."

"I told Susan that I thought Judy used to look pretty good when we were young", said Tom.

"What", said Will, "are you crazy"?

The organ began to play softly and Judy walked slowly down the aisle. Judy looked wonderful and she felt good. All eyes were looking at her and heads were nodding in approval. The royal purple was a good choice of color for her and her hair made her look much younger.

Then "Here Comes the Bride" was played and down the aisle came Carol, as stunning and radiant as any bride, escorted by Will and Tom. Will and Tom walked slowly; one on each side of the bride and then each one kissed the bride on her cheeks and handed her over to Paul. Tom was staring at Carol's forehead. They bowed toward Paul and went to sit with their wives. Tom said, "Now I know what bangs are." Susan just stared at him.

After the ceremony everyone headed for the Monponset Inn. The small function room had a large picture window that viewed the pond and the tables were set with cream colored cloths and bowls of purple and cream tulips. The tiny lights on the trees outside were beginning to cast reflections onto the glass of the windows as the sun finally set. It made the room look magical. The meal was delicious. Bob gave a nice toast, wishing them the best, and they all danced until midnight. Isabelle and Will surprised the newlyweds by arranging for a real limo to come and pick the bride and groom up at midnight and take them to the airport. They had an early flight to catch and were booked to stay at the airport hotel.

At the hotel Paul and Carol did not hesitate to make love. They had never been vain or conceited. They always knew their looks had imperfections and blemishes. This was good because now that they were older, they didn't have any anxiety about what to expect. They loved each other as is and unconditionally. They were two beautiful people.

They both had been married before so they knew the ways of making love. They were not shy with each other anymore and so their first act of passion together was done with respect and right away. Paul and Carol did not fool around. They were two kindred spirits. They were happy in each other's arms and becoming one.

Carol and Paul were lying in bed at the hotel. It was their wedding night. They had just made love.

Paul said, "Carol, did you know that the term "package" refers to a man's private parts?"

"What?" She answered.

"Yeah, I was talking with Will and Tom one time about when Will was at a nudist colony and he said he didn't care if people saw his package."

"Will was at a nudist colony?"

"Yes".

"Does Isabelle know?"

"I don't know," said Paul. "Anyway, they made fun of me for not knowing."

"I told them that my mother, God rest her soul, used to say, "Paul don't forget to cover June, July and August" when I would go to the beach.

"She did?" asked Carol.

"Yes, she was a very funny woman" said Paul.

Carol said, "My aunt always called them Tommy and the twins."

She went on, "I suppose if you're speaking about the penis and the two testicles, they are a whole package. I think it's a polite way of saying it. I'm surprised Will was so refined."

"He's not," said Paul.

"I mean when men say things like "nice rack" or "what a set" you know they mean a woman's breasts. There are a lot of crude terms out there," said Carol.

Paul said, "I'm glad you don't talk like that."

"Judy could tell you plenty of nasty words."

"Oh, her, I bet she could."

"Once Judy used the word "prick" and I didn't know if she jabbed her finger with a needle, or was referring to a penis. She was actually referring to her first husband."

"Your sister scares me a little," said Paul.

Carol laughed.

In the morning they gathered their things and boarded a shuttle that took them directly to the international terminal. Carol and Paul went through all the necessary security checks, sent their bags to luggage land, had passports examined, were worked over by metal detectors and wands and finally they were allowed to wait at Gate 5. They boarded the plane and settled in for a long flight. They did not care they each had a walk man with different show tune CD's in them and ear plugs. When the passengers were told they could now turn on all electronic devises they turned them on and held hands and listed to the music. They each almost broke into song at different times. After an hour they swapped CD's and resumed their listening pleasure. They were in love. They were going on their honeymoon. They were going to Italy. Paul was in love and Carol would keep Victoria's Secret.

# CHAPTER TWENTY-NINE: WILL AND ISABELLE YEARS GO BY

The summer came, Paul and Carol, returned from their honeymoon and headed for Vermont. Judy had gone back to Vermont right after their wedding. She was worried about Cat. He'd not been well for months. She wished there was such a thing as medical insurance for animals. Maybe there was. She must research this on the net. She was going broke paying the vet. Kathy was visiting with her daughter who just had a baby, a boy.

Will and Isabelle had gone to a first communion, saw two grandkids go to proms all decked out, went to a high school graduation and a college graduation for two other grandkids. The Forth of July Party was enjoyed again, Will was getting the hang of washer toss and they went swimming at the local beach. Isabelle and Will kept busy and happy.

Isabelle was preparing for her annual Tea Party. She held this every year during August for her daughters, daughters-in-law, granddaughters and friends. The decorating was easy since through the years she had collected many tea pots and dishes. She sent out fancy invitations. The girls came in dresses, gloves and some even wore hats. One year Isabelle made several hats with lots of tulle and ribbon and silk flowers. Another year two of the little boys came and she got them top hats to wear. The best china, lace table cloths and trays were used. There were tongs for the sugar cubes, and tiny spoons for stirring. The little girls were always impressed by the wooden paddle in the honey pot. Three tiered serving plates held pastries of all sorts.

Fancy dishes held small sandwiches, made of thin crust less bread spread with butter and thinly sliced cucumber. There were scones and jam and butter. Ham and chicken salad made sandwiches on small rolls. They were all taught to lift their pinkies while raising tea cups to their lips. There were vases full of flowers. A different special cake stood on a pedestal plate as centerpiece each year. Little girls' white gloved hands were covered in chocolate from the chocolate covered strawberries. Candles were lit and stings of tiny lights were placed here and there. The cousins did not attend this. It was Isabelle's girls and friends close to her home. It was always enjoyed and many photographs were taken. What memories she had of theses times. Now her youngest granddaughter was getting older.

Isabelle wondered how many more years this tradition would last. Time passed. Change was good. She relayed all this to Will and he was eager to help her the first year he had married her. His enthusiasm continued and each year he would tell her it was another wonderful tea old girl. He said she should have them until no one wanted to come but he doubted that would happen. If it did, then she could make a tea party for just the two of them. He said he would wear a top hat and she could wear one of the fancy bonnets she made.

Will and Isabelle still spent quiet afternoons in their bird watching chairs and loved the peace and quiet of the garden. They were trying to distinguish the different songs each bird sang. Isabelle's son, Joe, had given her a book that made each bird's sound. There was a button beside each bird photo and when you pressed it the bird's sound was heard. Since their hearing was getting as bad as all their other senses, they had some difficulty figuring out all the bird's calls. Sometimes they debated over which was which. Sometimes they tried to imitate the sounds. But they enjoyed all this. It was a beautiful time of year. The grass was bright green, the flowers in bloom and yellow and orange butterflies flapped their wings gently while flying by. At night the fire flies twinkled in the darkness and Will and Isabelle watched a full moon through the skylight over their bed.

Will had painted the back steps. Isabelle had painted one of the bathrooms. They were always together; and still thought of themselves as young even thought they knew the truth. Isabelle and Will were hopeful.

Their first anniversary was approaching in August and Will surprised her with a trip to London. She was ecstatic. She had always wanted to go there and thought time was running out for them. It wasn't as easy getting around like they used to. They packed and planned. One night in the middle of August, with hundreds of stars shining in the sky their plane lifted off the run way at Logan Airport. Will and Isabelle were surprised the air line provided breakfast the next morning usually no food was served on flight. They arrived at Heathrow. They were taking a bus tour of London and then another tour around Great Britain. After picking up their suitcases at the claim area they looked around because they were told they'd be met by a representative of the tour company. The tour guide's assistant was standing holding a card with big letters naming his company and Will and Isabelle fell in line with all the other tourists on this trip. This was the way to go.

She had told Will about a trip to Ireland that she and Tim took and how everything had been arranged and it made things so easy. Will went to a travel agent and told her just what he wanted. Their hotel rooms were all booked, their luggage would be carted to and from these rooms by younger, stronger men; all the site seeing activities were planned and most of the meals were included. Since Isabelle and Will had slept most of the flight, they were ready to go. They climbed the stairs of the bus as quickly as people their age could and sat at the back. There was more room there. The bus took them to their hotel where the travelers could rest or go out. They were told to meet in the dining room for dinner at 8:00 PM, where tomorrow's itinerary would be explained by the tour guide.

They had already looked at the itinerary in the brochure and decided today would be a good time to visit the places they would not be stopping at tomorrow. They got a cab out in front of the hotel and told the driver to take them to the Thames where a cruise boat to Greenwich was docked. They boarded and went up the river to Greenwich, and looked at the Cutty Sark and put their two feet in two different time zones at the Prime Meridian. When they returned, to the banks of the Thames, they crossed the bridge, not the London Bridge but the next one over, the Westminster, and went to the London Eye. They got their tickets and went inside the glassed booth to ride the huge Ferris wheel and got the best view of London anyone could see. They were hungry when they got off and saw, of all things, a McDonalds on the hill diagonally across from the Tower of London. They each ate a cheeseburger, well Will actually ate two, and they split a chocolate shake. They used the rest rooms. They walked around looking at the Parliament Building and Westminster Abbey. Since they were getting a tour of Parliament the next day, they went to Westminster Abbey. Isabelle said she was more tired than she thought she'd be. Will was more tired than he wanted to admit. But admit it he did and the two of them hailed a black London cab and went to the hotel for a nap.

That night they did team up with the other tourists at dinner and got an outline of what the trip would be like. They introduced themselves to all and exchanged pleasantries with their fellow tourists. The guide told them that all the bags must be outside their rooms before they came to the dining room for breakfast promptly at 7:30 AM. Will and Isabelle headed for the bar. Will got a stiff drink and ordered something not so strong for Isabelle.

"We may have trouble getting to sleep tonight", he said. "I don't want us to be the two old farts, that hold everyone back because we're tired. I want you on time in the morning, Miss. You're never on time. You will be on time tomorrow, Miss."

"It's Mrs. Benton, to you," she said.

"I know. I'm one lucky man" he said gently and he stroked her cheek with the back of his hand. Then he raised his voice and said, "You've never been on time for anything in your life and on this trip you will be. I have spoken."

Isabelle laughed out loud.

The bus tour of London went on as scheduled. The tour guide was informative. The passengers got out at the Tower of London and were met by a costumed Beef Eater who took them all around the Tower talking about history, Henry VIII's wives, and showing the crown jewels. Then it was back on the bus and over to the Parliament building. They saw the House of Lords and the House of Commons in session. They were then left along the Thames to shop at stalls or buy a quick bite to eat. They only had one hour. Isabelle and Will grabbed two bottles of water, three sausage rolls and two Cadbury chocolate bars at a kiosk and they sat on a bench enjoying their lunch and watching all sorts of boats going up and down the river.

Will had changed US money for British Pounds at Logan Airport at a discount booth. He had a wallet full of cash and Isabelle had quite a bit stashed in each cup of her bra. Will thought this was hilarious but she told him there were pick pockets everywhere. He was carrying his wallet in his front pocket to be safe. The next stop was Buckingham Palace. The narrator on the bus was friendly and had a nice personality. Isabelle liked listening to her accent. Then they went onto Hyde Park, Piccadilly Circus and they even saw Sherlock Holmes place at 221B Baker Street. The tourists were deposited back at the hotel and told they were free until dinner.

Will and Isabelle went to the nearest tube station. They wanted to ride it and to see names like Victoria Station, Charring Cross or even the one Harry Potter used to go to Hogwarts, Kings Cross Station. They had no idea where they were going; they just wanted to be able to say the rode the tube and saw the signs that read "mind the gap" as they boarded. They rode the tube and they damn near got lost. They finally found their way back to the hotel, and had dinner with their fellow travelers. The food at the hotel had been good. They were amazed at all the cold cuts that were served at breakfast and pan fried tomatoes too. They found British meats were salty but tasty. At night they had a meat and potato supper and lots of vegetables. They were served water with their meals. Drinks of course were extra. Will and Isabelle tried the hard cider and loved it.

The rest of the trip was as mixed up in Isabelle's brain as it could be. She should have brought a note book to keep track of all the things they saw. All the days were running into each other. She knew they went to Oxford and saw the university, but she couldn't remember which day. She would consult her brochure. Will loved visiting the City of Bath and touring the Roman baths with a set of earphones on his head but he wasn't sure which day they did that. He'd ask Isabelle. They passed through the Cotswold Hills with quaint villages that had wisteria growing down the fronts of the stone buildings, and market squares with butter crosses.

In Stratford on Avon they heard all about William Shakespeare and saw the cottage of his wife, Ann Hathaway. The tour group ate at a nice pub overlooking the Avon River. There were brightly painted and decorated canal boats all lined up along the shore. There was a park where people were feeding birds; many swans were swimming right in front of them in the Avon. Then they all hopped back on board again and the bus took off. Will and Isabelle saw Stonehenge, and visited the Cornwall area where they dined on meat pasties for lunch. In Plymouth they saw where the pilgrims left for America. On the route back to London they stopped at Loo, a tiny fishing village that looked like a post card. There was a dark ancient pub there, filled with smoke, the smell of ale and dogs. These animals were welcome at the pub and came with their owners, the patrons. Will and Isabelle sat and talked with these interesting locals. They were friendly. One woman opened her wallet to show Isabelle a row of photos of her dogs.

The weather held out pretty well but it was England and so they came prepared with rain coats and umbrellas. They saw the rocky terrain in Dartmoor, it made them think of the "Hound of the Baskervilles." Castles and Cathedrals dotted the scenery. Isabelle and Will had a cream tea at a farm, right in the farmer's kitchen. The scones were fabulous, the jam homemade, the double Devon cream rich and the tea hot. The hedgerows were as high as the bus, and the gardens impeccable and everywhere. The tour guide had a great personality and hurried all the passengers along without them even knowing. The bus finished up on the last day and left its charges at their hotel. They were tired but they made love that last night. They wanted to be able to say they did it in London. How childish they were becoming. They slept late the next morning; their flight was late in the afternoon. They were taken to the air port by a shuttle and began their long journey home. They were talking about how much they had seen and saying it was amazing they had packed so much traveling into just ten days. It had been a vacation of a life time and the best anniversary they could have had."

Will told Isabelle, "Now we can say we made love in another continent."

"Always striving for greatness, aren't you" she said.

They both laughed.

When they got home, Will and Isabelle rested for about a week. The fall arrived and with it Halloween, they dressed as Minnie and

Mickey Mouse that year, and at Thanksgiving, they pigged out. At the Christmas party Will made and drank eggnog and the following week he was the cookie sampler and on Christmas Eve he picked up all the torn wrapping paper and filled trash bags with it. Isabelle basked in the glow of the Christmas lights and loved just sitting looking at the lit tree with all the other lights in the house turned off. All the other family gatherings at holiday time went on as usual. The decorations went away, more came out. The fir tree went up and the fir tree came down. Decorations went into their tubs and pine needles into the vacuum.

Winter came and Will and Isabelle went to visit Jack and the family again. They found the air travel tiring. This time they toured the Lake Pontchartrain area. Jack, Jr., Dave and Nina were getting big just like Isabelle's grandkids. Will still told Nina a story before bed and played games of checkers with the boys. Isabelle worked on a jig saw puzzle with them.

Isabelle tried to get the kids interested in the birds from their area and encouraged them to write Papa letters describing and naming them. She suggested that they be pen pals. Secretly she was thinking that they would be learning about the birds, a little science and improving their writing skills with the letters. Jack Jr. said "Isabelle we can e-mail you it would be easier."

She said, "Jack, you're right, I must keep up with the times. We will expect many e-mails from you and Dave and Nina".

They took walks with the children and had long talks with Jack and Marilyn. It had been so good to be in the sun for two weeks and spend time with Jack's family. Will was lucky to have Jack just as she was lucky to have her children. The rest of their vacation flew by and good byes were made, bags were packed and miles flown to get home.

When they returned Isabelle's eye doctor told her she had a cataract in her left eye; and two weeks later she had it removed. Will worried about this but she was fine. They celebrated St. Patrick's Day, hid Easter eggs and went to another First Communion. The years raced by, each one seemed to be going at a faster speed. Life was rushing to an end and Will and Isabelle were trying to make the most of it together. Each night they held each other close always mindful of how fate had brought them together for a reason, growing old together.

They still enjoyed the bird watching and sitting in the yard. They still held hands and sat close. They loved spending time in each others company. One day Isabelle was sitting reading and she looked up and saw Will just staring at her.

She said, "What?"

He said, "I'm glad you danced."

She said, "Me too".

Then they went on to talk about family and friends and all the fun they had in the past two years.

"I wonder if the cousins and friends would get together again in Vermont," asked Isabelle.

"We should ask them", said Will. "Paul and Carol have already gone there for the summer". Isabelle was feeling nostalgic and romantic. So was Will, at least he was feeling romantic. She could be easily swayed. He was still her charming, funny, handsome wonderful Will.

Their romantic mood continued and Isabelle and Will decided it was a good night to be frisky. They hadn't done it in a while and remembered their first time together. They shared with each other all the fears that ran though their minds that night. They laughed out loud.

"Have you ever been on top" Will asked?

"I tried it a couple of times but I don't like it and now that my knees hurt with arthritis, it's hard to get in a comfortable position," said Isabelle.

"I like being on top", said Will. "So I guess that's good. I just thought I'd ask."

Isabelle said "I never had sex with a condom. I was always a Catholic, who got pregnant and now I don't have to worry about that. I'd like to try it with a condom just to see what it's like. Do you mind?"

"You kinky thing", said Will, "OK."

He had to find the box of condoms that he bought so long ago for that first night. He did. They got themselves ready. It takes a while in your seventies although it was easier now that they had been together so long. She didn't have her glasses on and almost used the BenGay instead of KY Jelly. Thank God she noticed just in time. That would have burned like hell; talk about a Hot Mama. The lights were out except for the soft light of several lit candles. The bed was full of love. He was all ready and clad in latex. Then the thunder rolled outside, loud, and the lightening blinked like the paparazzi flashing their cameras. They could see it through the sky lights, bright like a spot light, quickly tuning on and off.  The rain fell; torrential rain. There were big rain drops, making noise as they bounced off the air conditioner, and splashed on the windows. Then it was pouring through the skylights onto the bed. The bed was getting wet. Will was getting wet. Will jumped up to find the pole to close the sky light. He had been ready for sex, really, really ready, hard and ready. He must have bought the wrong size condom because it was rolling down his penis like a fat lady's panty hose. Isabelle stared at this. Did he have on the wrong size? Did they come in sizes?  She was amazed. It looked uncomfortable. Will asked where the pole was. She got out of bed and rushed to the hall to get the pole. She had KY Jelly dripping down her legs. She had put too much in since she didn't know how much jelly a condom needed. Just then the smoke detector went off. Beep, Beep, Beep, Beep.

"It probably just needs batteries", said Isabelle.

"Just give me the pole", said Will, "the bed is getting wet".

The phone rang. Isabelle answered it and said, "Hi, Jeanne. No we still have electricity, I think. Well maybe we don't. We didn't have any lights on. Let me see."

"What do you mean you didn't have any lights turned on?  It's 8:00 PM. What are you doing in the dark?  Oh, please don't tell me; mental picture; too traumatic."

"If she only knew" thought Isabelle, looking at her wet legs and his rubber covered member.

"Well if you need any thing just call." Jeanne hung up.

The mood was kind of ruined. The condom idea was ditched. The jelly wiped. They just tried it the old fashioned way.  Hands were marvelous tools. They knew of ways to start some excitement. The magic juices came out of retirement and all of a sudden it was as if someone shouted "attention" to Will's Willy. Up it went, in it went and everyone was happy.

# CHAPTER THIRTY: KATHY AND JUDY

The following spring, the doctor sent Kathy for tests. She had not told anyone. He did not like the sounds he heard in her lungs. She was laboring for breath last week when she had been at his office. Today she returned to talk to him about the results. She was sitting on the examining table with a Johnny on.

"I'm not going to beat around the bush. You have emphysema. It's in the early stages and frankly I'm surprised it's not more advanced. If you stop smoking now, it may not get any worse. I cannot make any promises. I'm not going to preach and tell you I've been saying this for years. It never helps. What's done is done. Let me listen to your breathing", said the doctor.

He placed his stethoscope on her chest. "It's not too bad today", he said. "Last week you had me quite worried."

Then he listened to her lungs from her back.

"You may have had a cold or an allergy last week that inflamed the lungs. I want you to try this newer stronger patch. I know you tried one before and it didn't work but this time you must give it a little bit longer to kick in. It will make you not want to smoke. Toss out all your cigarettes. I mean it."

He looked at her. He had seen this expression before. He had many patients who were addicted to tobacco.

"You will be wearing one of those oxygen masks with tubes up your nose and carrying a tank with you all the time if you don't stop now. And Kathy, the tanks don't come in black with sequins."

His attempt at humor did not work. Kathy was scared. She did not want to laugh.

He handed her two prescriptions, one for the patch and the other for pills that would help her breathing. He said, "The directions will be on the bottles the meds come in. Read them carefully. I know this is hard but think of it as a second chance. It's all up to you. Good Luck."

He left the room. She got dressed and left.

She went to the CVS near her home and had the prescriptions filled. While she waited she bought a lottery ticket. She won five dollars. She said this is good luck and immediately bought five more lottery tickets with the lucky money. Four were losers but the last one was a winner for fifty dollars. She cashed it in and used it to pay for the pills and patch. When she got home she got rid of all the cigarettes in the house. She soaked them in the sink and then put them in a zip lock bag and tossed them in the trash. That way no matter how desperate she got; even desperate enough to go through the rubbish, they would be soaked and ruined.

Well Isabelle and Will are taking a second chance on each other; this will be my second chance at living. I won fifty dollars today so things are looking up. She took a pill, put on a patch and started a jig saw puzzle.

In Vermont Judy was holding Cat down while the veterinarian gave the animal a shot.

"He's not in any pain except for a little in his arthritic rear legs, said the vet. "But his heart and other organs are wearing out. If I thought it would be better off to put him down, I'd tell you. Let's see how this shot works. Bring him back in a week."

Judy said, "OK".

The pet doctor patted Cat on the top of his head and said, "I think you still have some life left in you old boy."

Judy went to the front desk, paid the bill and put Cat in her car.

On the way home, Judy said, "Cat you're my precious pet. I hope this shot works."

The first day the cat did not want to eat and did not purr when she tickled his neck.

The next two days she watched him. He caught a mouse on the second day. This was a good sign.

Early in the morning three days later, Judy went to let Cat in as she always did. She called him. Cat was on the doorstep. Cat did not move. Cat was dead.

Judy sat on the floor beside him and wept. Two hours later, she grabbed her garden spade and dug a hole in the back yard. She laid the animal in it and covered it with dirt. "You were a good friend to me; I will miss you" is all she could manage to say.

Judy phoned Kathy. She was crying and said "Where is my sister? I've been trying to reach her for an hour."

Kathy said "Carol and Paul went to the Norman Rockwell Museum in Stockbrige with Bob and Esther. They're staying overnight they should be home tomorrow. What is the matter?"

"Cat is dead. I buried him in the back yard and I'm taking the 12:45 bus to Boston. I don't want to be alone and I don't trust myself driving right now."

"What time does the bus get to Boston", asked Kathy.

"Around 5:30 PM", said Judy.

"I'll be there," said Kathy.

When the bus arrived, Judy got into Kathy's waiting car. Her eyes were swollen and red. Kathy said nothing. Judy would talk when she was ready.

They drove in silence for about twenty minutes.

Judy told her about all the trips to the vet. She told Kathy that she never wanted another cat. She said that she was too old. Then she just sighed.

Kathy said "You're not the only one who's lost something you love. I have lost my cigarettes. I have emphysema".

Judy looked at her and reached over and squeezed her arm.

The rest of the ride was silent but each of them thought of their losses. It would sound silly to someone who was not a pet lover or someone who never smoked, but the losses were real.

Kathy took her out to supper at Wendy's. They stopped and bought lottery tickets and booze for martinis and headed to Kathy's house.

"Hell, we need something to cheer us up", said Kathy.

"God damned right", said Judy.

They went home to Kathy's scratched tickets, they were losers; and drank martinis; they were good. They talked about being roommates. Judy said she never wanted to because of all the smoke. Kathy said she never wanted to because of Cat. Well now things had changed. Their losses were changing their lives. Should they do summers in Vermont and winters in Massachusetts like Paul and Carol did. They should at least try it. That way if things don't work out they'd still have their own places to return to. They would have to sit down and discuss finances when they were sober. Think of how many jig saw puzzles we can do and the games of scrabble we can play. We both like the same television shows, and the Red Sox.

"Neither of us loves to cook so we can have sandwiches and pizza even if it's frozen", said Kathy.

"I could bake those blueberry muffins we like and the brownies. I'm good at that." said Kathy

"I can bake potatoes," said Judy.

"There's a plus", said Kathy.

They were both feeling pretty good so they decided to go to sleep before they passed out. When they woke up the next morning, they had headaches and spent the day in the back yard dozing in the sun. Two days later they called everyone over for a card party.

When Paul came in he went over to Judy and said, "I'm really sorry about Cat". He thought he saw tears start to well up in her eyes but she made a valiant recovery. He was grateful because he had no idea how to console Judy. He couldn't bring himself to put his arms around her. He couldn't even hug her. Should he shake her hand? Judy was a complex woman. She was kind, tough, maybe even borderline insane, Paul thought. Judy said, "Thanks, Paul. I know you liked Cat too." He just backed away, now too afraid she might embrace him.

Bob and Esther came in and sat with Will, Susan and Isabelle at one end of the table. Carol, Paul, Kathy, Judy and Tom sat at the other end. There are ten of us so five cards will be the biggest hand. They shuffled and dealt, bid and played, trumped and took in books. Everyone was enjoying themselves. "Why did you lead that?" "You know the rule, third man high". It's an overbid what do you mean it's an overbid?" "I can't believe you threw that card". All these phrases and much more were yelled at each other. That was part of the fun. The scores were tallied and Judy won, again. They came, they played; they lost. Judy always won.

Bob told Esther he would practice Scotch Bridge with her and she would get better. Will told Isabelle she always bid too low. She said that she always liked a sure thing like him. He kissed her hand.

Kathy served brownies one of her few culinary accomplishments and Judy made a pot of coffee.

Susan said, "These are not from a mix are they? They're too good."

Tom said, "Kathy, I see you're not smoking tonight. You haven't quit on me have you," he asked while puffing on a cigarette.

Kathy pulled up her sleeve and showed them the patch.

"I have emphysema."

They all looked at her. Carol and Paul were shocked. They knew about Cat but not about this.

At the end of the card party Kathy said, "Judy and I are teaming up. We're going to live in my house in the winters and in Vermont in the summers. We are a lot alike and will become even more so as the years go by.  No, Judy will not be wearing black all the time but I will not be smoking."  She then told them about her emphysema and the whole story about Cat.

They all made sympathetic gestures to Judy; and gave words of concern to Kathy.

Paul thought teaming up with Judy would be down right scary. He'd never say this to Carol, after all Judy was her sister. How could the same parents have such different daughters? He remembered how lonely he had been before he married Carol. He thought of Judy and Kathy again. Maybe it would be good for them; Judy a teammate, Judy a friend. Judy did dry his shirt. Paul had liked Cat. Then he remembered Judy had had two husbands. Boy they must have been brave men.

# CHAPTER THIRTY-ONE: STILL IN LOVE

The months and seasons passed by and even though they were getting older, Will and Isabelle still felt young. They wanted to make the most of what time they had left. They did fun things. They kept up with the cousins and friends and Isabelle's family too. Isabelle and Will dressed as hillbillies on Halloween, Will carved the turkey at Thanksgiving, and Isabelle set up her Christmas Village. The decorating was less flamboyant and the turkey and the tree smaller.

Their love making was less frequent than when they first married but not less ardent. Will still kissed her breasts and lips each morning. She still longed to lie naked beside him each night. He called her Sweetheart. She still called him Big Guy. When they walked it was almost always hand in hand. They never argued, well almost never. They secretly worried about each other's health. They did not like to talk about dying. But they did have some serious conversations about it. Will said if he died first and although she had a large plot at the cemetery, he did not want to be buried with her and Tim. Three's a crowd he told her. He wanted to be cremated and some of his ashes were to be scatted on the lake where they had met and she and Jack could decide what to do with the rest. She said she would respect his wishes.

"All I ask" said Isabelle is "if I have a stroke or some debilitating ailment, you make sure my hair is colored and my moustache is waxed."

"What a vain woman I married", said Will.

"Look who's talking", she replied.

When January had come and they finally put away all the festive regalia of Christmas, Will and Isabelle decided it was time to head south. They flew to Louisiana again. It tired them more than they thought it would. This time Jack and his family went to Baton Rouge with them to see the state capitol sites. Marilyn suggested they visit New Iberia to see its peninsulas and all the beautiful scenery of the region. Isabelle and Will drove west toward New Iberia listening to a

James Lee Burke mystery CD, called the "The Glass Rainbow". The area had much vegetation and even a jungle garden on Avery Island. They visited the Bayou Teche Museum, The Grotto of Our Lady of Lourdes and Main Street. They saw many Victorian style homes. Isabelle told Marilyn that they had brought a few of Burke's mysteries on CD to listen to for the trip. Since all his stories take place in Louisiana, they thought it fitting.

They stopped at roadside eateries and dined on shrimp. Will and Isabelle loved the area, and went fishing and saw sugar cane fields. They went on a swamp tour and saw some of Louisiana's untamed wilderness. There were many gardens with flowers they didn't know the names of and birds they had never seen before. They returned to Will's family and spent time with Jack, Jr., Dave and Nina. How big they were getting. The children were all on basketball teams and Will and Isabelle cheered at their games. They introduced Jack and his family to Scotch Bridge. They got the hang of it right away. Jack thought this was great. He told his dad that not many families did things together anymore and this was a fun game that they could all play. Will agreed. Things were better between Jack and Will. Their visit with Jack and Marilyn was longer than before. They had stayed almost a month in Louisiana; the southern sun was warming their old bones. When they returned to Massachusetts it was like spring. What a joy not to be here in the snow, Isabelle said when their plane landed at Logan and she viewed the skyline and smelled the city air. This was home.

Once at home, they unpacked, did laundry, settled in; read mail, and paid bills. They both had doctors' appointments. This time, Isabelle's eye doctor found a cataract on her right eye. She had treatment ten days later to remove it. A few days later she was as good as new. Will's doctor told him to lose weight and increased his cholesterol medicine. Isabelle had a filling in one of her teeth replaced and Will's skin doctor removed a small melanoma from his back. They were remembering when they were young and hardly ever saw a doctor and now they had so many.

When the good weather finally came, Easter was upon them. The decorating queen had buckets of silk forsythias all over the house. The table cloths for Easter dinner were pastel plaid. A row of pastel colored candles from Christmas Tree Shops were lined in a row as a centerpiece with jelly beans scattered at their bases. Dozens of pastel eggs were filled with candy and money and then hidden all over the house. She delegated that job to the Easter Bunny, Will. Isabelle filled her candy jars with jellybeans of all colors. A large basket sat in the middle of the kitchen table filled with solid milk chocolate chicks, marshmallow peeps, and small toys. On the bird watching window sill stood two pots of daffodils, one lily and a hot pink hyacinth. Her tiny Easter Village with even tinier bunnies was set up on the fireplace mantel in the living room. Ceramic bunnies of all shapes and sizes were adorning the rooms.

The back yard was colorful with stately tall orange and red tulips blooming, yellow forsythia branches swaying in the wind, and buds of azaleas and rhododendrons showing their pink and purple buds. Birds had returned from their winter's journey and were washing at the bird bath or eating at the feeders. A family of red cardinals was living in one of the bird houses. Squirrels were scampering up and down trees and all over.

Ham was baked with red cherries and pineapple slices. There were scalloped potatoes, Caesar salad, green bean casserole and glazed carrots to be eaten. Jen had given Isabelle the éclair ring recipe and it looked elegant covered with plastic wrap on a doily lined tray in the fridge. Tea and coffee were poured into cups. Bunny cup cakes and macaroon cookies stood on tall tiered plates, waiting to be eaten. It was a family day and they all enjoyed being together again. Love was given, fun was had, food went in, and decorations came down.

A few weeks later they attended a graduation, a month after that the Fourth of July Party. This time Will did win the washer toss tournament. The cousins and friends were together except for Tom and Susan. They always went to their daughter's home in New Hampshire. When August came Will and Isabelle went for a picnic at Webb Park. One of Isabelle's grandsons got engaged. Little Gerry got his driver's license. They went to Tricia's for a bite of her birthday cake. Every night they shared the bed that was now their end of the day comfort zone. How Will loved holding her in his arms and Isabelle loved his shower of kisses on her face. This bed was their heaven on earth.

One day when Will was sitting in the back yard bird watching, Isabelle came up behind him and put her arms around his chest.

She said, "You look so comfortable out here."

Isabelle hugged him and kissed his bald head.

She said "I love you my charming, funny, handsome, wonderful Will."

He held her hands and kissed them. He said, "If you love me so much; make us a cup of tea and come out here and watch the birds with me."

She said "OK."

When she came back he had the binoculars up to his eyes.

He said, "Isabelle, look there's a red tailed hawk".

She looked up and saw it flying away in the distance. She placed the tea tray on the small table between their chairs.

When he saw the plate of cookies he said, "You've out done yourself."

She laughed and sat down beside him. They sipped tea and munched cookies for a few minutes. They were quite when they bird watched. He pointed out the purple finch at the thistle sock. She showed him the blue jay at the feeder. A squirrel was trying to walk the wire Will had hung across two tree branches. The squirrel kept falling but his motions freed the feeder of seeds and the doves were waiting below on the ground for all the feed to fall.

Isabelle said "How lazy they are" pointing to the doves.

They had so many simple pleasures like this. They dozed in the sun. They were truly happy.

Another autumn approached and the pumpkins were bought, the pots of mums stood at each side of the entrance. Isabelle no longer climbed furniture to decorate. She had an old fake tree about ten feet high that was once new at Tricia's wedding. It had been stationed in the dining room for years and then it was put in the back yard with tiny lights on it.

One day she accompanied Will to Lowes. He was buying washers to fix some of the faucets, light bulbs for the recessed light fixtures, and leaf bags and a new rake. She had an artistic idea. She added three cans of spray paint to his cart, red, orange and yellow. He gave her a questioned look but all she said was, "You'll see". Isabelle went to the back yard when they returned home, rested the tree on its side and took all lights off the fake tree. She then began spraying it red and orange and yellow with no rhyme or reason, like Mother Nature painting fall foliage. She turned the tree on its other side and did the same. She paid particular care to the top part since once it was stood up, she'd never be able to reach it. She asked Will to help her stand it up and she continued her work making sure it looked like an autumn masterpiece. When she was done, she said "Come on Big Guy let's go in the kitchen and have lunch." They ate chicken salad, grapes and hot tea.

A few hours later Big Guy brought the tree indoors and they tested the lights; and put all those that still worked back on the tree. Isabelle resurrected two plastic owls that were in the side yard supposedly scaring away woodpeckers from her wood shingles. She washed them off and fastened them to two of the lower branches of the tree. Then she and Will together hoisted the entire tree on top the marble topped buffet that she usually climbed on top of. They stood back to look at their creation. The owls looked back at them.

"There" she said. "We made a new Halloween centerpiece, what fun!"

Will took her in his arms and kissed her.

She said "I think you and I will be Cowboy and Cowgirl for the party."

He said, "This is what keeps you young".

She kissed him back and then said, "Go fix the faucets".

Thanksgiving and Christmas came and went. Will told Jack that air travel was getting to be too much for them. Jack said that he and Marilyn talked about coming to Boston next summer. Would that be OK? Will said that he'd be delighted. Isabelle and Will thought long and hard about this and decided to make the Xbox room and the toy room into one, since the grandkids were almost grown up they didn't really need two play rooms. They could make the bigger room a nice guest room and Jack and Marilyn could be the first to use it. The kids can use the couches. Kids don't mind roughing it.

This was a good winter project for them. They didn't have to go outside too much. They'd buy all their paint and supplies before any storms came. Isabelle had her pen and paper; she loved making lists. They'd be sorting things out, getting rid of things, moving things, painting, picking out a bedroom set, and curtains and bedding. They could take their time. Isabelle was excited. They spent January sorting and discarding. They donated the diaper changing table, the high chair and various toys to charity. They tossed out a lot of old games, a ripped bean bag chair and much more into trash bags. In February they did the same to the Xbox room, washed windows, laundered curtains, had both carpets shampooed. They consolidated and organized the new kid's play room. It looked good.

During the last week in February, Will covered the carpet in old toy room and painted the ceiling. He was tall and did not need a ladder; the step stool was enough for him to reach the edges. Isabelle had chosen a pale green color for the walls. What was it with pale green thought, Will. Didn't Tom have to paint his dining room that color? Women! They all think alike. Isabelle was eager to paint. They were old but still able to push rollers and use brushes. Will proved to be a neater painter than she was. He did all the cutting in. She used the roller. Within a few days it was done even the closet. The plastic drop cloth was removed and the carpet was still clean. Isabelle had ordered the bedroom set on line and it was delivered the following week. The mattress came the next day and she and Will went to Bed Bath and Beyond, because she had two coupons to use and a set of sheets and a comforter to buy. She used the same sheer curtains that had hung there before and got pillows at WalMart. Isabelle had Will bring down the lamp from the wrapping room since she always used the overhead light up there and didn't need it. The room was finished and looked great and it was only the middle of March.

They ate corned beef and cabbage at Jeanne's on St. Patrick's Day. Will had never tried green beer but he liked it. There were hot scones loaded with fat raisins and slathered in butter. Two of the granddaughters entertained the family with their Irish step dancing talents. The Wolfe Tones, Liam Clancy and Celtic Thunder could be heard singing in the background. Everyone wore something green even Will. Shamrocks were hung on doors, and all the kids were trying to find the leprechaun with his pot of gold.

Will hid the eggs again for another Easter and Isabelle baked the ham. The birds still fed in the back yard and the old couple watched them. The years raced by. Isabelle and Will were older and slower but they're love grew stronger.

# CHAPTER THIRTY-TWO: QUEBEC

Before the heat of the summer, Isabelle and Will decided to make a long car trip to Quebec City. They asked the cousins and friends if any of them were interested. Carol and Paul said "Yes". Carol and Paul went to Vermont the weekend prior to the departure date. This would make their ride to Canada shorter. Paul did not like long rides. Will and Isabelle were to pick to them up at 9:30 A. M. That meant Will and Isabelle left Boston at 5:30 AM. Old folks don't like to drive in traffic and they wanted to get an early start. It's only a three hour drive to Carol's place in Vermont but there was coffee to be bought, bagels to be eaten and many bathroom stops had to be made. Will and Isabelle hated to admit it but they were slow. So on one morning late in May the four of them finally left Vermont at 10:00 AM heading to Canada. It was a Tuesday; there was less traffic. They brought along several audio books for the ride. Paul and Carol were not dressed alike and Isabelle was glad to see that Carol had kept her hair brown and bobbed. They had to stop every two hours to pee and get the cramps out of their aging legs; golden years indeed. Will had never been to Quebec. He brushed up on his French. He was going to impress the hell out of Isabelle. He did not. Paul had never been to Quebec and was afraid the Canadians hated Americans. They did not. He was convinced they would cheat him with the money exchange ratio. Carol didn't worry about any of that. Carol and Isabelle had been to Quebec before. They told the men that it was the most romantic city in North America.

Paul was thinking, romantic? What did that mean, romance languages, well French was. Did it mean candle lit dinners and soft music or European style architecture, Art? What were they talking about?

Paul was intelligent, educated and serious.

Will was thinking, romantic? What did that mean, brothels, sex toy shops; X rated films, surely they were not talking about that, at least not Carol.

Will was twisted, erotic, well he was Will.

They listened to an audio book on the drive north to make the ride pass faster. After two hours they stopped for lunch and a restroom. They got back in the car and headed toward Montreal. They spent the night trying their luck at the Casino de Montreal. They all lost except for Paul who had not tried his luck at all and considered gambling sinful. They got very plush rooms at Fairmount's Queen Elizabeth Hotel. It was very expensive but they did it anyway.

Paul looked at Carol and said, "I never knew Will and Isabelle were so extravagant".

"They're not; this is the only vacation they'll probably take this year. Why not go whole hog," she answered.

Will said, "Paul, next year none of us may be mobile enough to travel, we may even be dead. Let's enjoy ourselves."

"I know what you mean, I don't even feel that mobile now", said Paul.

"We have two beautiful women with us. Let's show them a fantastic time. A time they'll never forget", said Will. Then he added, "We can pick up some KY Jelly if you forgot it."

"Please Will, Carol might hear you."

"She'd be glad I mentioned it."

"I am and don't you worry, Will Benton, I came prepared."

"Carol!!" said Paul.

"Good girl", said Will.

The next morning after coffee and croissants, they boarded a tourist trolley and had a narrator tell them all about Montreal. It was a beautiful city with sites like the famous and busy St. Catherine Street, McGill University, Mary Queen of the World Cathedral, and the Planetarium de Montreal. They viewed the Quartier-International, St. Patrick's Basilica, Square Victoria, the Trade Center and Chinatown. The tour covered the entire city; the old and new sections. The St. Lawrence River and its Quays were pointed out along with the adjacent basins and the ships that were docked there were named. The Notre Dame Basilica was spectacular and the guide went to great lengths explaining all its history and that of some of the older buildings that housed banks and hotels. He also talked about several museums, the

City Hall, Marche Bonsecours, an imposing building which was once the farmers' marketplace. There was too much to take in and they hoped to get back to it someday and experience all that was there. The tour had been two hours long and worth it, but now they had to head to Quebec City.

They had checked out of the hotel and put their luggage in the car before going on the trolley and so all they had to do was eat lunch and head to Quebec. They found a restaurant that overlooked the river and ate sandwiches and drank beer. Then they headed northeast to their destination.

It took about three hours to get to Quebec from Montreal and they stopped only once for a bathroom. The ride had been comfortable and they all continued listening to the audio book on the way. The first thing Paul and Will saw was the Chateau Frontenac. They were amazed.

Will could only say, "Wow".

"I can't believe I'm not in Europe," said Paul. "This is so beautiful."

Isabelle showed Will where their hotel was. She had stayed there several times. It was called Hotel Bellevue. It was almost right next door to the Chateau Frontenac and faced the St. Lawrence River. It was better to stay there than in the castle type resort.

Isabelle said, "For one thing, if you stayed at the Bellevue you could look out your window and see the Chateau. If you stayed at the Chateau you could not because you were inside it. If you stayed at the Bellevue it was about ninety dollars per night and the Chateau was about three hundred per night."

Paul said, "Easy choice".

"Agreed", said Will.

They parked the car, checked in and went for a walk. They headed toward the front of the hotel where they walked through a small park which led to the huge boardwalk that flanked the west bank of the St. Lawrence River. The boardwalk, called the Dufferin Terrace was always filled with singers, violin players, mimes and even spoon players day and night. Musicians of all types, clowns, lovers, kiosks and happy people walked. It was a good place to people watch as well. Benches were lined up on both the sides and of course the landmark Chateau loomed above it. They walked to the railings and looked down at Old Quebec and the St. Lawrence; what a view.

They sat on a bench and looked up at the enormity of the Chateau Frontenac and people watched and listened to French conversations they tried to but couldn't understand. After a while they got up and made their way slowly with their stiff knees, through the cobbled stone streets to Anciens Canadiens Restaurant. They all had roast pork dinners with delicious brown wine flavored gravy and the best, freshest Brussels sprouts they had ever eaten. They viewed stoned archways, a bust of Winston Churchill, horse and buggy rides going by, and walked back to the boardwalk area. The performers were many with their caps lying on the ground upside down waiting for coins and bills to be dropped inside. At around 9:00 PM they were ready to call it a day. They went back to their rooms and despite exhaustion, both couples made love but in separate rooms. Quebec was a romantic city.

In the morning the two couples had breakfast at a sidewalk café that was diagonally across from the Chateau Frontenac.

Will tried out his French. "Bonjour", he said to the waitress.

Then he tried an entire sentence. It was bad.

He was trying to order toast, fried eggs, ham and bacon so he said "Rotie, pain, oeuf su la plat, et jambon et lard?"

Qu'est-ce? said the waitress.

Pain rotir, oeuf, et jambon, s'il vous plait.

Toast, fried eggs and ham she asked.

"Oui" said Will "avec lard".

The waitress said he made a good effort.

He said, "Merci".

"At least you got that right", said Isabelle.

Paul said, "Will give up the French".

Carol said, "The waitress was probably only looking for a good tip."

He said, "Well at least I tried."

The three laughed at Will.

They ate and then Will said, "L'addition, s'il vous plait".

The waitress said "Oui, monsieur" and brought back the bill.

The other three were a tiny bit impressed.

They all went for a stroll down the alleys to the left of the café to look at all the artists' work. Prints of all sorts, watercolors, pastels and even framed photos hung all over the walls and on easels with people standing beside them waiting for tourists to make purchases. Paul tripped on the cobble stones but Carol caught him. Will muttered something like damn those crocks to Isabelle. She ignored him.

It was warm and sunny and they turned back and headed toward the boardwalk where the Funicular stood waiting to take them to the lower city. The funicular is like an elevator with a glass front; and it glides down the side of the high cliff, from Upper Quebec to the lower city. The ride saves much walking especially for seniors and the view from the glass front is spectacular, showing the old buildings, river and cafés below. Carol did not like heights but climbing hundreds of stairs even less. They entered the funicular and Paul put his hands over Carol's eyes. Why she couldn't just shut them was beyond Will's comprehension. The box filled with people descended and glided down the side of the cliff. Paul said that he felt a little queasy. Isabelle assured him that the ride only took a minute. Paul kept Carol's eyes covered. Carol said that the feeling of falling always made her sick. Isabelle looked at Will. The elevator stopped. The couples got off and were delighted to see all the shops, old architecture and cafes.

They were near the river too. They walked toward the St. Lawrence, saw a cruise boat, bought tickets and boarded. It was a beautiful ride along the river. The recording was loud and narrated the history of old Quebec, pointed out the sites, like the Montmorency Falls, the skyline and of course the Chateau high in the background. When the cruise was done, the couples separated to look into shops and sites in the lower city. They agreed to meet back at the hotel around 4:00 PM.

Isabelle and Will walked along The Rue du Petit Champlain and visited the boutiques, art galleries and handcraft shops. They stopped at a bistro and had an omelet and salad lunch. They were impressed at the fine craftsmanship of the objects of art that were being offered. Isabelle picked out a few pairs of handmade mittens to give at Christmas. Will saw a wooden miniature of the Chateau Frontenac with a perfect photo inlay adhered to its front. It was really lovely and he said he wanted it for a souvenir. She told him that's why she loved him so;

his thoughts were loving and meaningful. She wanted to kiss him right then and there. She did. He said it would always remind him of this trip. He told Isabelle she was right about it being romantic and it was the closest thing to Europe, North America had.

Carol and Paul browsed in many of the shops and were surprised to see so much Native American influences. There were many leather and beaded handicrafts and books about legends and history of the Huron Nation. There was music playing in the background with Indian flutes and soft drums. Paul loved the sound. They bought the same CD to bring home. Carol saw a pair of brown leather slippers that were lined and looked comfortable. She purchased a pair for each of them. Hanging plants hung all along the streets on both sides, the sun was bright; the place was magical. They ate lunch at a side walk café that viewed the river and even had a drink of wine.

"This is a romantic place," said Paul. "Want to go back to the hotel room for an afternoon of delight?"

"I'll even risk the Funicular for that", said Carol and off they went.

At 4:00 PM Will knocked on their door. He heard a lot of giggling from Carol and commotion. He thought Jeez are they doing it?

Paul came to the door wearing only a towel around him. He said, "Um, Err, Ah we, I mean I was just taking a shower." His hair was dry and his body was dry.

Will knew Paul couldn't lie if his life depended on it and said. "We took the liberty of making a reservation for dinner at the revolving restaurant up town. I hope you don't mind. Isabelle says it's a good place and we can get a view of the city at day light and night time too if we go around 7: 00 PM. Is that good?"

"Sure, Sure", said Paul in a hurry to get back to his wife. "When do we meet?"

Will said, "How about 6:45 P M in the lobby. We'll take the car. There's parking"

"OK, see you then", said Paul and he closed the door.

Clearly Paul wanted to get back to whatever he was doing. Out of the corner of his eye, Will saw Carol peek from under the bed covers. Paul you sexy devil, thought Will, an afternoon delight.

When he went back to his own room he relayed what had happened to Isabelle and she said, "What a great idea."

Will, always eager to please, said, "I'm willing."

They enjoyed the revolving restaurant except for when Carol put her purse on the floor on the wrong side of the table. That part of the floor remained stationary and did not move as they revolved away from it.

"My money and our pass ports are in it", she said.

"How would they get back into the United States?" said Paul.

It took a while but the waiter located the purse and everything was in it.

The next day they went to watch the changing of the guard at the Citadel, the goat who was the mascot tried to butt Paul in the rear end a few times but one of the soldiers got the animal in hand. They were all impressed by the fort and walked back to the Rue St. Louis where they had lunch outside.

In the afternoon they boarded a bus to have a professional tour of the city and of the Isle d'Orleans. When you're seventy- something, it is easier to tour on one's seat rather than on one's feet. Their last stop was a quaint bakery which gave all the tourists a free cup of coffee and a slice of freshly baked bread, hot and spread with maple butter. The smell of the place alone was intoxicating. The bread tasted so good. Everyone wanted more. That was the idea. And loaves of bread were purchased. Jars of maple butter put into bags and second cups of coffee drank. One Japanese tourist bought a whole case of the maple butter jars, and maple candy leaves as well. They went to Mass late Saturday afternoon and thought of how different it was to hear all the prayers recited in French.

They checked out of the hotel on Sunday morning early and loaded up the trunk with their bags. It was raining and cool. They walked to a fabulous five room buffet brunch around 10:00 AM at the Chateau Frontenac. It was expensive but a once in a lifetime treat. It was the highlight of the vacation. Will and Paul pigged out. They had never seen such a variety of food in their lives. They had a table that overlooked the boardwalk with the St. Lawrence River behind it. Isabelle and Carol especially loved the dessert room, so much chocolate,

French pastries, cakes, mousse and every dessert imaginable. They all took their time with rests in between courses. They watched the activity on the boardwalk and the boats on the river. They didn't finish until 1:00 PM. What a time they had had! These were memories they would keep forever.

They headed back to the states. Rain continued for most of the ride. Crossing the border was easy; all their papers were in order. They drove right though to Vermont only stopping for bathrooms, after that brunch they said they'd never eat again. They would. Will asked Isabelle for Tums. Paul burped out loud. They finished the audio book about a half hour before they reached Carol's home. The windshield wipers moved back and forth and the car moved a little slower. They chatted about all they had seen and how happy they were to have made the trip.

Isabelle and Will stayed over night with Paul and Carol. This time they were allowed to share a room. The next morning they had breakfast at Sunnyside Up and Will and Isabelle took off for Boston. The sky was overcast but hopeful. They both vowed to diet and exercise when they got home and they promised to make each other keep those vows. They were fat.

# CHAPTER THIRTY-THREE: COUSINS AND FRIENDS

When spring was at its best, Judy and Kathy decided to have a hen party. They asked Esther, Carol, Susan and Isabelle to come for lunch. They agreed on a date towards the end of May and Isabelle arrived on time for once.

The site that greeted them astounded the guests. Judy had maroon hair and Kathy had a paler, orange version.

"What in the world have you two done" said Isabelle?

"Oh, we were having our hair done", said Kathy, "and the hair dressers cut our hair beautifully and the new girl passed them the wrong bottles of dye and voila here we are two weird looking women. We can have it changed back but we have to wait a month so we don't go bald."

"Yeah, we don't want to look like Will", said Judy.

"We'll have it fixed next month", said Kathy.

"You will", said Judy. "I'm going back to my natural color and cut. My beauty days are over."

"Your beauty days were over a long time ago" said Kathy.

"And while were on that subject" said Judy, "how I ever let you talk me into fake nails is a mystery. I almost broke a few of them off before Carol's wedding and that was only hours after they were put on. I did break two at the reception. And they looked like claws. I didn't find anything attractive about them. They got dirty. Do you know how much dirt I got under them? I was bleaching my fingers every night after I had them put on.

"That's probably why they broke off. The bleach weakened them", Kathy said.

"You should keep going to the salon and have your hair done and you don't have to get the nails. Your hair cut looked adorable", said Isabelle.

"Oh come on Judy", said Susan. "You may want a boyfriend. Remember how pretty you looked at Carol and Paul's wedding? I think purple is your color and you should not cut your hair too short."

They all chatted about news of each other families and gossip. Esther said, she and Bob went to Lexington and Concord and had a nice tour of the historic sites and they had tickets to see a show next month in a nearby community theater. Susan said her youngest daughter was pregnant and Tom was thinking taking photos again. He wanted to get some shots of the grandkids. Isabelle told them about her new guest room that she and Will had just finished. Judy told them about a bean supper she and Kathy attended and how they farted for days afterward and you know what that's like in the winter with no doors or windows open. Even Fabreze can't cure that smell. Kathy had some new photos of her grandkids that she passed around. Kathy said she and Judy were becoming regulars at Thursday night BINGO. They talked about how they spent their Easters. Esther and Bob of course went to Isabelle's. Judy went out to eat with Paul and Carol. Kathy went to her son and daughter-in-law's and Susan and Tom went too their oldest daughter's home in New Hampshire. Isabelle told them how Will loves filling and hiding all the eggs. He's really embraced this mottled crew I call my family and they like him as well.

Judy said, "I remember the first Easter I didn't have the egg hunt. My boys were getting older and I was a single mom. I put one big basket on the kitchen table and put some candy in it like their favorite things, and whiffle balls and decks of cards and a couple of CD's and shit like that and many boxes of condoms. The boys were quite surprised to see the condoms. A couple of them were young. One even thought the condoms were balloons. But it's never too soon to tell them the facts of life and how to practice safe sex. I told them they had to protect themselves from diseases. I told them I knew they were young and horny. I said I knew it was hard for a guy keep it in his pants. I told them I knew they had all those hormones and testosterone and whatever raging inside them. I let them know that if they got someone pregnant they would pay for that little bastard forever".

I said, "Don't listen to any girl who says she's on the pill. Girls lie. They try to trap you. It only takes a minute to put a rubber on; it takes a lifetime and a lot of money to support some illegitimate little fucker."

I told my boys they could discuss anything with me.

I said "The condom is the way to go".

One of the little pricks, the oldest, said "Ma, I love condoms. In fact I'm wearing one right now".

I slapped him upside his head before he knew it was coming.

They all laughed out loud.

Judy and Kathy put the cold cuts and breads on the table along with condiments. They had a bowl of chips and a dish of pickles. There was ice tea and wine. "Dig in," they said. "It's just a simple lunch." They all ate in silence. They were hungry. Then the conversations started again.

Kathy said, "I've given up my ballroom dancing lessons and my water color painting. I'm too old to dance and I have no talent for art. I had fun while I was doing it but I could use the money to go on a trip or fix something or buy a new outfit."

"Did you like the dancing," asked Susan.

"I did for a while. I was younger. I didn't start until I was a widow. I don't know why I really started. A friend of mine in work was going, so I went with her. She quit after two weeks but I enjoyed it at first and it was a little exercise. I wasn't really looking for romance which was good since most of my partners were gay. I didn't care, they were good dancers and I didn't have to be bothered with relationships. I just wanted a night out and a diversion from the bank and kids. It worked."

Carol said, "Have any of you ever danced naked?" They all looked at her in amazement.

"Alone or with someone", asked Kathy?

"Oh, with someone," said Carol.

Isabelle said, "No, Have you?"

She said "Yes and it's so liberating. You should all try it".

Susan said "This is a side of you we don't know."

"I'm surprised Paul doesn't find it sinful", said Esther.

"Oh, Paul says if we're married it's alright," said Carol.

"I don't want to know anything about this", said Kathy. "And don't think for one minute that Judy and I will be dancing naked. Not alone and definitely not together."

Isabelle burst out laughing.

Judy said, "If this is Paul the pervert's idea of foreplay, he can just stop hanging around with the Cappellos. All you guys are into some serious crap. I mean it borders erotic lunacy. We really don't want to hear about you and Paul doing it. I have to say though, while were on that subject, that when I was married, I used to think that if I was a guy I'd really feel sorry for my balls"

"OK", said Susan biting her lip and trying not to laugh. "Why would you feel sorry for your balls if you were a guy"?

"Well the penis gets to go in and do a lot of good stuff. The balls just hang outside flopping on the furry rug. I thought about this a lot, usually while we were having sex. And I came to the conclusion that they were probably just stupid, lazy little shits anyway and were perfectly happy on the furry rug."

Susan almost choked on her ice tea and Esther had tears running down her face she was laughing so hard.

Isabelle said, "I think I wet my pants".

Carol said, "Judy, don't you dare call Paul and me an erotic lunatics after relating all that to us."

Kathy said, "Ladies let's clean up the conversation. Our dear sainted mothers would be upset about this".

All the women laughed again and Esther said, "What fun we had when we all went to Vermont that time. It's been a few years now. I can't thank you girls enough for your hospitality and it was so nice to see your neighbors. I enjoyed the water and I don't even swim well. The concert was great, the cards and don't forget Mr. D'Arcy. We're all too old for that stuff now but aren't we lucky we made those memories."

They all nodded and agreed, looking at Carol and Judy.

"We could have another day at a lake" said Carol. "You could all come to see Paul and me here in Massachusetts. We could have a cook out and everyone could bring one thing so no one has to do too much. I'll talk it over with Paul and we will make some plans."

Isabelle said "Good for you Carol. We'd all be glad to bring something. We could swim, and row and Will could help Paul with the grilling".

"I know Tom would like that", said Susan. "He's such a stick in the mud. He's the oldest of all of us so he doesn't travel well these days. We'd just have to walk across the lawn and we'd be there."

Kathy said "What do you want me to bring, blueberry muffins or brownies. Those are the only things I do well? Oh, maybe pasta salad, I can do that too."

"Bob would love another card game and fishing too", said Esther.

Carol said "Let's not get ahead of ourselves. I have to talk to Paul first".

"Well talk to him while you're dancing naked; and he'll say, Yes", said Judy.

They all laughed and got up to leave.

The men were not to be outdone by the women.

Paul said "Why don't we hang out at my house while the ladies lunch. We could order pizza and drink beer and have a good old gossip."

The four men sat on Paul's back steps facing the lake. They had beers in their hands and a pizza box was on the top step with its cover opened.

Will said, "Bob did you know I went to a nudist colony?"

Bob said, "What, you went to a Buddhist colony? I thought you went to church with Isabelle now."

Will spoke louder and said, "Not Buddhist, nudist."

Bob said, "You went to a nudist colony. When recently? Does my sister know? Was she with you?"

"No it was a long time ago. I think Isabelle knows about it. She did not go.

"How did she feel about that?" said Bob.

"Well it was over and done with long before I married Isabelle," said Will.

Why did you go there?

Why do you think?

"I don't think the Catholic Church would approve of this. It would be putting oneself in a near occasion of sin, very near. Am I right Paul?" said Bob.

"Probably" said Paul "but Will was a little younger and he's not Catholic".

"Is it against the law?" asked Bob. "Did you get arrested"?

"Not in Louisiana" said Will. "I saw some very interesting things there. Some folks don't mind prancing around naked but they have to wear shoes. Others, women mostly, wore nothing but jewelry, lots of jewelry, beads and shit. I saw one guy wear only flip flops on his feet and another wore only a cowboy hat."

"That was probably you, Will, so the ladies didn't know you were bald", said Tom.

"No, it was not me. I had on the Red Sox cap."

"Yes and the string around your waist to hold your wallet," said Paul.

"I could never do this", said Bob. "I need pockets".

Tom burst out laughing.

"What's so funny", said Bob, "It's true; I need my reading glasses, my inhaler, my handkerchief; my cell phone, my wallet, my compass, my pen; my small pad of paper, and my tiny flash light."

"You carry all that stuff with you in your pockets" said Tom.

"Yes, I need them."

"I think it's a good idea" said Paul.

"You would" said Tom.

"But Will", said Bob, "where would a guy like me put all that stuff"?

"I saw one guy wear a fanny pack and the pack part was at his side so he could show off his goods. You could get something like that if you went", said Will.

"Well I'm not going, Will Benton and I hope you don't suggest this to anyone, especially my sister." said Bob.

I did but she said "No."

"She said "No". Thank God." said Bob, "Paul she hasn't lost her faith".

"Just her mind" said Tom, "She married Will".

"Ha, Ha" said Will, "very funny."

"Anyway at this nudist colony they had a baseball game", continued Will. "You guys would have loved it especially watching the girls run the bases. They flopped all the way from first base to home. All you could see were boobs bouncing up and down. It must have been painful. It would have been for Isabelle."

"Please, Will that's my sister you're talking about." said Bob.

"How about your old ball sack", said Tom, "Didn't your boys hurt as they did the flop around to home plate"?

"Oh, I never played. I was too old. I just watched."

"Let's change the subject", said Bob.

They each grabbed another slice of pizza and ate while the sauce, cheese and olive oil dripped down their fronts. Napkins were niceties they did not need. Paul told them about the great time they had in Quebec. Tom said that he and Susan had been there years ago and it was a beautiful city. Bob told them he went with his mother and Carol's parents when he was younger. He thought it was nice but didn't understand French so it was hard to communicate.

Tom told them he was going to start taking photographs again and said he saw so much still life on the lake yesterday he was ashamed he hadn't thought of this before. Why did he let himself get away from it? He liked photography and today everything is digital and can get hooked right up to your computer. He had learned how to use a new camera and it was very interesting. He wanted to compare the old and the new. He was going to have fun with it.

They talked about the Red Sox game yesterday; the kind of fertilizer they liked best for the lawn; the new restaurant at the Mall and politics. The men said they hoped to get some fishing in this year. Will told them about making a guest room and how he painted it pale green. Tom asked him why women like that color. He said that he had no idea.

Bob said he and Esther went to Lexington and took a narrated tour in a small bus and they were told all about Paul Revere's Ride, the Bunker Hill battle and the Revolutionary War in general. They saw the bridge the troops marched on, Louisa May Alcott's House, and Walden Pond. He said it was very informative and there was a museum and a beautiful old tavern where they had lunch at. It was a good take and he recommended it.

Paul said since they came back from Quebec and listened to the CD of Native American music, he and Carol have been going to Indian Pow Wows. They are quite interesting. There was one in Canton with costumes and dancing and there was one at Bridgewater College where they had all sorts of publications, and handcrafted items on sale. Traditional foods and music were there as well. We are now reading Tony Hillerman's books, the Leaphorn series, about two detectives in the Navajo Nation.

"I've read them" said Tom "They're great".

"Me too" said Will. "I liked them a lot."

"You know", said Bob, "Channel 2 made three of those books into a series for TV. They're going to be on next month. I'll look at the flyer they sent me and let you know. You'd probably like them."

"I'll remind you" said Paul, "I'm really interested."

They drank their beers and Tom lit up a cigarette. Will got another slice of pizza and Bob did too.

Bob said, "Will when you went bald did your hair come out fast or did it take a while? I have this bald spot and it's gotten much bigger in the last few years."

"Yeah" said Paul, "I don't remember you starting with a bald spot. You lost the hair in the front first. My bald spot isn't that big but a lot of hair goes down the drain when I wash."

Will said "I remember it well. I was only twenty-six when my hair started falling out and a year later I was almost totally bald".

"Did you cry? It must have been traumatic for you", said Tom sarcastically.

"Fuck off", Tom. "How would you know what it felt like? You're almost eighty years old and you still have a full head of hair, how come?"

"You guys need more testosterone; especially you Will. I'm virile", said Tom.

"My testosterone is just fine", said Will.

"Mine too", said Paul

"What, wine too?" said Bob.

They all looked at him.

Will said, do you guys remember when I got my first divorce and got a transfer to a post office in Maine to get away from everything?

"Yeah", said Paul. "You were a mess. First Isabelle dumped you and then you married a child, who you found in bed with another guy. I don't blame you for wanting to get away."

In all fairness to the other guy, he married Jill, so I never had to pay alimony to her. I wanted to pay the child support for Jack and I did, but when I left Massachusetts to go to Maine, I was in a bad way. I still thought of Isabelle all the time even though I knew that was over. I thought of Jack and I knew I could only see him on weekends. I was screwed. But more importantly how was I going to find another girl with my bald head. It's not easy to be almost totally bald at twenty-seven. I never told you guys this, and don't tell the girls, they'd never let me live it down but I bought a wig when I was working in Maine. I moved up there on a Saturday. Jill and Charlie had taken Jack to meet Charlie's family and she said she would let me have Jack two days the following week. I agreed. I told her I needed the time to move anyway.

I went to a store that makes toupees and wigs and tried many of them on. I figured my old hair wasn't that great anyway so I tried for a new look. First I thought the curly dark hair would be good, but I looked like someone in the Mafia. I tried a blonde beach boy wig, it kind of hung on my forehead but it was too youthful for my face. I put on a reddish regular medium cut with side burns and I looked awful. Then I found a light brown short regular man's hair cut. It was kind of like my own hair used to be. It suited me best. So I paid the guy. It cost $1,200.00. That was a lot of money in those days but I was a vain desperate man. I started work the following Monday and I wore the wig. I didn't have to move around too much since I was delivering mail then and anyway we had a hat as part of our uniform. No one noticed it was fake hair.

Well I made a date with a girl, who worked inside the post office, who I saw every day when I picked up my mail bag, bad mistake. Never date someone you work with. If it doesn't work out, and it didn't; you have to face her every day. I took her to dinner. Every time I looked down at the menu the damn hair piece slipped down onto my forehead. The first few times she didn't notice but when if fell into my spaghetti she laughed right in my face. In fact she laughed so loud waiters came to the table and then they laughed. We didn't even finish the meal. She couldn't stop laughing, she really made a scene and I was humiliated. I paid the bill and took my marinara sauce covered wig and left.

The girl, I don't even remember her name, said "Please let me walk home by myself". I did.

She shouted as she walked away, "And don't ever ask me out again". I didn't.

I washed the wig when I got home. I used regular shampoo. I didn't want it to smell like tomatoes and garlic. I had paid a lot of money for it. It still smelled and now it shrunk and looked like a hairy yarmulke on top of my big bald head. I had to face that girl everyday for the next six months. She laughed every time she saw me, the bitch. I wonder how good she looks now. I tried to return the wig at the store and the guy looked at me and said, "You can't really expect me to take a shrunken, garlic smelling wig back." He was right of course. I had to throw it away. What a waste of time and money. At the end of the six months time I transferred back here even though I had to work the night shift again it was better than facing that bitch at the post office every day. You'd think she'd just let it go but she didn't.

"You've lived an unusual life, Will Benton, I don't know why my dear sister, Isabelle, married you." said Bob.

"I'm all choked up and ready to cry, I feel so sorry for big bald you", said Tom

"You were stupid to buy a wig; I never would have paid that price. You should have just been yourself", said Paul.

"Screw all of you. I think it's time to get our wives, Bob. Let's leave these two insensitive bums."

# CHAPTER THIRTY-FOUR: ISABELLE AND WILL AT HOME

In early June, Will and Isabelle took a drive to Newport Rhode Island. They toured one of the mansions, the Breakers. That was her favorite. They took a harbor cruise and let the wind blow in their faces. The waves were choppy but not rough. The sun was strong but it was not humid. He had his arm around her as they sat in their seats looking at the sites. When the cruise ended they went for lunch. They were enjoying a nice meal at a waterfront restaurant. They didn't eat that much anymore. He was having a bowl of sea food chowder and she was eating a salad plate with avocados and pears.

"Remember when we could actually walk the Cliff Walk?" said Will.

"Those days are gone", said Isabelle. "I'm lucky to walk around the house and I noticed Tom going down stairs the way I do the other day, with two feet on each step before heading to the next. You're lucky your knees still work, Will".

"Yeah, Tom's got arthritis like you. I told him about the gel shots you get in your knees and he's going to ask his doctor about it but to tell you the truth, I think his are worse then yours. He really needs new knees and he's too old for the surgery."

The waitress came and asked if they wanted coffee or dessert. They said "No".

Will paid the bill and they left.

When they got in the car they drove to another beach, Brenton Point, and watched all the kites flying high over the rocks. Will drove through Fort Adams remembering the time they sat at the picnic table on the hill and ate sandwiches and coffee. Isabelle thought of the time they came here in the winter and viewed the Astor's mansion and went to a huge flea market at the Viking Hotel. She reminded Will of the time they came to the Vanderbilt's mansion during the Christmas season and saw how it had been decorated in earlier days when there were no mini lights and certainly no LED lights. There were candle sticks with holly and ivy around their bases and candles lit everywhere. People dressed in period costume, offered them Wassail Bowl punch and someone played the piano. Other actors asked them to dance. They were portraying how the holiday had been celebrated in the early nineteen hundreds. He told her he remembered it. It was nice that they had made so many wonderful memories.

They headed home and Isabelle said, "Will, let's get ice cream cones at Newport Creamery".

He said "Yes, why not".

They did, butter pecan and chocolate chip. She bit the end off the cone and sucked out the ice cream. He gently patted her shoulder she gave him one of her best smiles.

On the last Monday, of the month, Jack and Marilyn arrived in Boston with their children. The kids had never flown before and were excited. It was quite an experience for them.

"It was nice of your Dad to send us the plane tickets" said Marilyn, "he's a generous man".

"He probably figures I'll get his money in the end anyway", said Jack,

"That's not kind", said his wife.

"I think he misses the kids", Jack replied. "Let's get our luggage and rent a car".

The family from Louisiana arrived at Isabelle and Will's in time for dinner. It had been a hot humid day but Jack and the rest of them were used to this. Isabelle and Will greeted them with open arms and told the kids to put their bags in the kids play room and showed Jack and Marilyn their room. Marilyn commented on what a beautiful home she had and Jack shook his father's hand. Jack noticed that Will and Isabelle looked older and maybe frailer. It bothered him but there is nothing anyone can do to hold back time. It just keeps marching on.

Because of the heat, Isabelle had prepared a cold supper. She made her famous chicken salad with cranberries and walnuts, a plate was full of sliced ham and had another with a salad of sliced hard boiled eggs, spinach, sliced pepperoni, olives and sliced red peppers. There was a bowl of store bought potato salad, rolls, and chips. There was peach cobbler for dessert. Isabelle had just put it in the oven and she had vanilla ice cream to go on top. They all ate as if they were starving.

There was small talk at the table. The flight was on time and went smooth. The kids were excited at the airports.

"This was a very generous gift you have given us" said Marilyn to Will. "We could never have afforded the price of five air fares and we really wanted to see you both."

"My pleasure," said Will.

Jack said, "I'd like the kids to see the lake while we're here if that's OK. Do Tom and Paul still live there?"

"Yes" said Will "I'm sure they'd like a visit from you. Perhaps you could stop there on the way to or from Cape Cod".

Jack and Marilyn planned to take the children to Cape Cod at the end of the week for a few days to see the sights. "Sounds good" said Jack.

"Maybe you could come too and we could fish," said Jack.

"My days of rowing and getting in and out of small boats are over", said Will, "but I could certainly teach the boys and Nina how to cast from shore and we could catch a few that way."

"I'll call Tom and Paul and see what day is good for them OK?"

Jack looked at the kids and said, "What do you think of going fishing on a lake with Papa".

"Cool", said Jack Jr.

"Sounds Great", said Dave.

"Thanks for including me Papa" said Nina.

Will smiled at all of them, they were getting older; Nina was not the little girl who played with dolls anymore.

"I have a surprise for you", said Will.

"I got us tickets to a Red Sox game. Tickets are hard to come by so I was lucky to get seven. There not the greatest seats but we're going to have a great time. You can even get a cap like mine."

"That's great" said Jack, "but what an expense. You've already done so much".

"Please, if we went to Louisiana we would have spent money. Let's have a good time together," said Will.

Marilyn was looking out the bird watching window and said "What a nice view you have of the birds".

Isabelle answered, "We love to watch the birds. The garden used to be tended to better. I used to plant new flowers and divide old ones every year and I weeded all the time. My knees don't work as well as they used to so now I can't be bothered."

"If there's anything you'd like us to do in the garden while we're here, we'd be glad to help" said Marilyn.

"Oh for heavens sake", said Isabelle, "this is your vacation. I want you to be our guests and have fun. I've learned that all my years of hard work on the garden have been wasted. The birds and particularly the squirrels love disorder. The small twigs are grabbed by the birds for nests and the overgrown shrubs provide hiding places. God made these weeds so He must love them. Who am I to question, birds, squirrels and God Himself?"

They all laughed.

When they finished eating, Isabelle told the children they could use the Xbox and the TV in the kid's play room if they wanted to. She said that she only had one guest room which their parents would share and they could choose whatever couch they wanted in the TV room or the living room. There's even a couch upstairs near our room and the wrapping room. It's in the balcony and there's no real privacy but Papa and I will not be looking at you. There's a bathroom on each floor so there are three. We won't have any problems taking showers or whatever. Please make yourselves at home. The sleeping bags and pillows are on the couch in the living room.

Nina said "I want the balcony."

She got her bag and said "Mom, will you bring the sleeping bag and pillow. I want to see the wrapping room".

Marilyn said "Me too".

The girls went up stairs with Isabelle slowly bringing up the rear. The girls were impressed by the wrapping room. Once again there was a half finished centerpiece. A village scene being repaired and all the great stuff women would want in gift wrapping paradise.

"This is awesome", said Nina. "Do you let the grand kids come in here".

"Not too often" said Isabelle, "There are secrets in here. I shop all year round so they might see their birthday or Christmas gift or someone else's. These days I give money most of the time but I like to give a little gift with it as well. Everyone likes to open a gift."

Nina and Marilyn looked lustfully at the wrapping room. What a great place.

Isabelle enjoyed having children in the house again. She liked the sounds of laughing and yelling even the sibling spats. It reminded her of how things used to be. Will was a bit overwhelmed. He liked when he visited Jack and Marilyn even when he lived with them. Jack and Marilyn had rules and the kids obeyed them. They were usually at school or out side. But this was his haven; his love nest, his and Isabelle's. He really didn't want intruders living there. He told Isabelle how he felt that night in bed. She said "You surprise me Will Benton" and then kissed him.

On Tuesday morning they all boarded the commuter boat to Boston, arrived at Long Wharf and went to the Aquarium. Jack Jr. and Dave were amazed that there were divers who swam with the sharks while feeding the other fish. Nina loved the penguins. When they were through with learning about living under the sea, and watching dolphins perform; they decided to take a real tour of Boston.

They boarded the Bean Town Trolley and they were given a professional's view of the city. The walking was getting to Will and Isabelle so they were glad to sit for a while. The narrator told them about so many wonderful places, and talked about the importance of this city in Colonial Times and its subsequent history. They looked at landmarks, buildings, churches, the Freedom Trail, the Boston Common, the Constitution and many other sights. When the trolley was near a stop in the North End, Will told them all this was the one to get off at and they all went for a nice Italian meal.

They walked back to the commuter boat very slowly, Isabelle was hot and tired. They stopped at a bench for a rest when they reached the waterfront park. Will was fanning himself and Isabelle with his baseball cap. They sat for a while and then headed to Long Wharf to catch the boat home. No one wanted much for dinner so they picked at the cold cuts and the boys had sandwiches with their dad. Nina and rilyn had the left over peach cobbler and fought over the ice cream. ll and Isabelle went to bed.

On Wednesday they drove to Easton, Massachusetts in two cars with Will in the lead. It was about an hour's drive and they saw a Civil War Re-enactment. There were cannons, and people dressed like soldiers and they had all sorts of weapons. The cannons went off with loud bangs and clouds of smoke. There were men on horses portraying the cavalry. Some men pretended to be shot dead or wounded, others carried on the good fight. A huge man, about Will's age, was the general who stood by the sidelines speaking to the crowd watching this spectacle. He had an impressive uniform with a satin sash at the waist, a fancy hat and a sword in his hand. The general narrated the battle to the spectators and the fighting continued.

When the battle was over they were able to speak to the participants. The general told them that he not only belonged to a Civil War Re-enactors group but a Revolutionary War group as well. He said that he played the grandfather of the civil war general when he was in his Revolutionary War show. His persona in one was an engineer and a doctor in the other. Jack thought it was fascinating. The boys wanted to see all the weapons and the horses. Nina, Isabelle and Marilyn wanted to look at the women's dresses and see how one lady was making kettle corn and another was making butter. There were stalls set up where you could buy things and it was interesting to walk around and look at them. One of the soldiers had carved the top of his trunk so well that it looked like real articles were sitting on top of it like the soldier's cap, a rifle, a powder horn complete with leather strap. What an artist he was.

On the way home they stopped for pizza. The kids said they felt like they were getting spoiled.

Isabelle said, "Why not, we don't get to see you enough."

They went home and sat in the back yard with the kids and named all the birds that came to feed and use the bird bath. Jack and Marilyn sat in chairs drinking lemonade. They were marveling at Isabelle's hill. Her back yard was small flat piece of land. About fifteen feet from the back of her house then it became a garden filled hill. It was unusual but it was hers. At one time she had different levels with many flowers and vegetables. But as the years passed she became old and her knees more arthritic. So she stuck to perennials like day lilies, peonies and irises and let them come back all by themselves each year. She started to plant evergreens and boxwoods and tulip bulbs and things that didn't need tending. She told them that it was a sand pit when she and Tim first bought the house and how both their mothers hated it. But Tim made levels with rocks and I planted and now it's this. I told you I'm too old to make it orderly any more; I just let God grow what he wants there now.

"What's at the top of the hill, Isabelle" asked Nina.

"A cemetery", she said, "So they're nice quiet neighbors".

They all laughed.

The boys passed the binoculars back and forth and Nina said she thought the squirrel was greedy. Will agreed.

Marilyn said "I can understand why you like it out here; it's so peaceful, there's no one looking in at you."

Thursday was Red Sox day. The game was in the afternoon. Will didn't think he could stay awake long enough for a night game. Jack made a trip to Dunkin Donuts for coffee and muffins. When he returned he said, "We don't have Dunkin Donuts in Louisiana and Marilyn has become addicted. It is the best coffee in the world".

Isabelle surprised them all when a limo pulled up at noon and drove them all to Fenway Park.

Will said, "Isabelle you sly girl. I had no idea you arranged this."

She said, "The driving is tough, the parking expensive and my old legs are grateful for the door to door treatment. So let's enjoy it."

They did. The hot dogs were great, the beer cold, the peanut shells got thrown all over. The Red Sox beat the White Sox 6 to 4 and the kids got tee shirts and caps.

Later, lying naked in bed that night, Will said "Thank you for showing my son and his family such a good time today. The limo was a big surprise and a treat."

She said, "Oh, Will you are always great with my kids and grand kids. We're all one big happy family now."

They slept front to back that night, like two spoons. His arm was across her shoulders his hand cupped her breast. Thank God she married me and said let's dance. I love her so much thought Will. Thank God his whole body is right up next to me and he has those big hands thought Isabelle. Will and Isabelle were still in love.

On Friday at 6:00 AM Jack was prodding his family to get into the car; he was bringing them all to Cape Cod. "Come on you guys before the traffic to the Cape is bad" he said. His little family dragged themselves into the car and off they went. They had booked a room in a hotel near the beach in Yarmouth. They told Isabelle and Will they would meet them at Paul's house next Sunday around noon time. Will and Isabelle waved goodbye and told them to have a great time and lots of fun.

"Take photos" said Isabelle.

Will and Isabelle took it easy that day. It was hot and muggy. They rested in the back yard or in the house with the air conditioner running. They listened to a new audio book and watched the news. On Saturday she did laundry and he helped tidy the house. She washed the bathrooms and he unloaded the dishwasher. She folded the laundry and he vacuumed. They went to bed tired.

On Sunday Isabelle and Will arrived at Paul and Carol's around 11:30 AM.

Isabelle brought a dozen large sub sandwiches of all varieties; and cookies and cup cakes.

Carol said, "Will and you are so generous to provide lunch; these must have cost a pretty penny."

Isabelle said, "Please, this is Will's family, we should provide food. Look how generous you and Paul always are and I still remember that vacation to Vermont when you and Judy and Jen outdid yourselves".

Carol said, "Well thank you for bringing these. I know Prevete's Market must have been expensive".

Isabelle replied, "I can't take it with me. So let's enjoy some of it."

They laughed. Carol said she had put a pot of coffee on. She said there was ice tea ready and lemonade. Carol said she also had soft drinks and beer in the cooler out side.

Will and Paul were talking. Will had brought his fishing rod and a spare he had. Paul produced two, along with his fishing duffle bag.

Will looked at it and said, "Oh, we surely won't need that".

Paul said "You never know."

Tom and Susan came over and Tom had three fishing rods.

"I thought the little girl might want to fish too, and this pink one used to be my daughter's old pole," said Tom.

"Thanks" said Will.

"Did you get bait", asked Paul.

"I did" said Tom, "shiners and night crawlers."

"You guys are great" said Will. "I was surprised Jack wanted to come here."

Susan joined Carol and Isabelle.

"So tell me Isabelle, what are Jack and Marilyn like" asked Susan?

Isabelle said, "Jack and Marilyn are good parents and I think they are a very close couple. The children, there are three, have good manners and are normal well adjusted kids".

With that, Jack's car pulled up and everyone got out. Introductions were made since Susan and Carol had not met Jack and his family. And then they all ate lunch sitting at Paul's Picnic table or sitting on chairs in the yard. Then the three women talked and drank coffee in the shade and sampled the sweets too.

Isabelle said "This is where Will and I met when I was thirteen years old and he was fourteen. My parent's cottage was over there" she said "pointing to the other side of Paul's land, Paul's family's beach was here, then Tom's parents lived over there, then Will's folks place was further on. We were all friends. My brother and cousins were here too. What great summers we had as kids."

Marilyn said "Jack told me that you knew each other when you were young. I had no idea you knew each other then".

"Yes, Will was my first boy friend and I left him to marry Tim. It was a chance meeting at a restaurant that brought us together fifty years later"

"That's really quite romantic", said Marilyn.

"It always was romantic with Will and Isabelle", said Carol.

"They were in love then and they are now", said Susan.

The kids were eager to start fishing. They listened to Papa and Tom and Paul give advice. Jack, Jr. was casting and Nina used the net to pull one in and Dave hooked a large mouth bass. Tom showed Jack Jr. how to bait a hook. Paul showed Dave.

Jack said "I have taken them fishing before but we've not had much luck. The boys think you old guys are pros".

"We are" the three said.

Will was showing Nina how to fish with the pink pole. She wasn't really that interested so he grabbed one of the empty buckets they used for their catch of the day and walked to the edge of the lake with her and they found a turtle. It was not a snapper but a sun turtle with a yellow belly. Nina loved it and played in the shade of the tree, feeding it by tossing grass and leaves into the pail. By 4:00 PM they had had enough.

They fished, swam and learned how to row. Will was helped into the boat by Tom and Jack. Will did indeed still remember how to work the oars. By the end of the visit so did Dave, Jack Jr. and Nina. Jack told his kids that Papa had taught him to row the same way he taught them, and in the same boat added Tom. They packed up the cars and Will and Jack sat at the driver's wheel of each vehicle. Many thanks were spoken and away they went to Isabelle and Will's house.

At home they played Scotch Bridge until bed time and they were all asleep in five minutes. The next day Jack and Marilyn and the kids packed everything up and headed for the airport. It had been the best vacation any of them had ever had. The kids kissed Papa and squeezed him tight. They did the same to Isabelle. She gave them each a small wrapped gift.

She said "Don't open them until the plane is almost home".

"Where did you get these," asked Nina.

"They were secrets in the wrapping room".

The pilot said, "Ladies and gentlemen, we are making our final approach to Louis Armstrong air port, please fasten your seat belts".

Nina said "Can we open them now?"

Marilyn said "May we open them now, and Yes".

They all got a lovely framed photo of Papa and Isabelle there was a note that said, "You are always in our hearts."

# CHAPTER THIRTY-FIVE: FRIENDS

The day dawned bright and warm. It was early August and the friends and cousins went to Carol and Paul's for a day outing. Judy brought a lot of booze. Kathy made blueberry muffins and brownies and pasta salad. Isabelle made chicken salad and Will brought hot dog rolls, hamburger rolls, finger rolls and lemonade. Bob and Esther brought a cold cut platter and pumpernickel bread. Tom and Susan brought hot dogs and potato salad. Carol had the hamburger patties and all the fixings and condiments and paper goods. They arrived at noon and had the chicken salad and the deli platter for lunch with rolls, pickles and chips and dip. They drank cold drinks; it was hot. They all came in swim suits with cover-ups. They brought their own towels and some brought their own folding chairs. Bob wore his hearing aid today and they were all grateful. They were comfortable. The conversation was easy and the laughter hearty.

They were feeling nostalgic. Paul had put some sixties music on the CD player on the back step. The memories started coming back.

"Isabelle do you remember that pink dress you wore to Will's prom, Kathy said.  Carol and I thought it was like something from "Gone With the Wind", with that big full skirt. You looked so beautiful. We were just eleven and twelve then and we used to run around with my mother's sheer curtains wrapped around us trying to be you"

"I do remember it" said Isabelle. "Granny and I went to Boston together to pick it out. She was such fun. I loved that dress."

"Oh I remember it too" said Will "and that hoop thing skirt almost went right over her head when she got into my car".

"I had one like that too," said Susan. "Me too" said Esther, "mine was blue".

"Bob, remember that big mouth bass you caught I think it was 1963. What a beauty. I don't remember another one that big being caught from this lake since.", said Tom.

"He was the best fish I ever caught", said Bob.

Tom said, "How is the hearing aid working out?"

"It's good today although I sometimes can hear the music better than I can hear you", said Bob. "It seems to pick up background noise before voices. Esther and I were at dinner the other night and I heard the complete argument of the couple seated at the next table but I didn't hear a blessed thing Esther said to me."

"That could be a plus" said Tom.

"I know what you mean" said Bob.

"What was that" said Esther.

"Nothing"

Isabelle sat in a comfortable chair staring at the familiar surroundings. It had been at least fifty-five years since all of them were all together here at the lake. Soft pine needles carpeted the ground. The tall trees created a canopy shading them from the heat. Little chickadees flittered from tree to tree with their tiny wings spread wide. The air was intoxicating. The fat trunk of the beech tree still had all their initials carved in it. Will's and Isabelle's were encircled in a heart. Brown spotted sparrows pecked the ground for food. Chipmunks scampered to and fro. How lucky they had been to enjoy this haven year after year each summer. But like every generation of teenagers, they had never appreciated its beauty. That was a time of their lives that was just for them; no worries, no responsibilities, just fun and boy they had had some good times.

Will had been looking at her from across the yard. He was sitting with Tom and Paul at the picnic table. She looked serene. He still marveled that she was his wife. After all those years, his beautiful sweetheart was his. It did not matter to him that they were old. It just mattered that they were together. How lucky he was. He had never loved anyone as much.

Isabelle saw him looking at her. She winked at him. He smiled back.

"I used to love to play whiffle ball in our yard," said Bob.

"That was one game Isabelle was good at", said Tom.

"What's that suppose to mean", said Isabelle.

"Well you stunk at horse shoes," said Tom.

"True," she said.

"You could hit the ball. You had a good swing", said Paul.

"I had good eyesight" said Isabelle, "I just followed the pitch and swung".

"No, you were good, Isabelle", said Bob.

"Thanks".

"I loved playing Scotch Bridge the best", said Judy. "Isabelle and Bob's father loved it too. He was patient teaching us. He even taught Carol and Kathy and they were just little twerps then".

"I was once little but never a twerp" said Kathy looking down at her long lacquered nails.

"Nor I", said Carol.

Our grandfather used to take us blueberry picking in the woods over near the cranberry bog, remember and he'd pass out empty Maxwell House Coffee cans and we were told to fill them," said Bob. Will and Paul came once. Kathy never did fill her can because every time it got two inches full she'd eat all the berries. She'd try to deny it but her mouth and face were wet with messy berry skins and juice."

"Well since Papa died the following December and I was eight then I'd say that was normal behavior for a kid my age." said Kathy.

"Well those berries were worth eating," said Will "and the pies and muffins your grandmother made were great."

"I still have her muffin recipe. That's what you're having for dessert later", said Kathy.

"We had an out house when our grandparents first bought our place" said Will,

"My grandfather called it the privy; my Aunt Doris called it Tilly. I never knew why".

"We had one too but my grandmother made my father get plumbing as soon as we could", said Isabelle.

"Our kids would be appalled. They take showers every five minutes for God sakes.

I took a bath and washed my hair in the lake every Saturday night", said Isabelle.

"I know, I used to watch you," said Will.

"You did?"

"Yep"

Paul said, "I did too."

"Really, where were you", asked Isabelle.

"I was behind the hedge", said Paul.

"I was on the dock pretending to tie the boat", said Will.

"I don't know what you expected to see I was wearing the same swim suit I wore every day." said Isabelle.

"We were sixteen. We were hoping" said Will.

Judy piped in, "OK, See this just another example of things that bother me about men. They always have to look. They don't even know if they're going to see any flesh but even if there's a remote chance, men look. And if they do see someone naked they look at it like it's something they never knew existed. All women have the same parts there are no new items. Why do men keep looking? I mean if there was a woman with three breasts or something then maybe. Lots of injuries are caused by this obsession with women's flesh especially the boobs. A low cut dress can cause whiplash of the neck. Bikinis cause men to get a hard on. Let me tell you if you're on Viagra that could last for hours and it's a bitch to get it down. They use needles. Butt cheeks exposed cause carpel tunnel because men involuntarily start squeezing their fists like those cheeks are actually in them. Breasts are mammary organs used to feed the young. They are like cow's udders only smaller. Do you see bulls walking up and down the dairy barn looking underneath the cows all day long checking those things out? Maybe men who have been breast fed don't have this obsession. I must find out if a survey has been done on this. Really, if a parade of naked men marched into this yard right now, I wouldn't even look up. I've seen enough of those ugly things to last a life time.

I mean really Will and Paul what did you expect Isabelle to do? Cast off her bathing suit and prance in the pond naked; and soap up her body and lather her hair in front of you?"

"Keep talking" said Will, "I'm getting excited".

Paul said, "You just don't understand the mind of a sixteen year old boy".

There was much laughter. This is just what they needed. They always felt better after a good laugh.

Esther said, "It sounds like you guys had wonderful times when you were young". They all agreed they did.

Judy asked, "How many times do you think we all peed in that lake?"

"What altogether, do you mean," said Bob?

"Yeah" said Judy.

"Millions" said Tom.

They all nodded.

Tom told a story about when Will and Paul and he went over to Isabelle's house one night and they went around to the other side where her bedroom was. They ducked down so they could not be seen and listened in the opened window and heard Isabelle and Judy talking. They weren't saying anything interesting. So they decided to scare the girls. The window was pretty big and the boys were crouched on the ground beneath it so the girls couldn't see them. The boys popped up like jacks in the box and yelled Boo in the window. The girls screamed. The boys really frightened them. They saw Isabelle and Judy were in their pajamas and they ducked quickly.

Isabelle's father came running to her room and said, "What's the matter"?

Isabelle said "Judy saw a spider."

"He would have killed us", said Will.

"He would have, said Judy "and you saw more of us in our bathing suits than when we were in our pajamas so looks like you three were losers once again."

"I want to tell the frog in the swim suit story", said Isabelle. "I know some of you weren't there that day but it was awful. I was fifteen and just got the first two piece bathing suit I ever wore. I thought I was hot."

"You were," said Will.

"You were" said Paul.

"Thank you, boys now don't interrupt me I'll forget where I was. I'm an old woman now."

"On that day fifty odd years ago, I walked over to Will's with a towel in my hand swinging by my side. I gave a nod and hello to Paul's mother and aunt who were sunning themselves on chairs on top of Paul's dock. When I got to Will's beach, everyone was sitting at the table where we played board games. It was long and it was near the water's edge under the tall trees. Will's parents, his aunt, Doris, and his grandfather were sitting further back but not far from where we were. Linda was standing with them and little George was sitting on the ground playing with a truck or something. Tom's folks were on Tom's side of the beach talking with friends. All were within hearing distance, which was a pain because we children would all have to watch what we said during the game. I think it was monopoly. All of us were seated around the table sitting in those old fashioned folding chairs with woven strips of nylon web. Will and I were at one end. Tom was at the other. Paul, Judy and Milton were on one side; and John Stanley and Hector were across from them. So I came sauntering over, thinking I looked like freaking Marilyn Monroe and sat down next to Will, as usual. The play money had been distributed and they were waiting for me to shake the dice. Something fell from one of the high tree branches right inside my bathing suit top. It was a frog. It was in my cleavage. I screamed so loud everyone heard me and looked in my direction. I didn't just scream AHHH. I screamed WILL!!!! My hero, the sixteen year old wonder, takes one of those huge paws of his and tries to back hand the frog out of my top. He flicked both the top and the frog into mid air with such force he probably killed the frog and ripped the strap on the swim suit top. While the frog and top were flying through the air, Will covered my boobs with his hands palm side down, of course. He didn't want anyone to see the boobs. Everyone was trying to see the boobs, well maybe not Judy she didn't care and anyway she'd seen them. I don't think Tom was looking because he was looking for the swim suit top or the frog. Will was saving my honor. He wanted to see the boobs and was peeking over his hands. These hands were very close to my nipples. I even felt the palm of his left hand brush over my left nipple. He didn't think I knew, but I did. I didn't care as long as the frog was gone. You must understand that this entire incident happened with in a matter of ten seconds. I was trying to grab for my towel to cover myself. I didn't realize I was sitting on half my towel. When I pulled it my chair fell. While I was moving trying to do all this and falling, Will and his hands followed me. It was like a dance with his hands in front of him, like when women did the Charleston.

While Isabelle was trying to tell this story; Will got up and covered her breasts with his big hands; and moved them around at the same time just as he had done all those years ago. Everyone was already laughing.

Isabelle continued her story. When my chair fell it knocked Will's chair over. He fell on top of me with his hands still in place one hundredth of an inch above the sacred boobs. I freed the towel and covered myself. Will got up and helped me up. I covered the whole front part of my body with the towel. By now Will's father and grandfather were standing up looking. His mother's jaw had dropped and she sat opened mouthed. I think his Aunt Doris was trying not to laugh. Tom's folks and friends just stared. I pulled my shoulders back and held my head high and silently tried to walk home with as much dignity as I could. It was then that Tom came over and handed me the top of my swim suit holding it away from him, between his pointing finger and his thumb like it was a dirty hanky. I walked home with the towel covering me and put it around my shoulders and hid the bathing suit top under it once I got behind the hedge at Paul's. I didn't want my mother to see the swim suit top or my naked top. I went into the house and changed into my old bathing suit. I never wore a two piece again. Later Will had asked me what my mother said about the incident and I told him I never told her and never would. I would have been punished. I'm surprised Judy never said anything.

"I was too interested in Milton Stanley at the time", said Judy.

"Really", said Tom, "he told me you were a good kisser."

"That jerk" said Judy.

Bob asked, "Will, did your parents say anything to you?"

"Oh they thought I was some kind of pervert" said Will.

"They were right" said Tom.

"I'll vouch for that", said Paul.

"No, I was just a kid. They gave me an hour sermon that night on being a gentleman and respecting women and shit like that", said Will. "I think my mother was considering some kind of counseling for me. I don't think they were comfortable with me dating anyone after that. My grandfather called you the Catholic Jezebel"

"Well, that was nothing new; he called me that every time I played cribbage with him on Fridays. I thought it was a joke", said Isabelle.

"I never knew that", said Will.

"Anyway fifty odd years ago at this lake, you were my hero keeping my scared breasts from being seen." said Isabelle and she have him a kiss.

The men all reached for another drink and Tom lit up a cigarette. Judy and Kathy had martinis and Susan, Esther and Isabelle poured more wine.

"I remember keeping nine turtles in that Coke cooler we had in the yard. I had it filled with rocks and leaves", said Carol. "One turtle had a shell that was about six inches wide in diameter and one tiny one was the size of a dime. Most of them were sun turtles with yellow bellies but one small one was a snapper. We were careful of him. I had to let them go on Labor Day weekend. I remember being sad about this."

"I remember our grandfather making us put up the flag every morning and taking it down every night and we had to fold it military style. He tried to make us walk on stilts once. He had made them. None of us could. I think it was a big disappointment to him", said Bob.

"Will's father was very generous to have let us use his boat all those years for water skiing. How much he must have spent on gasoline for the motor. We never appreciated it or thanked him. I feel bad about that", said Isabelle.

"I wonder what Will's folks think in heaven now that Isabelle is their daughter-in-law," said Carol.

"Oh, they probably can't believe he has another wife?" said Paul.

"They're worried that Catholic Jezebel is wife number four, said Bob.

"They think they should have sent him for counseling after that frog incident", said Tom.

"Ha, Ha" said Will.

"What a lot of memories we have" said Judy.

"I remember trying to teach Bob how to water ski," said Paul. "It was pitiful."

"That was a day", said Tom.

"How old were you Bob? I think you were about sixteen." said Will.

"That's about right" said Bob.

Paul said, "At the time we all goaded Bob saying he must learn. Why didn't he want to? Even Isabelle told him to try it. Bob knew he was a good swimmer so what was the deal. Bob put the skis under his feet; it took me, Isabelle and Will to hold him while Tom put his feet into the rubber foot holders. Bob teetered and almost fell down. He was standing in about five inches of water. We all prompted him and encouraged him. He told us he needed to wear his glasses because he was almost totally blind without them. That was a problem. So Tom got duct tape and taped the sides of his glasses all around the back of his head ear to ear. Tom must have used a quarter roll of tape. Bob said he wanted a life jacket just in case. Isabelle put it on him. Bob said he had sand in the rubber foot holders and he couldn't stand under his feet it. Tom took Bob's feet out of the holders got rid of any sand and put his feet back in the holders. We all guided him out a little deeper so he could lean forward with the skis pointing up and at an angle. Bob kept crossing the skis and couldn't keep still. We all straightened him out and held him in place. It took me, Isabelle and Tom to do this. Will got in the boat and started the engine. Bob yelled to us what about snapping turtles? Don't worry about the turtles we told him. You'll be going faster than they can swim Paul told him. But if I fall in they might be right there waiting Bob lamented. Will said that the turtles didn't go anywhere near speed boats. Isabelle said she'd be in the boat with Will. She would yell to him if he needed to do something. Bob wanted to know how he would get back into shore. We told him to let go when Will brought the boat close to the dock. Bob said that he was worried that he'd crash into the dock. The boat won't be that close they told him. We told him all he had to do was hold on to the handle of the rope. When you feel the boat pulling you, stand up and let the boat pull you around. You'll see. It's easy. The motor started. Bob held on to the handle of the rope. The boat went a little faster. Bob held on to the handle of the rope. Now Bob was under water skiing. He never stood up. He was crouched almost sitting on the skis with his head under the water. The boat went faster. More water rushed onto Bob's face. It was going up his nose and in his mouth. Isabelle screamed to him to let go of the rope, please let go of the rope. Bob could not hear her. Bob was drowning. Will cut the engine. The boat stopped. Bob sunk. Isabelle asked if he was OK. Bob wanted to know if he did it. She told him No but said that he almost drowned. He wanted to know if we could see any snapping turtles. Isabelle said that she could not. She wanted to know what the matter was with his glasses. They're just wet Bob told her. He thought he'd have a hard time getting all this tape off his head. He wanted to go back shore. We asked if he wanted to try again. He did not. Will helped him into the boat and back to the dock they came. He spent the next hour getting the tape off his glasses. The hair was no problem. Isabelle just gave it a good yank. He had a bald spot in the back of his head for the rest of the summer".

Esther said, "Well I'm proud of you for trying".

"Where was Judy when all this was going on", asked Bob.

"She was kissing Milton Stanley", said Tom.

"Really" said Bob?

Judy said, "Screw you Tom Neeley."

Paul asked, "Where were Carol and Kathy?"

"We were much younger than you guys. When Isabelle was fifteen we were only eleven and ten. We were making hook pot holders or coloring", said Kathy.

"Or reading comic books or maybe spying on Judy and Milton", said Carol.

"Shut up," said Judy.

"We had to wait until Isabelle was eighteen or nineteen, then we could hang out with you guys. Even though I was only thirteen, I was lucky because I always looked older", said Kathy. "I just sat there and listened I learned lots of shit."

Judy said, "Well you looked older because you always wore black; and you two got gypped because by the time Isabelle was nineteen she was dumping baldy over there and everything fell apart. Paul was off at college. Tom and Susan were getting married. Then Will went in the Army. We lived in Vermont by then and I went to college.

"Where was Milton Stanley" asked Tom.

"Shut your face about him", said Judy. "Actually what ever happened to him Will? He was your cousin."

"He got married, had a couple of kids and lives in Maine. He's divorced now if you're still interested."

"No, I am not" said Judy. "Remember going to the fire works at the Marshfield Fair"?

They all said yes.

"This makes me feel so sentimental. Will gave me my first kiss at the fire works", said Isabelle.

"Well he's given a lot more since then" said Tom.

"Well, that's what made him so good at it," she said and she smiled at Will.

"Oh you two", said Tom.

Most of them went for a swim the water was still crystal clear and it refreshed them on that hot afternoon. They splashed and frolicked and tried out all the swim stokes they had once been good at. They weren't any more. Some of them fished and small ones were caught and thrown back. No one used the boat. They were realistic about their limitations. Nonetheless they had a great afternoon.

They started the grill and had hot dogs with mustard and relish and hamburgers with ketchup and pasta and potato salads. They drank decaf coffee and had blueberry muffins and brownies for dessert. They told a few more old stories. Then the reminiscing old timers left for their homes early in the evening. They were all tired but had a great day.

Three days later Susan called Will.

"Tom has passed away. He had a massive heart attack this morning. Please call Paul and the others for me. I don't feel like talking right now" she said.

"Oh Susan, I am so sorry", said Will.

She hung up the phone.

Will was stunned. He had lost one of his best friends. It made him worry about his own mortality.

They all attended his memorial and some of his ashes were spread on the lake, where they all played as kids. Susan sold the house. She said she couldn't bear to be there without Tom. There were too many memories. Isabelle found this strange. When Tim died it was all the memories at home that comforted her. Why are we human beings all so different? What makes us grieve in different ways? Maybe it was better that we did.

A few weeks later, when Susan was leaving to move to New Hampshire, she gave Will and Isabelle a gift. It was a framed photo of a young Will and Isabelle.

Almost sixty years ago Tom took that photo. Isabelle and Will were sixteen and seventeen. Will was looking down at her with love in his eyes; she was smiling up at him. They had been walking from her cottage to where Tom and the others had started a card game. Will had his arm around Isabelle and she looked adoringly up at him. Both of them had special smiles on their faces. At the time Tom was really into photography. It was one of his courses at college. Susan remembered him taking the photo. Tom was entering a photo contest. He had taken second prize the prior year. He was shooting still shots of birds and frogs and even fish jumping and water scenes. Tom saw Will and Isabelle approaching and said to the others, "Look at those two". He grabbed his camera and began shooting. He shot at least six views but this one was the best. After he had developed the photo he asked all of them all to look at it and think of a good name for it. The photo entries in the contest had to be labeled. They all agreed it was a great shot. They were all kids and came up with the usual, Young Love, Big Guy and Isabelle, Love at the Lake, Kiss Me You Fool and other stupid things. Tom did not like any of them. Isabelle just stared at the photo; she loved it.

She almost cried when she first saw it.

Will loved it too.

Then Isabelle said, "I know what to call it Tom".

"What" said Tom?

"Magic", she said.

He did. He won. He got five hundred dollars.

That was such a long time ago and here it was still giving them joy.

Isabelle and Will wept again when Susan gave them the photo. This made Susan cry too. "He'd want you to have it", she said.

Will said, "He was my life long friend. I loved him and I will miss him".

They kissed her and she was gone.

# CHAPTER THIRTY-SIX: KATHY AND JUDY AND MOTHERS

Judy and Kathy had been talking a lot about their mothers and Isabelle's mother, Chickie, a lot during the past two weeks. Why were they doing this? Was it a sign of getting old? Were they expecting to die? Were they lonely? They talked about how close the sisters had been. The three sisters had been good mothers. They mentioned what great things they had passed on to their daughters. It all stemmed from Granny. She taught them and they taught us. Maybe all cultures were like that. Women were always handing down ideas and traditions from generation to generation.

Kathy said, "I remember your mother, Edna, was always entertaining and having many friends around. She loved parties. She got Granny and Chickie to help her make costumes for that play the parish priest ran during Lent before you moved to Vermont; and she was always in charge of the mother's club activities at our school when we were real young".

"She was always happy. She always wanted to learn. She got everyone involved, the more the merrier", said Judy.

"Yes", said Kathy, "and I think Isabelle is more like your mother, Edna, than either you or Carol are."

"Isabelle is nothing like her own mother", said Judy.

"No, but her Dad liked to have fun, said Kathy.

"He did", said Judy "I'll always be grateful to him for teaching me to play Scotch Bridge."

"Bob picked a wife like their mother", said Kathy.

"He did" said Judy.

"What about Chickie, she always came up with money if you needed it or she'd paint a room at the drop of a hat. Remember every year she and my mother would caulk and paint that tub of a row boat at the cottage and they had fun doing it. Oh and every time we had a wedding Chickie bought us all sweat shields so we wouldn't ruin our dresses. Did she think we'd ever wear those ugly bride's maid dresses again? And she took me to Disney Land once", said Kathy.

"Yes, she was cool. She was my god mother. I loved her. She always made sea food salad when she came to Vermont. We didn't get that up there. One time when Isabelle and me were going to the Marshfield fair with the kids at the lake she bought us new outfits. They were nice, tee shirts and matching jersey pants. I had purple and Isabelle had hot pink. We thought we looked great. Someone, I think it was Tom, said, what are you wearing, your pajamas? We were crushed" said Judy.

"And your mother, Rosemary, always had just the right pair of gloves for us, since she worked at Jordan Marsh's glove department. Remember the long ones we wore to our proms and the colored satin ones we had to go with some of those ugly bridesmaid numbers. No one even wears fancy gloves anymore. How times have changed", said Judy.

"I used to love the little things Mom did, like putting a train set on the floor that went underneath the Christmas tree", said Kathy. "We'd look at the tree lights and watch the train go around for hours. Remember that Santa that appeared every Thanksgiving to keep us behaving until Christmas. She loved our dog, Daisy too. She was kind and loving, I still miss her", said Kathy.

"Your mother could bake brownies and ham. She always brought Jordan Marsh's blueberry muffins to Vermont when she and Chickie came to visit. They were good but not as good as Granny's," said Judy.

Judy and Kathy didn't know why they had been talking about their sainted mothers so much? Didn't they just have a conversation like this just last week? They wondered if it meant that the mothers were thinking about them. Maybe they needed more prayers to get out of purgatory or something. Judy's mother had been dead for ten years and Kathy's mother died at least fifteen years ago so they still couldn't be in purgatory. Chickie had died before that. It must be twenty years ago that she died.

Kathy said, "You don't think they're still in purgatory do you?"

"I don't believe in purgatory," said Judy "either you go to heaven or hell".

"Don't let Bob hear you say that", said Kathy.

"I don't care if he hears me. I'm not afraid of him."

Judy and Kathy thought about all of this.

Then Judy said "We should go to a medium".

"A medium what", said Kathy.

"You know someone who can reach out and hear dead people".

"You mean a psychic?" said Kathy.

"Yes, someone clairvoyant who can tell us what our mothers are doing", said Judy.

"You want to know what they're doing", said Kathy?

"Yes" said Judy "and I want to know what it's like up there."

"Where would we go?

"There must be something on a web site about this."

Judy went to her lap top and researched.

Kathy sat in silence thinking.

"I found two", said Judy. "One is in East Bridgewater and the other is in Carver. Where do you want to go"?

"How do we know they're any good; or even for real"?

"When we call to make an appointment, we'll ask for credentials" said Judy.

"No one actually has credentials in that sort of thing. Isn't it a gift, like a sixth sense or something?"

"How do I know" said Judy.

Kathy said, "Well what do they do read our palms or our tea leaves?"

"No, I think we just sit in a room with other folks who are looking to hear form someone dead just like us. And wait."

"Wait for what" said Kathy?

"Wait for the medium to be contacted by dead people", said Judy.

"Is there a crystal ball involved" said Kathy?

"No, you're thinking of fortune telling," said Judy. "I think we just sit at a table or maybe just in chairs and we all think of a deceased loved one and the psychic gets some kind of vibes and hears things.

She'll ask us questions like does anyone know an Edna or did anyone's loved one have something to do with gloves. Shit like that."

"We're not getting ourselves involved in witchcraft or anything like that", said Kathy. "I mean I don't like hearing about covens and warlocks and potions and spells and that crap"

"What do you think we're in a Harry Potter book? No that stuff scares me too", said Judy.

Kathy said, "What are the names of these psychics"

"The one in Bridgewater is called "Voices from Heaven, Helen Overton, Psychic". The other one from Carver is called, "Messages from Beyond, Roy Curdle, Clairvoyant," said Judy.

"Why don't we go to one this week, and the other next week. We can compare what they said and if they agreed on several points then we can believe them" said Kathy.

"I'm going to call and set up appointments or see when the next happening will take place", said Judy.

Kathy said, "Find out how much it costs. I don't think we should go crazy.

We don't want to waste money. I wonder what Isabelle would say about this, and Carol. Should we tell them?"

"No, Isabelle would laugh and give us crap about wasting our money and Carol would give us a religious sermon and not approve. We can tell them about it after we go", said Judy.

Judy called the first psychic, Helen, and was told that Voices from Heaven was having a hearing tomorrow night and the fee was $25.00 per person. Helen told Judy that sometimes clients have to come two or three times before they get any news from their loved one. It takes time for an aura to surround the client and time for Helen to hear the voices. Judy said they would be there and gave Helen their names.

Well I'll go once, but if we don't hear anything we'll know it's a fake and just a money maker for Helen", said Kathy.

Judy called Roy Curdle next and he said that they could definitely have a place at one of his paranormal experiences the following Wednesday. He told Judy that all the clients sat around a table in a dimly lit room holding hands. He would ask each person at a time to mention one name and then he would wait to hear from the great beyond. He would relay any message that a loved one was sending. The cost was $35.00 per person.

Judy booked places for her and Kathy at next Wednesday's séance.

The next night, Friday night, they went to Voices From Heaven. The building had once been a small store in a strip mall. Now it was set up like a question forum with chairs lined in rows with Helen sitting on large wing backed chair center stage so to speak. Helen told all the guests to sit and meditate in their seats. There were only seven people there. Some were not clients but just folks accompanying friends to this meeting.

Helen greeted all of them and told them to be perfectly still for the next three minutes and not speak a word.

Helen said "I want each client, and by that she meant the people who had been foolish enough to have paid $25.00, to think of one word, the name of the loved on you wish to hear from. Do not speak at all. Don't think of any other word, just that person's name". Kathy wondered if the non payers closed their eyes and thought of a name too. Who could stop them? "Then close your eyes and in your mind repeat the name over and over in your head until I say stop," said Helen.

They all did what they were told. Three minutes seemed like a long time.

Then Helen said "Stop."

She looked around and asked if anyone knew a Frank.

A fat old woman wearing all black, not Kathy, said "Yes is it my darling husband Frankie".

Then that lady's companion, also fat and in black, probably Italian, put her arm around the other woman and patted her shoulder.

Helen said, "What do you want to ask Frank".

The grieving widow said, "Oh Frankie, my handsome Frankie, why did you kill yourself. Why, Why, Why," She was quite dramatic and the stage had lost out on her talent.

Helen was silent for a moment and then said "Frank wants you to know that he is sorry for all the pain he has caused and that he did not kill himself. His car skidded and slammed into the pole. It was an accident. He says he'd never kill himself because he still loves you, Ruth."

The grieving widow said "Ruth, Ruth, who's Ruth, I'm Anna. Either you have the wrong Frankie or he was a cheating bastard."

With that said, Anna and the other black clad figure, not Kathy, stormed out.

Helen apologized for this and said, "Sometimes these things happen. The aura around us has disappeared, we needed to start again".

They all closed their eyes and thought for three minutes of one name.

Helen said "I'm hearing flowers, no wait, a rose and a daisy. Does anyone here want to speak to Rose or Daisy or someone who worked with flowers?"

Kathy said, "Me. My mother is Rosemary and her favorite dog was Daisy".

Helen said, "Good".

Then she said, "Rosemary your daughter is here. She wants to ask you a question".

Helen said to Kathy, "What do you want to know? Only one question please". Kathy said, "Is she happy?"

Helen closed her eyes and touched her forehead and then said, "Yes, Rosemary is happy. She is with your father and her sisters. She said she is glad you stopped smoking. That is all she said."

Then Helen said, "I must go on there is another voice. It is Mabel, does anyone here want to speak to Mabel."

"I do" said a fat man wearing denim overalls. He looked like a farmer.

Helen urged him. "What do you want to say to Mabel?"

"You were the best cow I ever had".

Helen said, "Sir that is inappropriate".

"Why" he said, "she gave more milk than any of my other dairy cows. She was my favorite. I miss her. I loved her."

Helen said, "Please sit down sir, the Mabel I am referring to is a woman not an animal."

"Your ad in the paper said 'loved ones'"; "I loved that cow. I want my money back", said the man.

"You will have to put that request in writing", said Helen.

"I must ask you to leave."

He did.

"Now let me get back to this," said Helen. "Sorry, but we need to think silently for three more minutes. I am still hearing the voice of Mabel. Someone here knows a Mabel."

A very tall thin man with a crew cut and wearing dark rimmed glasses said, "Mabel was my girl friend."

"What do you want to ask Mabel", said Helen?

"Ask her where the money is?" He said.

There was a moment of silence and then Helen said, "Mabel said to look in the freezer in the ice cube tray."

He immediately rushed toward the door.

The aura disappeared again. Judy had never seen an aura and didn't even know what an aura would look like. Helen had the remaining clients close their eyes and think of one name again, for three minutes.

Then Helen said "Josh". "Is someone here hoping to hear from Josh"?

A tiny woman at the end of the row of chairs said, "I am, he was my son. He was killed in Afghanistan three years ago."

"He is here" said Helen. "He will answer one question".

The tiny woman asked if he was happy.

Helen said, "He wants you to know that he went out fighting like a good soldier and that he is very peaceful. He says that he looks forward to seeing you when you come there too, and it won't be long now."

The tiny woman beamed. "I'm so glad he's at peace", she said.

"I have another voice", said Helen, "someone named Ed. Does someone have a husband, father, brother, or son named Ed. Ed's voice is loud. It is saying something about salt and pepper shakers".

"Oh," said Judy, "that's my mother, Edna. That's who I'm trying to reach".

"Well she is here" said Helen. "What do you want to ask her?"

Judy said, "Ask her if she's just with God and the saints and angels or with people she knew when she was on earth?

Helen was silent for a long time. Then she said, "Your mother is with your dad, her two sisters, her parents and some other good friends. She said your two ex-husbands are there too."

"What" said Judy, "Little Prick and Fat Bastard"; No that can't be true. They would never make it to heaven. God's forgiving, but not that forgiving. Oh, no. Oh, no. Oh, this is terrible news."

Helen said, "I'm sorry but the voices have gone."

"Good because we're out of here," said Judy. She grabbed Kathy by the arm and they left.

All the way home Judy was not herself. She kept muttering. She was really upset.

Kathy finally said, "Why are you letting this get to you? Your two former husbands may have repented. There's always time for redemption. You should be glad their souls were not lost."

"Yes, but now when I go to heaven, I'll have to be with them for eternity. I might as well go to hell", said Judy.

Kathy said, "We were probably the most normal people there. I mean can you imagine trying to get in touch with a dead Cow? What about that guy who was only interested in the money? I think if I was in heaven and someone from down here asked me that question and didn't even ask how I was, I wouldn't have answered him.

"Well we did only get one question", said Judy. "I wonder how much money it was".

"The woman looking for Frankie was upset. There must be millions of Frankie's in heaven, why did she jump to conclusions", said Kathy?

"Yeah well Frankie sounded like a dirty rotten skunk to me, even if he was the wrong Frankie," said Judy.

Kathy said, "Well maybe the next medium will tell us your exes are not in heaven. This could be a lot of nonsense you know."

"Well how did she know you stopped smoking? You wore long sleeves so the patch wasn't showing. How did she know about the salt and pepper shakers? And anyway I'm not spending my one and only question asking about those two Jerks," said Judy.

During the next few days all the two women talked about was Helen and wondered what Roy would be like. Judy said she wanted to know things like, "how long it took to get to heaven?"; "Was purgatory just a long journey and not really fire? Were there really pearly gates; was St. Peter there waiting for you? What did he look like?

Kathy wanted to ask, "Did you see a white light? Did you see God? Do you become and angel?"

The two cousins thought about all of this and then went to Messages from Beyond the following Wednesday night.

They were greeted by Roy Curdle, a medium size man with grey hair and a handlebar moustache, who could have been the Wizard in the Wizard of Oz. He wore a long dark purple robe.

Kathy immediately said, "I thought there were no wizards; look at his robe, shit. I don't like this."

"You wouldn't mind if the robe was black. Anyway he's not a wizard, he's just getting into his role" said Judy.

"His role as what?" said Kathy.

Judy said "As a clairvoyant."

Roy told everyone to sit down at the round table. It held six. No one except clients could sit at the table. If someone came with you for moral support, they had to sit on the folding chairs that were lined against the wall. The room was large with big windows with their shades pulled all the way down. It was in the front of an old farm house. It was probably used as a parlor in the olden days. The lights were turned off and a single candle stood in the center of the table. It was lit and smelled like eucalyptus. Kathy thought she might fall asleep from the scent. Roy began by saying that he wanted them all to hold hands. He sat beside Kathy and reached for her hand, Kathy held Judy's and then Judy held the hand of a very fat hairy man about Judy's age. He had those gross hairy patches that sprouted from his ear holes and a long unkempt beard and moustache. He was dressed in a short tee shirt that exposed his protruding belly and naval and had rough knobby hands. His other hand was holding the hand of a slim young woman who had spiked blonde hair, and was wearing a lace camisole for a blouse along with a black leather mini skirt and very high heels. She had three nose rings in one nostril and a huge dragon tattoo on her right shoulder that reached all the way to her wrist. The eyes of the dragon were looking in Kathy and Judy's direction. Next to the tattooed lady was a small bent over man, with thick glasses, wearing his hair in the bald man's comb over style. He appeared to be clean but all his clothes were badly wrinkled. He held Roy's other hand.

Roy said, "Now we must not break this circle. Keep holding hands the whole while we are here. Do not let go of anyone's hand. I want to go in turns and ask each one of you something and then I will see if I get any messages from beyond."

He nodded to the fat man beside Judy and said, "Who would you like to reach from beyond.

The fat man said, "My father".

"What was your father's first name", asked Roy. "We do not use last names here".

"Earl" said the client.

Roy closed his eyes and said "I am getting something. Yes, I am hearing a voice". "Is that you Earl", said Roy. "Your son is looking for you".

Roy looked at the client and said "What would you like me to ask your father?" The fat man said "Ask him why he liked my brother better than me".

Roy waited a few seconds and then said, "Your father said that he loved both of you equally; but your brother needed more help so he was given more attention. He said you should have known that because you were so bright."

The fat man was crying and Roy said "Do not break the circle".

The fat man did not let his hand go. "Earl is gone now. Maybe he will come back later or maybe you can come another time to ask him something else".

Roy then said to the young woman, "Whom do you want to talk to tonight?"

She said "Marvin".

"Was Marvin a friend?"

"Marvin was my pimp".

"I see" said Roy.

"Marvin is not in heaven. I'd bet on that" said the girl.

"Well I don't know where my voices come from" said Roy. "I just hear them. Let's be silent for a moment and let me listen for Marvin"

"Marvin are you there", said Roy. "Yes I can hear Marvin. What do you want to say to him"?

The girl said, "Tell him I'm making more money on my own now and the best thing he ever did was to get shot to death"

Roy relayed this to Marvin and waited a long time.

Roy said "Marvin said he's sorry he worked you so hard and that you were a pretty little thing".

The woman said "Fuck Marvin."

Please continue to hold hands we don't want the spell broken. He then turned to the small bent over man.

"Who are you trying to reach sir?"

The small man said "My mother, she died last year and I want to make sure she is happy".

"What was your mother's name?"

"Bernice."

"OK" said Roy "I'm trying to hear Bernice. Bernice can you hear me". He waited. "Bernice". He waited. "I'm sorry sir but she's not here tonight. Why don't you come back in a few weeks", said Roy.

"I've been here twice before and she did not come. Why won't she answer me?" Roy said "She will when she's ready. Please continue to hold hands".

"Next" he said turning toward Kathy.

"Who do you want to speak to" asked Roy.

"Auntie Chickie" said Kathy surprising Judy. "Chickie" said Roy. "Was that her real name"?

"No" said Kathy "it was Eileen but no one called her that".

"Alright, Chickie whose real name is Eileen can you hear me", said Roy? "Chickie are you there"? "Yes, Chickie is here. Is your name Kathy?"

Kathy said "Yes".

"Good we have the right person. What do you want to ask Chickie"?

"Have you seen my husband up there?"

"Chickie did you hear that question?"

There was a pause and then Roy said "Yes your husband is there and her sister.

Your parents are there too. Chickie said they are never too hot or too cold and they are all very happy".

Kathy smiled.

Roy said "That is all from that voice. I want everyone to hold on; the circle must stay in tact. We have one more client."

"Who do you want to speak to? Roy asked.

Judy said "I want to ask my mother if she has seen God."

"What is your mother's name"?

"Edna."

"Alright, where is Edna; Edna with a daughter." "This Edna, I'm listening to has two daughters, Judy and Carol", said Roy.

"That's her, tell her it's Judy".

Roy said "Edna speak to me. Your daughter Judy wants to ask you something".

"What do you want to ask Edna?"

Judy said, "Did she see God"?

Roy closed his eyes and waited. Then Roy said "Edna has seen God. He is a not a human; but a spirit. His spirit fills you with such happiness you won't understand until you get here".

Roy said that was it for the night; and that they could stop holding hands.

Roy was totally exhausted.

"Well, what did you make of that" said Judy as they drove home.

"I don't know" said Kathy. "As long as they're all happy who cares".

Judy said "I mean Roy can't really be a quack, he said Chickie knew it was you and my mother mentioned both me and Carol as her daughters."

"Did you see that girl's tattoo", said Kathy.

"Yeah it was fantastic. I bet it took weeks to draw that whole dragon. How many needles would that take?"

Kathy said, "I don't know. Did you ever want to get one?

"No, but I'm glad the working girl stuck it to Marvin," said Judy.

"I wanted to get a small one on my back near my shoulders. I thought it would be sexy", said Kathy.

"Really what would you get, a rose, a butterfly or something like that", said Judy.

"No" said Kathy, "a black swan."

"You still could" said Judy.

"Maybe"

"I felt bad for the little guy. We should have told him about Helen", said Judy.

"I was glad the other guy got closure. Now he understands his father better. Some good can come from these things."

"Oh him, I couldn't get past the ear hair", said Judy.

"I knew that was bothering you", said Kathy.

They arrived home, kicked off their shoes and headed for the kitchen. Kathy made martinis and Judy got crackers and cheese.

They clinked their glasses together and Kathy said "Here's to clairvoyants and séances".

Judy said "And all paranormal shit".

# CHAPTER THIRTY-SEVEN: BOB AND THE CHOIR

Bob and Esther were at the waiting room of her doctor's office. It was just a routine annual checkup for her.  They were reading magazines until her name would be called. All of a sudden, Bob looked at Esther and she was stiff and seemed disorientated. He said "Esther, what is wrong". He could see that she could not speak. He called for help. The doctor and his assistant both came from examining rooms. The doctor said "Call 911 she's having a stroke". The receptionist called and an ambulance came within minutes. It was about a half hour ride to the hospital but the Emergency Medical Technicians were attentive and knew what to do. Bob followed in his car. When Esther was admitted, she was given shots and then moved to ICU. She was monitored for the next twenty four hours. Bob stayed there the whole time.

The next day he called Isabelle and told her. She and Will went to the hospital. Esther was moved out of intensive care and to her own room. Her eyes were opened and you could tell that her brain was working. She could not move her right side. She could not speak. She moved her left leg and her left arm. That was it. She wanted to communicate but she could not. Bob just sat and held her hand.  Her doctor came in with a specialist. He examined Esther more for responsiveness and reflexes. He looked into her eyes. He tried to move her right limbs and see if they would move on their own. They did not. He asked Esther to speak. She tried. She actually thought she was talking; her lips were moving but only sounds came out. She didn't know why we could not understand her. She made louder noises thinking that would make her speech better. It did not. She became frustrated and tears were falling down her cheeks. Bob kissed her forehead and told her to relax and that she didn't need to say anything. He got a pen and paper from one of the nurses and told Esther to try to write something.

Using her left hand she wrote with difficulty, "What's wrong with me?"

Bob told her she had a stroke in the doctor's office and that the doctors were trying to figure out how to help her. The doctors said the first forty eight hours are critical.

"You may recover" said her primary care doctor, "You may need therapy. We have to wait and see".

The specialist told her, "I see patients like this all the time".

"Let the medication work and we will go from there." I will be in to see you tomorrow. Bob stayed with her again that night.

The next morning Esther has another stoke. This time it was more serious. She died within hours. He called Isabelle and Will. They met him at the hospital and then went to the undertaker with him. Isabelle came to Bob's house and got clothes to bury her in and Bob got the deed to the grave for the funeral director. Will drove them back to the undertaker together and they made their final burial plans.

Two days later in the pouring rain. Esther was laid to rest with Bob and Isabelle's parents. Bob would be there too some day. She was a good woman and the best thing that ever happened in Bob's life. He would miss her dearly. It was a sad day for them all but death visits every family; it does not play favorites.

Kathy and Judy had the funeral luncheon at their home. It was catered and it was a final tribute to Esther and a kind gesture to Bob. When all the mourners had gone, Kathy smiled and said, "Bob, Judy and I want you to come here every Tuesday night for supper. We're not good cooks but it will be nice to have a guinea pig to try our recipes." He thanked her and said he would be there next Tuesday. Judy hugged him and said, "Chin up old boy, there's nothing else we can do sometimes."

Bob left and he did return on Tuesday. He was somber but was coping better than any of them imagined. Bob was strong in his faith and knew Esther was in a better place. Bob was always at Church on Sundays to sing in the choir and he went out for breakfast with some of the choir members after Mass. He had choir practice on Monday nights. Dinner at Kathy and Judy's on Tuesdays. He taught CCD at the Church hall on Wednesday afternoons and had supper with Carol and

Paul on Thursdays. Bob kept busy and everyone marveled at how he embraced his grief.

About a month later on a night when Bob had come for dinner, Paul and Carol told him they'd like to join the choir.

Bob said, "Can you sing?"

They said that they could indeed and after dinner they would put on one of their show tune CD's and have a sing along and he could join in if he chose to.

They ate their meal chatting about church music. Paul said his mother and aunt had always liked being in the choir and he didn't know why he hadn't thought about joining it before. They finished their coffee and dessert and went to the living room where show tunes were beginning. Paul told Bob that Carol had a sweet voice. He thought it had some volume too.

He said, "She could belt out "Memories" from "Cats" as good as Betty Buckley".

Carol said "I don't think that's quite true Paul, but you certainly sound like Andrea Bocelli sometimes".

Bob was impressed by these comments. He wondered how the choir director would feel. After all church music and show tunes were not the same. All of a sudden "The Man from LaMancha" was playing "Don Quixote" and Paul was bellowing the lyrics to the tune. When "Annie" came on, Carol was belting out "Tomorrow" for Bob. Bob felt like he was a talent scout and these two were auditioning for him. Paul and Carol urged Bob to sing with them and the three of them went on for about an hour singing the best of Broadway songs.

They asked Bob when a good time would be to join. Bob told them that practice was every Monday night at 7:00 P.M. Bob said that they didn't have to try out or anything they just needed a willingness to participate with the group singing at Mass, funerals and the like. Paul asked if they ever did solos. Bob told him once in a while they were asked to sing at a wedding or funeral but mostly it was group singing. Paul and Carol said that was great and they would look forward to meeting the choir master next Monday night. Bob was afraid that Paul and Carol thought it was going to be like going on American Idol.

The following Monday night Paul and Carol showed up, this time they were dressed alike, and had a tambourine and a ukulele with them. They met the choir director and some of the other members of the choir. There were about twenty-two singers, all over sixty, counting Bob. The choir master told Paul and Carol to sit with their appropriate voice group. Carol said she used to be a soprano but now that she was older she couldn't hit the high notes. She was told to sit with the altos. Carol could not harmonize. Carol needed to sing the melody. Carol did sing the melody only in an octave lower than all the other sopranos. This confused both the sopranos, and the altos she was sitting with. Paul was a tenor and he could carry a tune but he was always one note behind everyone. So when Paul sang Amazing Grace with the rest of the choir, it would sound like, Amazing Grace how sweet the sound sound, That saved a wretch like me me. The director was going to correct them in the nicest possible way, but since there weren't too many interested in joining the choir, he just admired their enthusiasm. He was a kind man. He gently pointed out their flaws. Paul said that he'd try to keep up with the others. Carol said that she'd sing with the sopranos and just omit the real high notes. They sang again. It was a little better.

Carol and Paul waited until all the other choir members left and they cornered the director. They showed him their skills with the tambourine and ukulele, not impressive. They told him that they could spice up the church music with these instruments. The director said they usually used the organ and sometimes guitars if they were singing a folk Mass for teenagers. He also said at high Masses, like Christmas and Easter they had a professional trumpet player come join them. He was as polite as he could possibly be but he said that right now there is not a need for a tambourine and ukulele. He said he would consider it though. The man wanted to get home. Paul and Carol said they had other ideas as well but they could wait until next week. The couple said that they would be on time for singing on Sunday morning. They parted and the choir master, whose head was spinning, said to himself that he couldn't wait to thank Bob for bringing "Stevie Nicks" and "Arthur Godfrey" to the once normal choir.

On Sunday morning the singing went pretty well. The songs that were sung were old familiar ones. Carol, to her credit, did sing soprano in the right key. She mouthed the high notes. Why didn't she just skip them? Did she thing this was like lip syncing and people were actually watching her? Paul did well until the closing song when all the congregation could hear was, "Let there be peace on earth earth and let it begin with me me." Paul was loud if nothing else. Of course Paul and Carol stayed after to speak with the music director suggesting songs and types of music.

"We thought this choir needed new blood", said Carol, "and we have lots of ideas".

Paul said, "I think when the choir sings "How Great Thou Art", just the men should sing and try to impersonate Elvis. He did such a rendition of that song. It would wake folks up". It sure would and probably kill some of the old men in the choir, was the choir master's thought; why Jim Beaton was at least eighty; he could never sing like Elvis.

"How about introducing new music like the songs from the Shout to the Lord CD", said Carol. "You know those folks in the mid west and bible belt, sure know how to sing. We watched them on television one night and the whole church was singing young and old, even teenagers. You are familiar with that score of music aren't you?"

He said that he was and he would think about it.

"What about a cappella asked Paul? Once when we went to Aruba the people at church sang in a native language called Papiamento without music in four part harmony. It was as beautiful as the African music in 'Lion King'." Since Carol couldn't even harmonize in two part harmony, how did she think she'd accomplish this and without music, thought the director?

I also think "Jesus Christ Superstar" would be very rousing especially during Lent. And the songs from "Godspell" are never used at Mass. I think they should be", said Carol. "These songs need to be belted out. It would keep the congregation from falling asleep", she said.

The choir master told them they certainly gave him a lot to think about. He was a kind man. He told them he had a breakfast engagement, a lie; and that it was almost time for the next Mass, true.

The next night Bob came to practice early, the music director said "Bob, your cousin and Paul are certainly exuberant. They have all kinds of ideas for this choir." He then told Bob about these ideas. Bob laughed at the "Stevie Nicks" and "Arthur Godfrey" reference and thought of all the men in the choir impersonating Elvis. There were only eight men in the choir, all over sixty, altogether they could not rouse enough talent to sound like Elvis singing anything. He never saw Carol play a tambourine or any other instrument; it was difficult to imagine. Did she think she was a gypsy? And if so how did that remotely belong in church? Bob was trying to think of one religious song he knew that would be improved by a tambourine. He could not think of one. And what was Paul thinking? A ukulele, thought Bob. Did Paul think there was room for Hawaiian music at Mass in Massachusetts? What holy song could be played on a ukulele? Bob was sorry he encouraged them to join.

The other choir members started coming in to practice and finally Carol and Paul entered decked out in green sateen robes with gold trim.

Carol said, "How do you like these? I made them for Paul and me and I'm going to make twenty more for all of us. There is more ordinary time during the year than any other season so I started with green. The priests wear green during ordinary time too so I thought it would be good if we all wore the same color as the priest's vestments while we sang Mass. What do you think?"

There was silence. Even Bob was speechless. Carol and Paul looked like two seniors who just passed their high school equivalency tests and their school colors were green and gold.

The music director said, "I think it is a very nice gesture but it there is too much time and expense involved."

"Oh, the material is cheap and light weight" said Carol, "I could whip these up in no time".

"I helped", said Paul, "I'm good with the scissors. I put the cloth on the pattern and cut the pieces out."

"We were thinking red ones for Christmas and Confirmation and White for Easter and First Communion" said Carol.

"We could make Purple for Advent and Lent", said Paul.

"What a great idea", said Carol.

"We could store them here in church and we'd always be ready", said Paul.

The choir master figured if they're busy sewing they can't get any fantastic ideas for changing the music. He said "I think I'd like the red ones made first. Then we would be ready for Christmas."

"No problem" said Carol. "One size fits all."

The practice began and this time Paul was on time with that last note. Carol sang with her soprano group and managed to hit a few high notes. They really could carry a tune and they did have powerful voices. The choirmaster said "He had a new song for them to learn, it was called "Shout to the Lord". He had had this music for weeks in his brief case. He had been practicing it on his piano at home. He liked the sound of it and it would be just the change they needed. Of course Paul and Carol thought it was all their idea and he let them think that. He was a kind man.

At the end of the session Bob stayed behind to see if Carol and Paul would once again corner the director. They did.

Carol said, "You know if you ever think of having a variety show we would be glad to help."

"Why we know all the show tunes and we could help with costumes and settings,"

said Paul. "I was thinking "Oklahoma" would be a good one to start with."

The choir master was astounded. He told them that he thought most of the choir members were a bit long in the tooth to put on a show. He looked to Bob for help. Carol and Paul said that they would scout the parish for young blood. Oh my God, thought the music director. Well he'd give this some thought he told them and of course he'd have to discuss this with the pastor.

"In the meantime", he said, "why don't you two get started on the robes?"

"Oh sure, sure", said Paul.

"You know I bet there is a lot of musical talent in this parish", said Carol, "We just have to seek it out". Also I forgot to mention that I really like the southern Christian songs like "What a Friend I Have in Jesus" some of the black choirs sing this beautifully perhaps we could keep that one in mind. The funeral music in New Orleans, the dirges send powerful messages. What do you think? Perhaps we need a jazz influence or a saxophone, just for the funerals, I mean."

"Well I don't know. I will do some research on this", said the director.

Paul said "I recently got a CD with Native American flutes and drums. Do you think any of the choir music could use that sort of accompaniment?"

I will surely want to consult the pastor with all of these new ideas.

"We love all sorts of musical entertainment," said Paul.

Bob remembered that Esther told him about Carol telling the women how she and Paul danced naked. He laughed out loud.

Paul said, "What's so funny".

Bob said, "Oh nothing, I just never knew how talented you two were."

# CHAPTER THIRTY- EIGHT: OLDER AND STILL IN LOVE

Years passed, nine to be exact. Will and Isabelle still had toast with peanut butter for breakfast and watched the birds from their window. They didn't travel far any more. Jack and his family visited them every the summer. Isabelle was almost seventy-nine. She looked like an old lady now, even though her hair was still ash blonde. She had had pneumonia last year and a melanoma removed from her arm last month. Her arthritic knees still hurt but she refused to go under the knife. She had heard lots of horror stories of surgeries and infections and didn't want to go there.

Will was eighty. He could still get around but he moved very slowly. He learned he had prostate cancer but it was in its early stages and it was a slow growing cancer especially for a man in his eighties. The doctor told him he would not die of this. Something else would get him first. Great, thought Will. His blood pressure was very high and his medication was increased. He needed stronger glasses and his hearing was not as good, golden years indeed.

They saw Isabelle's family often. She still adored them all and doted on the younger ones especially. She was awaiting the birth of her first great grand child. How excited she was. She felt babies were always good news.

It was Halloween again, and Isabelle and Will were going to be an angel and a devil. This year she had long cloths that looked like they had been soaked with blood stains hanging from the fish lines. She was too old to get up on the marble topped buffet but one of the grandsons obliged. She had them all over the place it looked like a slaughter house. There were spiders all over the walls and a flashing strobe light. Labels were being made to place on the food platters like "bat wings" for chicken fingers, and "maggots in sauce" for macaroni and cheese. Isabelle and the granddaughters took pizza dough and made bread sticks that looked like witches fingers with colored slivered almonds for fingernails. The strings were strung, the donuts attached, the biting began. There was "Monster Mash" playing in the background. A magician came and tricks were performed. A good time was had by all.

At Thanksgiving the front of the house was bedecked with cornstalks on either side of the entry and big orange bows tied at their middles. A wreath of fall leaves was hanging on the door and an orange bow was tied around the lamp post. The house smelled of good food cooking. Some of the family went to the high school football game; some stayed home and watched the Macy's Parade on television. Everyone ate until full at dinner and still had room for sandwiches later on. Cider was cold, pies were hot; and everyone was thankful.

At the Christmas Party Santa took the year off and Carolers came instead. It was a nice change, and Bob and Paul and Carol sang along with them. It actually turned into one big sing a long. The tree was up if not a little smaller, but falling over because it had so many ornaments on it. Will made a Wassail Punch and Isabelle made a huge chicken pot pie. There was a chocolate Yule log from the bakery. There were cup cakes and pastries. The coffee urn stood at the ready with cream and sugar waiting. Isabelle wore a green blouse and Will wore a red sweater.

On Christmas Eve all the gifts were unwrapped and the spirit of holiday enveloped the whole family. The two youngest grandchildren, Eileen and Liam, were thirteen and eleven. There would be new babies and generations coming. How wonderful life was. Will and Isabelle went to midnight Mass. It was peaceful in the dim lit church. They prayed for each other's health and the health and well being of all their family.

They hibernated in the winter and celebrated the spring. The back yard was welcoming the birds back and so were Will and Isabelle. A tit mouse was pecking at the thistle and a fat robin was pulling up a juicy worm. The leaves were just beginning to leaf their yellow gold of spring. How good it was to see this new season, a hopeful season. Will and Isabelle sat in their chairs outside with warm sweaters on. They had hot cups of tea on their little table and gulped lungs full of fresh air. Life was good even if they were old.

In June they went to a play one week and met some friends for lunch another. The air was getting warmer and their old bones loved it. When the Fourth of July came they went to Gerry's party, looking at how old Isabelle's children looked. Isabelle was a great grandmother now. Her grandkids were becoming adults; they looked older.

She told Will what she was thinking, and he said, "I wonder how we look to them?"

She laughed and said "Ancient".

Judy and Kathy came to the party. Bob came with Carol and Paul. Will told Joe he was too old for washer toss but was he was told he had to play since he was a one time champ. He played but was out the first round. Carol and Bob wore the same Statue of Liberty tee shirts they had worn years ago just to be funny. Bob and Judy got a card game going. Kathy and Isabelle talked about the gel shots Isabelle got in her knees. Carol and Paul told everyone about joining the choir and asked Kathy and Judy if they'd like to join since they were in the same parish. Kathy said she might start going back to Mass but that was as far as it went.

"Can you sing" said Paul?

"I can sing alright, I guess. I sing in the shower" said Kathy.

"Not well" said Judy.

"OK, well there you go, Paul, the choir can do without me".

"How about you Judy", said Paul?

"I can't sing at all", said Judy.

Carol said, "Didn't your first husband teach you how to hum"?

All the women laughed. The men looked confused.

Judy said "Humming doesn't count but I may go back to church".

Even though it was passed their bedtime, the old timers stayed for the fireworks and they were as impressed as the toddlers at the colorful explosions bursting in the sky. They had a great time and this time Paul and Carol stood up and sang, "God Bless America" with the grand finale. Everyone joined in.

# CHAPTER THIRTY-NINE: PLAYING CARDS

Kathy and Judy decided to have a card party on a Friday night in August. Isabelle, Will, Carol, Paul and Bob were coming. The guests arrived within seconds of each other and Judy served each one a drink, wine for the girls; beer for the boys. Bob told Judy he was sick and tired of her winning at cards and tonight was going to be different.

Bob said, "You better prepare to lose."

She said, "In your dreams".

OK well there are seven of us so the first hand is seven cards.

Will won the first hand, Isabelle lost.

The next hand was six cards. Bob and Judy both got their bids.

Paul and Carol got their bids for the hand with five cards and Kathy lost.

The four card hand was an overbid. Isabelle liked these she was good at getting rid of cards.

The three card hand was an underbid Paul lost.

Only two cards this time, Will won.

The final hand was one card, with diamonds as trumps. Judy had the king of diamonds. She thought this was a great card to bid on because each player only had one card and probably not diamonds. It was her lead. She led her king of diamonds, Will threw a two of spades, Isabelle tossed in a jack of hearts, Kathy followed suit with a queen of diamonds, Paul threw a nine of clubs, then Bob slapped the Ace of diamonds on top of the king and Judy lost. She was mad as hell.

They played another game. This time Judy won. Then they took a break for decaf and brownies.

Kathy was telling them that she had been so embarrassed today. She went to the store to get milk, eggs and a lottery ticket. When she got in line a nice young man told her she could go first since he had a cart loaded with food. She thanked him and then the cashier tallied up Kathy's two items. She reached in her purse to get out her wallet only to find no wallet. She remembered she left it on the counter this morning when she was fishing through her purse for her glasses. She had held up the line, inconvenienced the young man, her order had to be voided and she had to go home, get the wallet and repeat the process all over again. She felt so bad for that nice young man. If this is what getting old does to a person; I'll pass.

"Well you found your way home", said Judy, "so everything is OK."

Carol and Paul sat down with their drinks and joined the conversation.

Isabelle said, "We all have had embarrassing moments. Once when I was about forty-five we went to a square dance at church. It was a fund raiser for the school and after I bowed to my partner and bowed to my corner; then I did the promenade left and then I Do-Si-Doed with my corner around the circle. He was an old man to me then, probably about our age now. He had his hand on my back and we were holding hands in front like square dancers do and my bra hook popped. Let me tell you, that old guy felt the pop and the boobs were loose and they were not Do-Si Doing they were floppy flopping. The poor old man knew what had happened and was quite amused. As soon as the music stopped I had to leave. I could not have done any more of that without injuring my self."

Judy said, "You could have gotten black eyes."

"Thanks", said Isabelle.

Bob said, "Once after my mother died I was so distracted trying to change title of the house, the car and writing to her life insurance company I was absent minded about everything else and wore grey glen plaid pants and a navy pin striped jacket to work with one brown shoe and one black one. That was embarrassing."

Paul said, "When I had my office over on Main St. me and two doctors shared waiting room space. I went to use the men's room and when I came back all the people in the waiting room were staring at me. It was about 10:00 AM. I just smiled back. After lunch my receptionist told me that I had about a yard of toilet paper stuck to my shoe and I had been trailing it around since this morning. It was still on my shoe. No wonder they were all looking at me. Not good for business."

Judy said, "One time my mother in law, my second mother in law actually, was cooking the guts of some animal she had just killed. She wanted me to learn how to make stew. They were strange people. She had all this blood and guts all over the table. She asked me to pass her the heart. She was chopping these bits and pieces up and throwing them in a stew pot. I didn't want to learn how to do this. I used a spatula and passed her some bloody thing and she looked at me like I was as dumb as the floor. She told me I passed her the liver."

"She said, "you don't know the difference between the heart and the liver do you"?

I said, "Yes I do, you try not to get your heart broken and when you do; you pickle your liver in alcohol. She laughed out loud. That's the only time I ever saw her laugh."

Will said, "Once when I was between wives, I was trying to get to know this young pretty girl at a bar."

Paul said, "Watch it Will, Isabelle's here".

"No, No, she won't care. Anyway, I was chatting with this pretty young thing." About a half hour later she said "What did you say your name was again?"

I said, "Will Benton".

And she said, "Oh wrong guy, the music is so loud I thought you said, Bill Denton. I'm supposed to be meeting my grandfather's friend here to return his book and you look about his age. I don't think I could have possibly looked old enough to be her grandfather."

Paul said, "Yes you could".

Carol said, "Well once I had to go to a rep meeting for the phone company in New York. The Boston shuttle to Kennedy was delayed; the cabs were scarce so I got there just in time. I had to go to the bathroom so bad I didn't even care if I was late. I ran to the ladies room and I was in such a hurry, I meant to tuck my blouse in my skirt and I tucked my skirt in my panty hose. The front was OK it was just the back part. I looked in the mirror before I left the ladies' room. It was a full length mirror. I looked fine from the front. I sped to that meeting room and marched right down that aisle to the front row where my seat was and everyone got a view of my rear end covered with pantyhose and a skirt stuffed inside. I heard a lot of laughter, but I didn't think it had anything to do with me. Luckily when I went to sit down a lady beside me fixed my backside. But I tried to be the last one to leave that day. I didn't want to face them."

"We have to get back to cards", said Judy. "We need to play the tiebreaker."

Bob said, "Don't even think you're going to win. Tonight is my night."

Bob was right, he beat Judy.

She was such a sore sport.

She said, "It's too bad we don't have a trophy for you. It's the last time you'll ever win".

They all laughed and said it was time to call it a night.

Isabelle and Will had had a great time playing cards. They arrived home exhausted and went to bed. Their years for sex were over they were content to lay naked in each other arms. Pillow talk time was one of the best times of the day. They talked about the card game and laughed at the jokes and comments that had been made.

"I hope this becomes a habit", said Will. "We had fun tonight."

"Let's try to arrange a card party every week", said Isabelle. "It's more fun when Judy's there. She's a character. I'm glad she lives with Kathy now"

"You didn't win any games tonight, sweetheart, I'm surprised you're saying you had such a good time," said Will.

"Well that's because I'm not lucky at cards, I'm lucky at love." They laughed and then they kissed.

"I had fun just being there. I'm so glad you asked me to marry you, I'm so happy. You were right; this is the best dance anyone could have. I love you Will Benton."

They kissed again and were asleep in five minutes.

The next morning Will knew when he saw her face that she was gone. She was cold, bluish and not breathing. Thank God her eyes were closed; he did not want to see them if the stars had gone out of them.

He kissed each breast and then her lips, and remembered her last words were "I love you, Will Benton".

Then he got up and called her children.

# CHAPTER FORTY: THE LAST CHAPTER

Isabelle's children and grandchildren were seated at the front of the church. Carol and Paul were in the rows behind them with Bob, Judy and Kathy.

Will's son had come up from Louisiana to stay with him and then bring him home.

There were many others in attendance. It had been a lovely Mass and now Will was giving the eulogy. He stood on the altar at the pulpit and spoke.

"We are celebrating the life of a good, beautiful, happy woman who made all of us happy. No tears please." said Will. Even though he said this, his lips quivered and he stood at the altar with tears spilling down his cheeks. Isabelle had said one of them would be like this someday. He told their story. Will said they had both fallen in love at first sight sixty-seven years ago. He told of their chance meeting fifty years later and how he wanted whatever time they had left to be spent together. He said he was relentless in his pursuit of her hand. He kept saying I hope you'll dance. She took a long time to be persuaded. He told the congregation how he explained to Isabelle that even when one of them died, and yes the other would be devastated, at least they would have had this dance. He asked her to marry him forty times before she said yes. He told her she'd be sorry if she didn't dance, much more, sorry than if they never danced and then died. Many days he would start the day with his proposal just to get it over with, hoping he got her at a weak moment and she'd say yes. Will said he never wanted them to regret not marrying. He proposed to her by e-mail, by phone, in person and by letter. Finally, one day he had to go back to Louisiana for business. He was discouraged that she had not accepted his proposal. He thought she would not have him. A few days went by and there was a letter for him. Most of her letters started, "Hey Big Guy" and ended with "Love you, Isabelle". This letter did not. It was a plain sheet of white paper. All that was written on it was "Let's

Dance" in huge letters. Will still had the paper and held it up for all to see. Will said he took the next flight to Boston and they were married the next day.

"Oh, how I will miss her." he said. He spoke of their happy ten years together and of all the joy and love they gave each other. I will never see those eyes with the stars in them again. I will never see her smile. Those were the happiest years of my life and I know I made her happy. I will remember how wonderful it felt to hold her in my arms, my young arms and my old arms. He told all present that when he looked into that eighty year old woman's face he still saw the beautiful thirteen year old girl he fell in love with. He told them all to cherish the ones they love. Before he walked out of the church, he kissed the casket and said, "I will love you forever Isabelle, I'm glad you said "Let's dance"."

# EPILOGUE

Will went back to Louisiana to live with Jack and Marilyn. The only things he took from Isabelle's home were his clothes and personal things which he had brought when they married, the photo Tom had taken of them and the wooden Chateau Frontenac. Will missed Isabelle but he knew he had been lucky enough to have had ten years with her. He was glad she did not have to endure the pain of the loss he was enduring. He thought about her all the time. How he had loved her, as a girl and even as an old woman. He was too frail to do much these days. He was eighty-one. He felt eighty-one but on certain days when the sun was bright he would fall asleep in the garden and dream of a young Will driving a motor boat and pulling Isabelle on her water skies, or the pink dress she wore to his prom, and their first kiss under the fire works. He poked around the yard at Jacks house and enjoyed the company of his grandchildren.

Sometimes he would doze in a chair in the back yard and in his mind's eye he would see an older Isabelle hanging bats from the ceiling, laying on a blow up raft beside him in Vermont or wearing a fancy hat at a tea party with her granddaughters. He remembered romantic Quebec City, how bad she was at horse shoes, her smile. Will had memories of the Swan Boat ride, the library incident, Newport and playing cards. He had loved her completely and she had loved him totally and unconditionally. He was glad they had danced.

Two months after Isabelle's death he had a cerebral hemorrhage and died instantly. He had left instructions with Jack as to what was to be done. Jack had his father cremated and sent the ashes to Massachusetts to Paul. Jack told Paul that Will wanted half of them tossed into the lake so part of him could be with Tom and where they had all met. The rest were to be put in the ground near Isabelle's grave. He left all his worldly belongings to Jack except for two. He gave the wooden Chateau Frontenac to Nina with a note telling her that she should go one day to see the beautiful castle that he and Isabelle went to in Quebec. The other was the framed picture of young Isabelle and Will called "Magic" along with the note that said "Let's Dance". He had these sent to Tricia, Isabelle's youngest. She was the most sentimental of all her children and he knew it would be passed down for generations.

Before Will died he had remembered what Paul had said about heaven and hoped that his heaven would be Isabelle and Will for eternity. He was glad they had danced.

Made in the USA
Lexington, KY
15 November 2012